VALUE SWEEP

VALUE SWEEP

MAPPING CORPORATE
GROWTH OPPORTUNITIES

MARTHA AMRAM

Harvard Business School Press
Boston, Massachusetts

Printed in the United States of America

06 05 04 03 02   5 4 3 2 1

Requests for permission to use or reproduce material from this book should be
directed to permissions@hbsp.harvard.edu, or mailed to Permissions, Harvard
Business School Publishing, 60 Harvard Way, Boston, Massachusetts 02163.

Library of Congress Cataloging-in-Publication Data

Amram, Martha, 1957–
     Value sweep : mapping corporate growth opportunities / Martha Amram.
          p. cm.
     Includes bibliographical references and index.
     ISBN 1-57851-458-4
      1. Valuation.   2. Corporations--Growth.   3. Investment analysis.
     I. Title.
     HG4028.V3 A5 2002
     658.1--dc21

                                                                    2002004560

The paper used in this publication meets the requirements of the American
National Standard for Permanence of Paper for Publications and Documents in
Libraries and Archives Z39.48-1992.

Contents

Preface

I suspect that most business books are sparked by moments of pure frustration. My own experience was the clash of four worlds.

First, my modern graduate school training in valuation and the pricing of risk was breathtaking in its vision and elegance. The powerful ideas I studied changed public policy and financial markets. But, as I later discovered, these concepts have not been deeply applied in corporations.

A second world was strategy consulting. Working with large corporations on important and risky decisions, I used a toolkit that was rich but confusing to clients. Sure, the method could provide good answers to hard questions—Build the chemical plant? Switch technologies on our key product? Set a price for that piece of intellectual property?—but the tools became black boxes after the consultants left. Risky projects were the key to growth, but their value remained unclear to those who owned the opportunity.

Third, in my work with startup companies I've noticed a profound disconnect between the startups and more established firms. Experienced entrepreneurs and venture capitalists use a language about risky growth that helps everyone to quickly identify the key drivers of value and to quickly dismiss business ideas that don't have enough value. This language, shared frameworks, and tendency to act would have helped my corporate clients.

This has been a fragmented and frustrating experience, but also a struggle at the conceptual level. The fourth and last force in my colliding worlds has been watching managers struggle to understand and quantify the value of growth opportunities. Managers really don't like the hard work required by our current valuation tools; they are very genuine in their intent, yet very frustrated. The managers I've met gave shape to the vision of this book: a method to create easy-to-use and credible valuation tools that can be used to compare growth opportunities across the sweep of value.

This book is about a new approach to valuation, one designed to meet three objectives:

- *Benchmark and compare the value of growth opportunities.* With a clear picture of the economic landscape, we can better assemble the scarce resources required for strong corporate growth.

- *Align the value of private growth opportunities with public-market valuations.* This opens the door to innovative ways to finance, insure, and monetize growth projects.

- *Replace complex calculations with simple and transparent methods.* People and financial resources gravitate toward growth opportunities with a credible and well-understood value proposition.

Who Should Read This Book

This book is written for managers who don't want to be valuation experts; strategists who want to weigh alternatives with a set of simple calculations; CFOs and business unit heads who want to compare the varied initiatives clamoring for their approval; and M.B.A. students who are trying to grasp and use high-powered ideas. Real people require credible, transparent, and easy-to-use valuation methods that work across the sweep of growth opportunities.

Readers of this book share a bias toward action; they have jobs that help to nourish and grow new products, new markets, and new companies. While the industries and job functions are quite varied, the needs are the same. The more detailed look at who should read this book includes:

- *Managers at the crossroads.* This includes CEOs, CFOs, business unit heads, and those who head growth initiatives and other new ventures. Managers at the crossroads must make the tough choices—"Do I put money into this project or that one?"—and need a way to compare the value and risk of growth from business as usual with the value and risk of new initiatives.

- *The staff who support managers at the crossroads.* Your boss read this book, and he dropped it in your lap. (Of course you should read it, too!) There is a language and a method here that brings the value and risk of growth to life. You can use this book to shape alternatives and to quickly summarize opportunities. Use the Web site, www.valuesweep.com, to make this process easier.

- *Equity analysts.* Many analysts write schizophrenic reports. They use a simple quantitative model to obtain a target stock price. Meanwhile, significant and interesting growth opportunities are described in the text surrounding the number—but they are never directly translated into value. This book is aimed at giving analysts a way to quantify growth opportunities in a quick and sensible way.

- *Managers who speak to equity analysts and investors.* Your company has some innovative early-stage projects and is performing well in its current business. The innovative projects might not hit, yet the pipeline deserves some value credit. How can Wall Street's expectations be set? Meanwhile, the analysts will react harshly if the current business fails to meet its projections. Are they overreacting? The framework of this book helps to communicate your answer to these questions.

- *Finance staff.* Companies want to do the right thing, to select the strategic investments that increase shareholder value and to reject all others. The problem is that their valuation frameworks have not kept up with the complexity of new business opportunities. The quantitative analysis drags on and on, and out of frustration, critical decisions are made for strategic reasons without regard to value. Often, because growth projects are so exciting, a frothy optimism prevails.

As a remedy, this book offers a hard cold logic about how growth strategies translate into value. Armed with context, transparency, and intuition, finance staff can help to speed up and make credible the tough decisions about growth opportunities.

- *Investors.* At the peak of the Internet boom, nearly 20 percent of the firms traded in U.S. stock markets were not profitable. A wider range of investors must now do what angel investors and venture capitalists have been doing for some time— quantify the value of preprofit growth opportunities. The framework in this book allows reverse-engineering of stock prices, and the examples show periods in which the market over- and undervalued firms rich in growth opportunities.

- *Those ready to contribute financial resources to growth opportunities.* Value is opaque in many private markets. Consequently, there are widely divergent expectations about value that frequently slow negotiations or, even worse, kill transactions. The methods of this book create a common point of reference for those who own growth assets and those who can bring innovative financing to them.

- *Auditors.* This book provides a framework to align private assets with valuations in the public markets, the mark-to-market of growth assets. Intangible assets constitute the majority of corporate value, and growth opportunities are a large portion of intangible asset value. There's much debate but no clear and well-accepted method for the valuation of intangible assets. My hope is that this book is a solid step forward.

Real Options: Beyond Pioneers

Three years ago, I wrote a book on real options, *Real Options: Managing Strategic Investment in an Uncertain World,* with Nalin Kulatilaka of Boston University. We saw real options as a powerful way of thinking and a useful valuation framework for managers. *Real Options* was written to serve as a bridge between academic literature and managerial concerns. (For more information on real options, see www.valuesweep.com.)

Our book, along with others written on real options, hit a nerve. The concept of real options straddles strategy and finance, and a common reaction from managers was, "I just knew there was value in this project. Now I see that it has embedded real options."

Unfortunately, new ideas are often too complex to be widely applied, and this was the case when real options met the business world. In some companies, real options advocates have asked managers to spend time working through the partial differential equation that underlies the foundation of option pricing. In other companies, detailed, handcrafted, and highly opaque real options models have been used to justify investment decisions. Eyes glaze over for everyone but the author of the report. Real options has suffered from what I call the "second date problem": It's great as the subject for a workshop or first project, but real options fails to take off inside the company. There's no second date!

After the publication of *Real Options*, I benefited from working side by side with the practitioners of decision analysis at SDG (formerly the Strategic Consulting Division at Navigant Consulting). For years, this group of consultants has helped companies make high-quality strategic investment decisions in the face of risk from product markets, technology, and managerial inertia. The folks at SDG helped me learn what is really new about real options and what had already been learned by another field, decision analysis.

From these experiences I drew two strong conclusions about real options. First, in many applications, real options is not the right tool. I'll raise this issue throughout this book and show how to combine real options with other perspectives. Second, decision analysis (and decision analysis coupled with real options) is quite an expansive approach; it can handle a lot of detail. Often, however, the detail overwhelms the rationale. A consistent theme in this book is that to be used, real options must be understood. This requires simple calculations and a strong story line. In sum, I see *Value Sweep* is a natural follow-on to *Real Options*.

Expectations Investing

This book speaks to many of the same issues as *Expectations Investing*, written by my book-writing colleagues Michael Mauboussin and Al Rappaport. *Expectations Investing* sets up a clear valuation framework (used in Chapter 3 of this book) and shows how to find the expectations embedded in stock prices. *Value Sweep* focuses on growth opportunities and uses market expectations to better value private assets. It has been my great pleasure to collaborate with Michael and Al on initial drafts of Chapter 4, which overlaps with Chapter 8 in their book.

Acknowledgments

I'd like to start with my editors, Kirsten Sandberg and Jacque Murphy. Their vision and support for this book have been unwavering and valuable. They seem to have been to that special school where editors are taught how to delicately switch between carrot and stick—and have mastered the lessons with grace. Many thanks.

In the years since the publication of *Real Options,* I have had the wonderful experience of sharing and growing the ideas that Nalin Kulatilaka and I wrote about with an insightful and energetic group of people. Many of those conversations and experiences are reflected here. Thanks to Nalin, John Henderson, and Cyrus Remezani and to my former colleagues at Navigant Consulting— Jim Matheson, Jeff Foran, Udi Meirav, Jerry Caciotti, Rishi Varma, and Dave Macway. Special thanks to David Fishman, who continues to be a terrific sounding board and reliable reader on concepts and issues.

My deep gratitude also goes to Alan Jung. Alan has been part of many of these conversations, has worked with me closely in building real options applications, and has carefully read earlier drafts of this book. A group of anonymous reviewers also provided early and helpful feedback.

During the writing of a book, there is often one conversation, one lunch, that significantly changes how the book's content is presented and organized. Thanks to Blake Johnson for that special lunch. Blake's comments, which span the range of his own unique perspective (from Stanford professor to founder of a startup), have made this book more useful.

Laura Martin, who collaborated on the original work for Chapter 10, continues to be a delight and a delightful challenge. Her energy and enthusiasm for innovative valuation methods is wonderful and much appreciated. Her insatiable curiosity, her willingness to go one level deeper, and her Wall Street–style sense of impatience have kept me on my toes. The book is better for it; many thanks.

Michael Mauboussin has been a strong and thoughtful voice for real options on Wall Street. Writing books opens doors, and I'm very glad that my earlier book has caused our paths to cross. Al Rappaport, Michael's coauthor of *Expectations Investing*, carefully read an early draft of this book and provided an important editorial wake-up call. My deep thanks.

During the writing of this book, I was fortunate to be assisted by Vera Scalia, who with great competency and humor helped with manuscript and graphics. Kyle Kim also provided research assistance. Richie Ganitsky stepped in at the last stage and provided steady assistance, with incredible attention to detail. Marc Igler and Jennifer Cray generously gave me last-minute editorial support. Jane Bonassar at Harvard Business School Press patiently coordinated production. Thanks also to the companies, individuals, and former clients who heard draft presentations of the material in this book, including Ron Beaver and Bill Poland of Pharsight, David Avny of MIPS, Paul Germeraad of Aurigin, and the staff of In-Q-Tel.

A special group of people have come to represent for me the raw and elegant beauty of a growth opportunity, those folks who surround a young startup, Vocomo Software. Special thanks to Mitsuru Oshima, Mike Inman, Luke Hohmann, and particularly Danny Lange and Nick Arvanitidis. In this group are three book authors and three Ph.D.'s. Their patience and understanding of my bookwriting is greatly appreciated. As Oshima told me, "It is a privilege to have the opportunity to write a book." He's right, and it's also a privilege to work with this group.

Families bear the highest cost of authorship. My children, Oz and Aurelle, have been cheerleaders and enthusiasts, despite many inconveniences. My husband, Yosi, who has taken two companies from idea through IPO, is quite familiar with the marathon of business growth yet continues to bring fun and personal growth to our lives. Yosi's helpful and encouraging advice has been "Just finish the darn book!" (See how he gets things done?) Many, many thanks for all that and more.

VALUE SWEEP

1

One Map of Value

The modern corporation faces a wide range of growth opportunities, from business as usual to e-commerce to corporate venture capital. Large companies make 2,000 to 10,000 capital investment decisions each year, yet fail to credibly value growth projects. This chapter argues for a transparent approach to valuation that works for all types of growth opportunities and that aligns internal corporate valuations with financial market pricing of growth. A new approach to valuing growth leads to meaningful comparisons: Let's put the sweep of corporate growth opportunities on one map of value.

Three Companies, Three Questions

In the spring of 2000 a large part of the market value of Procter & Gamble (P&G) evaporated. Selling diapers, soaps, and other consumer household products, P&G is typical of an established firm. But in early June P&G announced that for the third consecutive quarter it would not meet Wall Street's expectations for sales and profits. P&G also announced that it was changing CEOs and changing strategies. It would no longer promise a flood of new products but would focus instead on growing sales and profits from current products. P&G's market value fell 35 percent.

How can the value of growth from new products and innovations be compared to the value of executing the current business?

The year 2000 was rough for Internet consulting firms. One firm, Viant, saw its market value fall from twenty times annual revenues in spring 2000 to less than one times revenues a year later. During the year other Internet consulting firms experienced similar drops in value as Wall Street changed its expectations about Internet-fueled growth. KPMG and Accenture went public in 2001 at valuations just under one times revenues—the firms would have been hugely more valuable one year earlier.

Was there any rationale behind the valuations based on Internet growth expectations? Is there a way to identify and track the changing value of growth?

MIPS Technologies creates and sells its intellectual property. MIPS doesn't make anything we can actually touch; its microprocessor designs are embedded in the products of other firms. MIPS's designs are in electronic games, handheld devices, and networking equipment. There is no "price" of a microprocessor design; the company instead shapes and crafts the terms and conditions of its intellectual property licenses. Revenues in 2000 were $89 million, and the company's market value throughout the year was never less than $1 billion.

What's the value of intellectual property? What is the value of business models built around selling of ideas?

The issues in these three vignettes are typical of the varied growth challenges facing the modern corporation. Also typical is the conceptual fog around their value. And while the examples seem to come from distinct high-tech and low-tech industries, the issues cut across the separate worlds. At P&G, licensing officers wrestle with the value of P&G's intellectual property; at MIPS, managers worry about how financial markets will value their R&D pipeline; and at KPMG, top managers study the shifts in technology and how it will drive value in the next wave. Growth comes in many forms, and we need a way to compare the value of varied opportunities; we need a single map of value across the sweep.

Valuation Models Are a Language and a Lens

Here's a simple exercise that demonstrates the importance of growth opportunities in corporate value. Pick a public company and get its current earnings. Assume the earnings stay at that level forever. Calculate the value of the no-growth company using your favorite valuation model. Compare how much you are willing to pay for a share in the no-growth firm with the current stock price. Typically the calculated no-growth value of the firm is one-fourth or one-fifth its market value as a growth company.[1] The vast majority of the market value represents the value of future growth opportunities.

> *Can you tell a story about the growth opportunities*
> *that supports the value of growth? Can you include*
> *reasonable numbers to back it up?*

Although simple, this short exercise is often difficult. Growth opportunities are uncertain. They need to be managed in a dynamic environment. Growth depends on assets in place, the caliber of the management team, and a number of other factors that can't be seen from outside the company. No valuation method can lift this cloud. But suppose there were no cloud; instead there was complete information. Would you then be able to tell the story about the path to growth? Probably not. Growth opportunities are a huge part of value, but we lack a lens to see their structure, a language to describe their features, and tools to quantify their value.

Problems with the Current Valuation Tools

Valuation tools structure information and establish the requirements of a good valuation result. Our current tools fail in both aspects. They ignore key features of growth opportunities, and they don't provide a framework and process for credible answers. Here are some of the key problems:

- *The most important uncertainties of growth are ignored.* In one company I worked with, the finance staff was increasingly excluded from the strategic decision-making process. Their analyses, impeccable when applied to mature businesses and stable markets, were irrelevant when it came to new markets, new products, and incomplete technology.

- *There are too many dense, opaque, and specialized models.* Ask an e-commerce consultant how to value an investment in supply chain infrastructure. Then ask a specialist on intangible assets. Then ask a corporate finance professor. No doubt, all answers will appear rigorous. The reports will be dense, but the answers will be different and hard to compare.

- *There is no connection between growth projects and shareholder value.* The complex and technology-driven project in front of the team feels like it is on another planet, with no potential impact on stock price. Even worse, each project feels like it's on its own planet, disconnected from other growth initiatives.

- *There is no alignment between the value of growth opportunities and pricing in the stock market.* Think of growth opportunities as children and teenagers, on their way to adulthood. If the stock price of the mature sustainable business changes, shouldn't that ripple through to the firms and projects that are still growing up?

- *There is no benchmarking.* Deal by deal, we'd like to compare the value of the transaction at hand to those done before. For example, think of the value of licensing transactions in chemicals when the industry is at the top of its cycle, compared to the value of the same transaction when the industry is coming down. The comparison should meaningfully account for change in stock market valuations, progress by the company, and so on. In the long run, the valuation tools and data should be calibrated and updated in an open manner, one that makes sense to all parties.

The Wrong Lens Hurts Growth

No lens and bad tools are more than just a modeling problem. Without credible valuations, there is simply less growth: The ability to attract the resources—financial and otherwise—to execute a growth opportunity rests on all parties understanding the story of how value will be created. For example, several companies studied later in the book, such as MGM and Anadarko Petroleum, have attracted new financing after making bold moves that clearly demonstrated the value of their growth opportunities. In other cases, financial instruments have been developed that rest on a clear understanding of growth opportunities. For example, rock star David Bowie has issued a bond whose payments are made from future song royalties. (See Chapter 11.) This process of securitization increases the funding of growth opportunities, ultimately spurring growth itself.

A clear example of how the lack of credible valuation tools hurts growth comes from the venture capital industry. After several boom years, venture capitalists simply stopped funding new companies in 2001. One venture group blamed its halt on not knowing the value of the candidate startups. But more often, venture capitalists reacted to the decline in the stock market and offered low valuations to entrepreneurs. The entrepreneurs, more emotionally tied to their endeavors, felt the deal was unfair when compared with recent financings.

A transparent valuation tool, such as the one described in Chapter 8, would allow a rational discussion of the link between stock market value and venture capital valuations. Without the discussion prompted by that or other similar frameworks, deals are not done. No deals, no growth.

In short, we lack a shared language for describing the structure of the largest components of current value: expectations about future growth opportunities. We lack a lens to see how features of growth opportunities lead to measurable value. We lack a way to identify the common features of growth across the many different types of opportunities. Without a credible framework, we fail to make wise choices about growth projects.

The Value Sweep Vision

This book sets out a practical, rigorous, and transparent valuation method for growth opportunities. The goal is to illuminate—through language, images, and quantitative tools—the structure of value across the sweep of growth opportunities that arise in our modern economy. The results must be practical: The world does not need another idiosyncratic black-box tool. The results must be rigorous: Holes in logic will cause monetary losses. The results must be transparent: The valuation method must tell a story of growth that can be understood by many different kinds of users.

Figure 1-1 illustrates the value sweep vision. The vertical bars represent the growth opportunities before the modern corporation. The variation in width and color indicates their diversity. The height of the boxes indicates value; the diverse opportunities can be compared. (The heights shown in Figure 1-1 are illustrative.) Figure 1-1 is a simple picture, but the results cannot be achieved without a change in how growth opportunities are valued.

To place growth opportunities on the same page, or onto one map, the two dimensions must be carefully organized. On the horizontal dimension, the valuation tools must match the type of growth opportunity. As Chapters 2 through 5 will show, certain features of growth can be valued with one valuation tool but not another. On the vertical dimension, the valuation results must be transparent and aligned with valuations in the financial markets. This alignment is known as updating an asset's value to market value, or "mark-to-market."

Focus the Process of Valuation

How can this vision be made to work? Most of us would be appropriately skeptical of a new approach to valuation that came out of nowhere. But there is no need to reinvent the wheel. We can assemble and extract from the rich resources already available. Here are the steps in a valuation process focused on growth opportunities:

- *Target the value of growth.* Extract from existing valuation tools only what is needed to solve this narrow problem. The toolkit includes discounted cash flow (DCF), real options, and decision analysis—and a combination of the three. All have strong pedigrees.

- *Take a look through the lens.* Valuation tools provide a framework to describe value. They organize data into a structure

Figure 1-1 The Value Sweep Vision

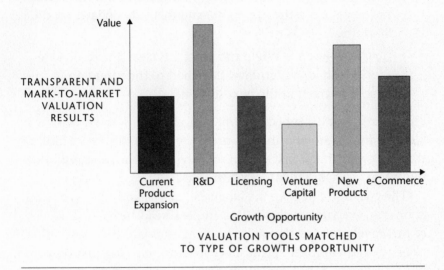

and highlight the drivers of value. They clarify what is required to achieve project success. Chapters 2 through 5 lay out three ways to see growth opportunities.

- *Replace an infinite number of variations in models with a limited number of templates.* Most valuations of growth opportunities are dense and idiosyncratic because the analyst attempts to extend a valuation tool. Replace these black boxes with an array of precalculated valuation templates and preassembled data sets. Replace opaque modeling efforts with a moment of transparent choice: Match the growth opportunity to a valuation template and data set. The tables in the Appendix and on the Web site (www.valuesweep.com) are the tools of the new approach.

- *Identify benchmarks, logic checks, and comparables.* Most often the purpose of valuing a growth opportunity is to take action—invest, sell, buy, or finance. To be credible, the valuation results must have points of comparison with other assets, other transactions, other companies. These data and logic checks should be built in to the process, anticipating the need to communicate value to others.

- *Update the data sets*. Assemble the data sets needed to support the mark-to-market orientation. Update as needed. Sample tables are in the Appendix, and there are updates on the Web site.

- *Codify the process*. When the process is clear, the results are more credible. A high-level flowchart of the valuation process is given in the next section.

The process just described is fairly typical of the way know-how is codified into a product in software or service industries. Think of this book as a similar first step in solidifying and articulating valuation know-how for growth opportunities.

The goal is to integrate the language, image, and process of valuation into everyday business life. Simple spreadsheets—think back-of-the-envelope—are the right level of software for most valuations. (Avoid complex spreadsheet macros and plug-ins; they are not transparent to senior management.) A manager should be able to calculate his or her own answers. There will be room for pros, but the role of the nonspecialist should be a lot bigger.

A Look Ahead: Valuing Webvan

To provide a flavor of how a revised valuation process would work in practice, let's walk through an example. In July 2001 Webvan ceased operations. The quick rise and fall of the Internet grocer illustrates many features typical of growth opportunities, as well as the valuation logic behind Internet-fueled growth opportunities. The valuation method used in this example is the subject of later chapters, and a spreadsheet summarizing the calculations is available from www.valuesweep.com.

In the spring of 2001, Webvan was a growth opportunity, a company not yet able to self-fund its business growth. Typical of many e-commerce prospects, it had its feet in both the Internet and physical worlds. Webvan's sales were running at an annualized rate of $300 million, and it promised Wall Street profitability by the second half of 2002. The company also said that an additional $25 million of capital was needed to achieve this milestone. What was the value of Webvan at that time?

Begin the analysis by throwing out the standard valuation tools such as price-earnings ratios, price-earnings-to-growth ratios, and DCF (also known as net present value [NPV]). In all of these methods, value is driven by near-term positive cash flow. But Webvan expected near-term losses! Instead of assuming the issue away, use valuation tools that directly account for value creation while incurring losses.

The first step is to calculate the value of Webvan at maturity when further growth can be sustained by internal funds. What will the business model look like, and what is its value? The mature Webvan might have been somewhere between a grocery store and a delivery business. In spring 2001 the stock market was valuing companies in those markets at one to two times annual sales. Webvan told the financial markets that it would be profitable in three U.S. metropolitan areas by the end of 2001, with annual sales of $300 million. As a rough cut, the value of Webvan in three profitable cities could be put at $600 million (2 × sales).

But there was a significant risk that the firm might not cross the profitability threshold, as it had yet to make a profit in any market. The value of Webvan was less than $600 million, but how much less? One answer is found in the data provided in Chapter 8, which presents a specialized valuation template for valuing venture-funded startups. The template strikes a balance: It is built on the common principles of valuation for growth prospects discussed throughout this book and yet is tailored for the types of firms funded by venture capitalists.

The template shows that the historical venture capital valuation for a firm at the same stage of development (shipping product but not cash flow positive) is about 20 percent of the value of the business once profitable. Webvan's value would then be $120 million (20% × $600 million). Notice how the valuation result is aligned: Webvan's value is expressed as a percent of the current stock market valuation of the mature business. As the market value of the mature business changes, so will the value of the growth opportunity.

What about Webvan's other markets? These are follow-on opportunities that the company may pursue once it has proved its viability in the initial three markets. Assume, in back-of-the-envelope mode, that Webvan might double sales by opening up two additional markets. Using the method given in Chapter 7, the value of this follow-on opportunity is shown to be only 15 percent of the current value of the company, or an additional $18 million (15% × $120 million). This result is typical; follow-on opportunities capture our imagination but are seldom large in value.

The total value of Webvan is then about $138 million. This is the value of a company that is currently losing money, but which has a near-term growth opportunity and a follow-on opportunity. The valuation is based on the current stock market value of similar mature businesses.

The Four-Step Process

Figure 1-2 summarizes a four-step process to valuing growth opportunities such as Webvan.

Step 1: *Define and calculate the success payoff.* The success payoff is the answer to the question, "What is the scale and value of our sustainable business?" Webvan's success payoff was three profitable markets. The value of the success payoff is determined by the size of business at maturity, type of business, and the value of that type of business in the stock market.

Step 2: *Select the valuation template.* Valuation templates are built on rigorous valuation principles and industry-specific data. They are tailored by type of growth opportunity, and their transparency allows all parties to understand the structure of growth value. A venture capital valuation template was used for Webvan, and a number of others are developed in this book.

Step 3: *Calculate.* Valuation templates make this task easy: Just find the right number on a table and multiply. When the inputs are highly visible and the process is extremely simple, the results can be more clearly communicated. In fact, the calculations are so quick that management attention naturally wanders back to steps 1 and 2. And that's great, because most valuation errors arise not in the calculation stage but in how the problem is framed. Use the extra time to check that logic.

Step 4: *Write.* For a further check on the frame, complete two sentences: "The path to sustainable growth is . . ." and

---

Figure 1-2   The Four-Step Valuation Process

- Define and calculate the success payoff
- Select the valuation template
- Calculate the value of the growth opportunity
- Write the story

"A pessimist would say . . . " For Webvan, the path to sustainable growth is to bring the first three markets to profitability and then to grow the other markets, probably using some sort of outside financing. A pessimist would question whether the profits can be made in any markets. Pessimists would also point out that additional financing is unlikely until the first markets prove out. As of the spring of 2001, more than $800 million had been invested in Webvan. Pessimists would question the purpose of an additional $25 million! The two descriptive sentences bring together the upside and the risks to the investment, fostering consistency between the business plan and the valuation. Seeing both descriptions on the same page helps users of the valuation results better understand the risks of and the requirements for project success.

Here's how one experienced manager does the narrative. Geoff Moore, author of *Crossing the Chasm* and other books, is now affiliated with a venture capital firm. Moore has a Ph.D. in English, so it is not surprising that he screens startup business plans by their plot development. He treats a business plan like a novel: How might the plot unfold to a successful outcome? Which side character (business partners or technology) must move first? How does the central character (the company) move to center stage? Moore argues that a complete plot line is part of a good business plan.

An Overview of the Book

This book has an ambitious objective for valuing growth opportunities, yet the calculations for valuing Webvan require only simple multiplication. No doubt some readers are saying to themselves, "Why does this take a whole book? I could make up these numbers myself!" Here's a reply: The point of the valuation templates is to make the act of valuation exceedingly simple. This is key to aligning decisions and value, and to opening the door to monetizing growth assets. But while the process is simple, the prepared templates are rigorous. Information and models are codified, and the burden of complex calculations is taken off managers.

The objective of this book is to change how growth opportunities are valued. The first part of the objective is to create an alignment, a mark-to-market mentality, between private assets laden with growth opportunities and financial market valuations. At the conceptual level, this is like motherhood and apple pie—there's just no debating it. At the operational level, there's likely to be disagreement about implementation. The second part of the objective is a transparent layout of the valuation models—one designed for continued improvements. What's described in this book is the start of a process of refinements and updates based on experience and benchmarking.

The central topics in this book are rethinking the valuation process, codifying rigorous and defensible valuation models, and marking private assets to market values. Chapter 2 sets the stage with the introduction of new images and a vocabulary of growth opportunities. Two types of risk are defined. Private risks are those uncertainties unique to a growth opportunity, and market-priced risks are the uncertainties that also influence the price of traded securities. The type of risk determines the valuation tool.

Chapters 3 through 5 comprise the first main section of the book and introduce an expanded valuation toolkit. Chapter 3 provides a brief overview of the DCF valuation model. It may seem surprising to include this old-world valuation tool in a book about growth, because it so obviously fails to capture so many growth risks. But DCF is the right way to capture the value of the growth trajectory of a mature company.

Chapter 4 shows how to use the real options approach for valuation—a method that applies financial option pricing models to real or nonfinancial assets. The chapter includes the valuation of real options at Amazon.com. Chapter 5 introduces decision analysis, also known as decision trees. Only decision analysis can value private risk in some growth opportunities. An example from pharmaceutical drug development illustrates how to quantify the value of investments to acquire information that better defines the prospect of success.

The book's second section develops several valuation templates. Chapter 6 shows how to value growth opportunities that contain both market-priced and private risk. Oil exploration is a clear example. It has market-priced risk from the uncertainty about oil prices, and it has private risk from the uncertainty about geological formations. Chapter 7 focuses on the valuation of staged growth opportunities, including the valuation of sequences of real options. What is novel in this chapter is the use of option value lookup tables for option sequences, which makes the calculations very simple. Chapter 8 constructs benchmark results from the valuation of companies funded with venture capital. These results provide insights for other settings, including corporate growth opportunities and stock price analysis. Finally, Chapter 9 tackles a topic of great current sentiment: Why bother to align private valuations with stock market valuations if the stock market is so irrational? It's a challenge to write a book about the value of growth during a landmark decline in the stock market, and this chapter tackles these important issues.

The book's third section dives into the detail of four different growth opportunities. Chapter 10 takes a new look at the value of film production and at the film studio business model. A key lesson from the movie business applies to growth opportunities in many other industries: While it is difficult to predict which movies will be profitable, the drivers of studio profits are clear and must be proactively managed. Chapter 11 lays out the challenges for valuing intellectual property and looks at the performance of two firms that compete solely on their ability to create fresh and valuable intellectual property, MIPS Technologies and ARM Holdings. Every method has its limits of applicability, and Chapter 12 argues that for a number of reasons, information technology (IT) investments won't have crisp and tidy valuation results. Instead of investing time and effort into detailed valuation models, IT managers can more reliably create value by developing strong processes for IT project selection and project management. Chapter 13 takes a close look at how several Fortune 500 companies wrestled with achieving full corporate value for their growth projects. Examples of the balance of initiatives, financing, and dedicated resources are taken from P&G, Anadarko Petroleum Corporation, and Cargill Dow.

The fourth section of the book, the epilogue, is a direct statement from author to reader. My own experience has shown that growth opportunity value is just a number on paper until the management team delivers. Chapter 14 is about the people who lead growth initiatives. Most often value in a growth opportunity is created because of the charisma, drive, and smarts of one or two people in the organization, so how do we pick them and what do we want them to do? Chapter 15 concludes the book with a short list of takeaway thoughts for using the tools and perspectives presented here.

Using the Web Site

There is a natural tension between detail and accessibility in a book about valuation aimed at a broad audience. To grab the attention of busy managers, the book's story line must be clear and uncluttered. At the same time, sufficient detail is needed to start the process. Fortunately, in the age of the Internet, the book is not the author's last word. The associated Web site, www.valuesweep.com, contains more detail on the concepts and examples presented in the book. Here's what you'll find on the Web:

- *More examples.* The calculations in this book are frameworks that make the point; additional examples and more detail are posted on the Web site.

- *A longer glossary.* The glossary in this book is a sample; the Web site has the full version.

- *Pointers to other researchers.* I've tried to acknowledge other researchers and prior work in this book, but references have been kept to a minimum. The Web site has a more complete listing.

- *Updated data.* A mark-to-market analysis requires updated data. You'll find templates for easy updates on the Web site.

With these resources in place, the book has been written to introduce the key concepts as clearly as possible. How should you get started? Read this book in stages. Check the resources on the

Web site. Work through additional examples. Use both resources, with the book as a starting point.

The Cool Idea: There's Just One Map

There's usually one idea that makes the author get up in the early morning to write a book. For me, this has been the notion that the value of private assets can be transparently linked to market values. This connection opens the door to growth itself: A strong link aligns strategy and value; a transparent link spurs outside financing to growth opportunities; a rational yet easy-to-use framework speeds the negotiations for private assets. Most important, transparent alignment with market values makes comparisons across growth opportunities clear. Suppose each growth opportunity shown in Figure 1-1 is a glass house. Mark-to-market is about how tall each house is in the city of value. The valuation method allows us to see inside, to the architectural structure of the house. Now the value and structure of growth can be compared across the sweep of corporate opportunity.

Takeaways

- The current toolkit fails to credibly value growth. Either the tools don't match the features of the growth opportunity, leading to a misvaluation, or the results are too complex to be easily understood by managers.

- The goal of this book is to develop a method to value growth opportunities based on valuation templates that are easy to use, yet rigorous and credible.

- Growth opportunities can be compared if both dimensions of Figure 1-1 are addressed: The valuation results must be transparent and mark-to-market, and the valuation tools must be credible, easy to use, and matched to the growth opportunity.

2

The Look and Feel of Growth Opportunities

Often we don't have a clear image of the growth opportunity and thus can't even begin to value it. This chapter identifies the features of a growth opportunity that most affect value and introduces a new verbal and visual language to describe them. The description of growth opportunities focuses on three diagnostic questions: (1) Is the growth opportunity sustainable or does it need funding from external sources? (2) How does the interaction of uncertainty and investment affect growth value? (3) Which investment strategy most effectively reduces risk?

Growth opportunities are always risky, and consequently, they stir our emotions. Conversations about growth opportunities often stall. Suppose I'm your boss. As I talk about my growth vision, you get nervous, waiting for me to ask you to make a risky career move, to support a risky project, or to attempt a stretch goal. Your reactions will shape the outcome. Growth opportunities are a volatile combination of risk and people. There's no avoiding the emotions of risk. An objective look at growth opportunities can help to defuse tension.

Here's another example: My karate instructor says you can't anticipate how a fight will unfold, that the best defense is a repertoire of moves that can be unleashed as needed during the clash. Some corporate strategists hold a similar view for business planning in an uncertain world, arguing that preparations to maintain flexibility are key. In contrast, a CEO I have worked with employs an operating style for entrepreneurs that could be called "focused march to risk reduction and increased value." He's somewhat flexible, but he also sets clear objectives two stages ahead to reduce wasted time and money. Which strategy is best? Without a shared understanding of growth opportunities, it's hard to begin the debate.

This chapter introduces the language and images of growth opportunities so that we may begin the valuation exercise with a shared view. The Glossary at the back of the book lists all the new terms.

Three Components of Growth Value

The Market Value Balance Sheet

Figure 2-1 is a stylized accounting statement, known as a market value balance sheet. The value on the right side is the sum of the market value of debt and the market value of equity. The value of the left side is the sum of the assets-in-place and the present value of growth opportunities (PVGO). The phrase *present value* indicates that the number is in terms of what someone would be willing to pay today to acquire these assets.

The market value balance sheet makes the dynamics of growth opportunities clear. Assets-in-place and debt change slowly, while changes in PVGO quickly ripple to changes in equity and vice versa. Typically, PVGO is estimated as the difference between the firm's market value and an accounting estimate of assets-in-place. PVGO can be huge: A recent study found that on average PVGO is more than 75 percent of firm value.[1]

A New Look at Total Assets

To take a closer look at the structure of growth opportunities, divide the total assets (the left side) of the market value balance sheet into three components. Each of the three components is a

Figure 2-1   The Market Value Balance Sheet

Assets	Liabilities
Value of Assets-in-Place	Debt
Present Value of Growth Opportunities (PVGO)	Equity
Value of Firm	**Value of Firm**

different type of growth opportunity and is matched to a separate valuation tool.

1. *Near-term self-financed growth.* The value of this component is easy to see. Revenues and profits are predicted with confidence; there is a working operational plan to deliver growth. The plan shows the size and timing of investments required, and the dates and dollars required are set in stone. (If you feel more comfortable writing the dates and dollars in pencil, see the third component of growth value.) There's some uncertainty about the future, but no one expects an outcome that would require a change to the plan. *Near-term* is usually three to five years—the time horizon in which everyone is comfortable setting the fixed plan. *Self-financed* means that the planned investments can be funded from the cash flow produced by the business.

2. *Long-term self-financed growth.* Seldom is there a clear story about this component of growth value. It is the years of business-as-usual, self-funded growth after the near-term horizon. This component is also known as the terminal value. By definition, not enough is known to make a confident forecast of revenues, profits, or investments; it is simply assumed that the long-term is a stable growth trend. Typically, the lack of information creates a feeling of caution, and the expected annual growth rate is lowered to 3 percent. (3 percent is a rough estimate of the long-term U.S.

economic growth rate.) Shareholders are not expected to received a superior return, such as from competitive advantage or fast-growing industry.

The economic trends supporting the terminal value tend to be fairly persistent, but occasionally news will suggest a shift in the competitive landscape. For example, American Greetings had a sharp drop in the sales of greeting cards in 1999 and 2000.[2] Company executives and industry experts blamed the drop on the substitution of free e-mail greeting cards for the firm's paper product. When executives announced that earnings would be well below forecasts, the company lost nearly half of its market value in one day. The terminal value evaporated when it seemed that no assumptions could be made about business as usual.

3. *Cash-needy growth.* Most growth opportunities require years of investment before obtaining a return. R&D labs and startup companies are good examples. Traditional valuation tools, based on near-term cash flow and straight-line extrapolations, break down when applied to cash-needy growth opportunities, leaving their value unclear. When this happens, it becomes difficult to allocate funds to these projects within the corporation—and difficult to obtain funding for them from the outside.

An analogy can be made between the structure of cash-needy growth opportunities and financial options. For decades financial economists have used the term *growth options* to describe these business opportunities with future upside potential. (In this book, the terms *growth options* and *growth opportunities* are used interchangeably.)

Chapter 4 describes this analogy in more detail, but the distinction between *options* and *alternatives* illuminates a key issue for cash-needy growth. *Alternatives* are immediate choices (Should we lease building A or building B?), whereas *options* are choices to be made at a later date (We obtained the right but not the obligation to renew the lease in three years.). In everyday conversation, the word *option* is often used in place of the word *alternative*, but in the vocabulary of this book, options are firmly linked to future contingent decisions.

Summing the Components

Can the three growth components be summed to estimate the market value of the firm? Could this method be used to choose stocks? Unfortunately, the bottoms-up method doesn't work very well. Largely, this is due to trouble with estimates of the value of the third component, cash-needy growth opportunities. Ironically, words are needed to quantify cash-needy growth; there must be a story that articulates the value. Often, the story is not clear from an external vantage point.

For example, in theory the value of a company could be calculated as the sum of the value of products in the market and products under development. Typically, however, the sum is only 65 percent to 75 percent of the firm's market value. My own thinking is that the product-based estimates omit the value of the R&D labs and entrenched sales and marketing capabilities.

To summarize, three different methods have shown that the current tools don't fully capture the value seen by the financial markets. (The three methods are: the no-growth or analyst forecast model from Chapter 1; the sum of the three components of the market value balance sheet; and the sum of the products in market and in development.) The need for new tools and perspectives on valuation is one implication of this result. Another implication is a question for top management: How can your company show more of its growth option value to Wall Street?

The Tangle of Decisions and Uncertainty in Cash-Needy Growth Opportunities

Cash-needy growth opportunities take time to complete and require up-front investments for an uncertain payoff. Figure 2-2 shows the structure of a typical cash-needy growth opportunity: a series of investments followed by the payoff. The investments might develop and shape technology, or they might be simply payments to keep the project alive. For example, an annual tax

Figure 2-2   The Structure of a Cash-Needy Growth Opportunity

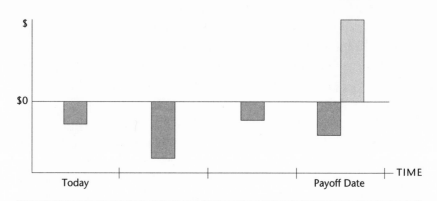

might be paid to maintain rights to a natural gas reserve. When gas prices rise, the reserve will be opened for production. The tax payment keeps the project alive; it maintains the option for later production.

A Clear Picture of the Payoff

The payoff is calculated as the sum of the value of near-term and long-term sustainable growth. A clear picture of the payoff meets two requirements. First, the payoff is defined in terms of value. Often inexperienced analysts forget to take the present value of the cash flow stream. Second, the final payoff—the one at the end of all the investments—should be self-funding. There is simply no way to value growth opportunities that never arrive at profitability. A valuable business need not be profitable today, but must be so at some point in the future.

Consider two Internet portals, Women.com and iVillage, which have since merged. Both companies searched for several years across paid content, advertising, and online retailing to find a sustainable business model. Sometimes these searches are necessary to find the winning formula, but while searching there is no clear payoff to investment. I don't know how these companies were credibly valued.

Luck and Failure

Two extreme outcomes—fantastic luck and clear failure—are intrinsic to cash-needy growth opportunities. For example, some Internet companies were started and funded by venture capitalists at the height of the boom, in late 1999 and early 2000. By the end of 2000 it was clear that the future stock market value of these companies would be low, and many startups folded—in some cases returning funds to investors—because no one could find a path to value creation. Two years earlier, these same companies might have gone public. Luck is a component of growth opportunity success.

At the same time the possibility of failure is always present. As one experienced venture capitalist puts it, "Most of the companies organized in Silicon Valley will become product lines of larger companies, features of product lines of larger companies, or they will fail."[3] Growth projects inside larger corporations should have similar failure rates. At first glance, it would seem that the possibility of failure only hurts value, but an opportunity to kill a failing project avoids further losses. Projects with an opportunity to abandon in the future are more valuable than projects that require completion.

Flexibility

In an uncertain environment, flexibility is valuable. For growth opportunities, this flexibility appears in the form of an if-then decision: "*If* we don't sell 500 units, *then* we'll shut down the test market project." This is known as a contingent decision and is the source of flexibility in growth opportunities.

The value of flexibility depends on the project-specific sequence of decisions and uncertainty, as well as the amount of uncertainty, the investment cost, and the payoff. Suppose you own a growth option. In two years you must pay $1,000 to obtain either $1,050 or $950. You can peek at the outcome before you pay. Even with a good outcome, your potential gain from continuing is only $50, so today's value of this future flexibility is low. But what if the payoff is either $2,000 or $0? With the greater potential gain and greater potential loss, there's more value in the contingent decision. The increased value of future flexibility increases the value of the project. A common real-world example of this result is a willingness to pay more for standardized technology because it creates the future opportunity to switch suppliers.

Flexibility is most valuable if it occurs after new information is obtained. Because the timing of contingent decisions is discretionary in most growth opportunities, projects can be designed to maximize the value of flexibility. This is an important feature of the "forced march" strategy described at the beginning of this chapter. Each investment is focused on reducing an identified risk, and future investment decisions are made after the information is revealed. Chapter 5 provides an example of how an information technology project rollout can be designed to reduce key risks early on.

Features of Cash-Needy Growth Opportunities

The following list summarizes the features in cash-needy growth opportunities that have been introduced in this section:

- *Value of the final payoff.* This is the value of sustainable growth, after all those cash-needy years.
- *Contingent decisions or flexibility.* In an uncertain world, there's value in waiting to decide.
- *The role of luck.* Even the best management team is exposed to the extreme outcomes of uncertainty.
- *The value of flexibility depends on the magnitude of uncertainty.* A wider range of potential outcomes creates an opportunity for a very large gain or a very large loss, making future flexibility more valuable.
- *The timing of decision points is discretionary.* Wait until information is revealed, then decide. Growth opportunities seem hazy because they are hazy; there's a lot of "wait and see."

Two Types of Learning, Two Forms of Uncertainty

To further characterize growth opportunities, let's look at the decision to kill a project. (Isn't it ironic that one of the keys to managing growth opportunities is knowing when and how to close them down?)

Passive and Active Learning

Consider an older model of a personal digital assistant (PDA), such as those produced by Palm or Handspring. Unless the product sells a minimum number of units each quarter, it will be discontinued. The marketing manager has tried all sorts of promotions to extend product life and is now just waiting for the end. He sits back and watches sales volume, engaged in *passive learning* about the market. The abandonment decision will be triggered by low sales volume.

Now consider the introduction of a new PDA model. The marketing manager engages in a series of pricing, packaging, and advertising tests. Some tests fail. But unless money is spent, nothing is learned. The test budget and subsequent evaluation are called *active learning:* Investment dollars must be spent to resolve uncertainty. The abandonment decision could be triggered by learning that potential sales will be smaller than previously thought.

The terms *active learning* and *passive learning* were first used by MIT professor Robert Pindyck. A classic example is oil exploration: There's passive learning about oil prices and active learning about geology. While petroleum engineers can sit back and watch oil prices move, there's no way for them to learn more about the geological structure of a prospect unless they spend money. In the oil industry abandonment decisions depend on both types of learning. For example, low oil prices and/or poor geology can kill a project.

Images of Learning

Figure 2-3 matches the two types of learning to the two types of uncertainty. Part (a) shows active learning. The current estimate of the payoff value is surrounded by a rather wide range of uncertainty about the estimate.

For example, the estimate of the value of an oil reserve is uncertain because of the lack of data about the geological formation. The magnitude of uncertainty is reduced by an active learning investment. After each round of investment, a new estimate is made of the payoff value. But not all news is good. After active learning, the result might be a lower estimate of the payoff, more confidently given.

Figure 2-3   Two Types of Uncertainty about the Final Payoff

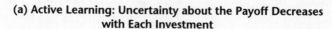

(a) Active Learning: Uncertainty about the Payoff Decreases with Each Investment

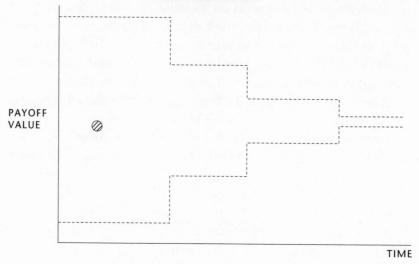

⊘ Current estimate of the payoff

(b) Passive Learning: Uncertainty about the Payoff Increases as the Forecast Horizon Lengthens

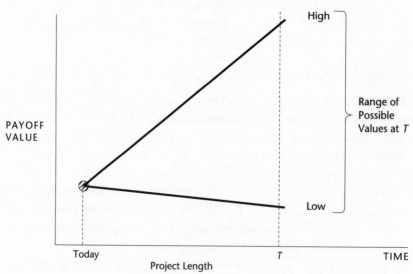

⊘ Current estimate of the payoff

Figure 2-3(b) shows passive learning. The two lines fanning out from the current estimate of the payoff value indicate that the longer the time horizon, the wider the range of possible payoff values. For example, the value of an oil reserve depends on oil prices and the reserve has a wider range of potential values ten years from now than one year from now. While the outcome is uncertain, the action plan for passive learning is simple: Just sit back and watch.

Is there really passive learning in growth opportunities? The answer is yes and no. When growth opportunities are technology-based, most of the time is spent thinking about the technical details, and the focus is on active learning. But often the value of a startup company, for example, depends on the value of mature public companies in the same industry. In this case the value of the startup growth opportunity depends on both active and passive learning.

In other cases, the payoff value is independent of stock market valuations. Think of a new sunscreen product from a large health-care products company. The payoff, after all scientific uncertainty has been resolved, depends on market acceptance. There will be test markets to learn about packaging, pricing, shelf display, and so on. All of these risks are private and project-specific. The financial markets see none of the specific uncertainties surrounding any single growth project, only the aggregate uncertainty about the company's entire portfolio of sunscreen products. The project-specific risk of the sunscreen product is not contained in the market-priced risk of the company.

In other industries, passive learning has a different form from that shown in Figure 2-3. Take the case of prescription drug development. In the final stages, the regulators issue a ruling about the wording of the product label. With a few more words on the label, the drug can be prescribed for a lot more people. The company experiences passive learning as it watches the regulators. The form of uncertainty is a one-time shift in the size of the potential market, not the smoothly growing range of uncertainty shown in Figure 2-3.

Market-Priced Risk: More Choices

Chapter 1 briefly introduced the concepts of market-priced risk and private risk. Active and passive learning can be connected with these concepts. The summary most often given by consultants and finance staff is:

- Active learning and some forms of passive learning are driven by private risk.

- Passive learning opportunities that depend on stock price movements are driven by market-priced risk.

A problem with this summary, however, is that it's a project-specific method to thinking about the structure of growth opportunities: "First let's create a long list of risks, then model each. We'll add market-priced risk at the end." The project-specific approach often goes astray, as the analyst overemphasizes private risk. An alternative is to start by searching for how market-priced risks influence payoff value.

Consider, for example, the wave of preprofit companies that went public after 1995. The result is that today a fair number of public companies are essentially startups: They are still cash-needy growth opportunities. And as we saw in Chapter 1, startups have a mixture of private and market-priced risk. But wait a minute—aren't these companies now public? That means that formerly private risks are now captured in their stock price. In public company startups, the entire bundle of private risk is now a single market-priced risk.

And knowledge of market-priced risk leads to more choices. For example, Enron was a pioneer in offering debt financing for oil and gas exploration.[4] As part of its loan package, an exploration company customer was required to put a contract in place that removed some of the oil and gas price risk. The deal was attractive because it made financing available when previously none could be had. Enron understood how to transfer the market-priced risk of oil and gas price fluctuations to others.

There are two approaches—market-oriented and project-specific—to identify risk in a valuation application. This book uses a market-oriented approach. First, look for ways to increase the visibility of how private risk affects the value of growth opportunities. Second, use the increased transparency to move private risk into market-priced risk through new securities, debt collateralized by growth opportunities, and insurance.

Takeaways

- Growth opportunities are often hazy images, and this prevents action. A new vocabulary and set of images that identify, define, and communicate the structural features of a growth opportunity can help to break the impasse.

- There are two types of learning. Passive learning has the flavor of "sit back and watch." Active learning requires investment to acquire information, such as doing a consumer survey to fine-tune a new product.

- Over time, more and more private risk is priced by financial instruments and insurance, opening the door to more transactions and choices about the financing of growth opportunities.

Part I

Expanding the Toolkit

T HIS SECTION introduces three tools useful for valuing growth opportunities. The approach here, with its emphasis on verbal reasoning, may be new to many managers. But when valuing and comparing diverse growth opportunities, there is a danger of losing the underlying business intuition. To build insight and to strengthen the quantitative results, this section:

- Introduces a vocabulary to articulate features of growth
- Highlights the logic of each valuation tool
- Displays calculations in easy-to-use valuation templates

Each of the tools introduced in this section—discounted cash flow, real options, and decision analysis—is the correct tool for valuing a certain type of growth opportunity. As the reference guide Figure I-1 shows, DCF best values opportunities without contingent decisions while real options and decision analysis best value opportunities with a larger amount of uncertainty and flexibility.

Figure I-1   Valuation Tools Matched to the Type of Growth Opportunity

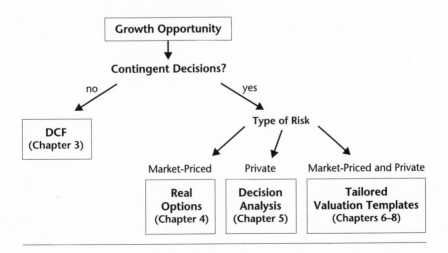

3

Discounted Cash Flow

Valuing Sustainable Growth

Think about restaurants, retail, and consulting. All are well-established industries with mature companies. New companies enter, but they use the same business models as the incumbents. This chapter is about valuing an established business using discounted cash flow (DCF). The purpose is to take a close look at the assumptions, and the misapplications, of this often used valuation tool. The IPO of KPMG provides an example of the challenges of using DCF in practice.

Why DCF?

This is a book about the world of growth opportunities—big ideas, big visions, big upside potential. So why is the first tool in the expanded, growth-focused toolkit discounted cash flow? For two reasons: DCF is the right tool for valuing certain types of growth, and DCF is needed to complement decision analysis and real options in other growth opportunities.

The DCF valuation method is based on three steps:

- Create a forecast of near-term cash flows
- Calculate a value of the business over the long term
- Convert the cash flows and the long-term value into their equivalent current value

The final result is also known as the net present value (NPV), and this is often used as the name of the method itself.

One goal of this chapter is to establish a high-level perspective of DCF. A few years ago I worked with a CEO who asked one of the business units to value itself in preparation for a spin-off. The CEO was trying to shake any false illusions held by the spin-off's management. In a stern voice he told them: "Show me a plan that makes sense. I can smell the numbers; I know when they're solid and when they're built on air." Let's acquire a similar impatience with quantitative flimsiness in a DCF calculation.

DCF Is a Strategy Road Map

The centerpiece of a DCF analysis is the projection of future cash inflows and outflows. What's often not recognized is that these form a strategy road map.

The investment plan is the result of an optimization; it is the best rollout (timing and amount) of investment, given the sales forecast. Sales and profit margins are uncertain, but the logic of the DCF model is that the investment expenditure plan is optimal within the range of expected outcomes. DCF does not include contingent decisions; its embedded strategy is "straight ahead."

This feature of DCF was tested in the spring of 2001, when a number of high-tech firms announced unexpectedly low revenues and lower earnings. But their most disconcerting news was "lack of visibility." The high-tech firms could not predict revenues and earnings for the following one or two quarters because of a confusing swirl of economic conditions. If these firms had more bad news, they would be obligated to announce it. What they were announcing was "we don't know."

How is the lack of visibility included in a DCF analysis? If the firms are committed to their previously announced investment plans, and their expectation is that these plans are still optimal given their current forecast, then DCF is the right valuation tool. But if "lack of visibility" implies a potential change in investment plans, now or in the future, then the DCF result will be wrong.[1]

DCF Calculations

Most readers are no doubt familiar with the mechanics of a DCF valuation, so this section is a quick review of the inputs and calculations shown in Table 3-1.[2] The top box lists all of the input data needed to complete a DCF valuation. The lower box, labeled "DCF Valuation Template," shows the calculations. The lower box is frozen, in that none of the formulas can be changed, but we can see what the formulas are. This is the template approach to valuation.[3] Resist the temptation to modify a template. Avoid the argument "my project is special." Templates provide opportunities to compare valuation logic and results across projects and to external benchmarks. These are lost when there is a mountain of opaque changes.

The Input Data

Let's briefly walk through the inputs needed to calculate free cash flow. Free cash flow is the cash available after all investments have been made to support the current business and the expected growth.

- *Sales in the previous year.* This anchors the sales forecast on the top row of the valuation template. The sales forecast is calculated as the previous year's sales times the sales growth rate.

- *Sales growth rate.* Often taken from historical performance at the industry or firm level, expected sales growth can also be inferred from stock price data.

- *Operating profit margin.* Another entry typically based on historical performance at the industry or firm level, this can also be expressed as a percentage of sales.

- *Cash tax rate.* The tax expense reported by a firm on its income statement is usually greater than the actual tax payment because of tax accounting procedures. The cash tax rate on operating profit is a better estimate.[4]

- *Fixed capital growth rate.* The key word in the name is *fixed*; fixed capital investment is irreversible (or reversible only

Table 3-1   A Sample DCF Valuation

($ millions unless noted. Totals may not add due to rounding.)

Inputs

Sales in previous year	$100	Fixed capital growth rate	10%
Sales growth rate	8%	Working capital growth rate	8%
Operating profit margin	22%	Cost of capital	10%
Cash tax rate	35%	Market value/Sales	1.5

DCF Valuation Template	2002	2003	2004	2005
CALCULATE FREE CASH FLOW				
Sales	$108	$117	$126	$136
Operating profit	$24	$26	$28	$30
less Cash taxes on operating profit	$8	$9	$10	$10
Net operating profit after tax (NOPAT)	$15	$17	$18	$19
less Fixed capital investment	$1	$1	$1	$1
less Working capital investment	$1	$1	$1	$1
Free cash flow	$14	$15	$16	$18
CALCULATE PRESENT VALUE OF FREE CASH FLOW				
Present value of free cash flow	$13	$12	$12	$12
Cumulative present value of free cash flow	$13	$25	$38	**$50**
CALCULATE THE TERMINAL VALUE				
Terminal value				$204
Present value of terminal value				**$127**
CALCULATE NET PRESENT VALUE				
Net present value				**$176**
Present value of terminal value/Net present value				72%

WRITE THE STORY

The path to sustainable growth is:	*"The plan is for business as usual."*
A pessimist would say:	*"The terminal value is the majority of the NPV. Can this business be sustained?"*

with large cost). One method for obtaining this input is to simply specify a growth rate, based on historical experience or analyst projections. Another method is to estimate the capital expenditures per dollar of sales increase from the firm's historical experience. For example, the first entry for fixed capital investment on Table 3-1 is calculated as: 10% × ($108 – $100).

- *Working capital growth rate.* As sales grow, so does the need for working capital. Again, there are two methods for obtaining this input. One is a simple projection of the growth rate; the other is a calculation of the change in working capital required per change in sales.

With the data in hand, free cash flow is calculated as operating profits less investments in fixed and working capital. Operating profits are often labeled net operating profits after tax, or NOPAT. The two additional inputs shown in Table 3-1, the cost of capital and the market-value-to-sales ratio, are discussed in the next section of this chapter.

The Value of Near-Term Growth

The second step is to calculate the present value of the stream of free cash flow, using the cost of capital as the discount rate. The cost of capital is the rate of return required by investors as compensation for the risk of investing in the company or project. The example shown in Table 3-1 has no debt financing, so in this case the cost of capital is the return to equity. Historically, equity returns have been 8 percent higher than the risk-free rate of return for U.S. government securities. The book *Expectations Investing,* by Michael Mauboussin and Al Rappaport, provides data by industry on the weighted-average cost of capital, which includes the after-tax return to debt. A 10 percent cost of capital is assumed in Table 3-1.

The cumulative present value of free cash flow shown in the middle of Table 3-1 increases from left to right. The entry in the final column is the cumulative present value for the near-term forecast period. This convention—the opposite of most corporate finance texts—is helpful when comparing the value of growth expectations in the DCF with the stock price, and when setting a target stock price, as done by equity analysts.

The Value of Long-Term Growth

The next step is to calculate the terminal value, or long-term growth component. There are two common ways to do so: the growing annuity method and the market-based multiple method. Under the growing annuity method, a long-term growth rate is set. It is applied to the last period's free cash flow. Typically, the long-term growth rate does not include returns to investors above the cost of capital, under the important assumption that the firm does not grow value in the long term.

This book uses the market-multiple approach for the terminal value to better align DCF valuations with current financial market pricing. In theory, the growing annuity method and the market-based multiple method give the same answer, but in practice they produce different results. The market-based multiple approach requires an additional input, the market-value-to-sales ratio, which is an industry average calculated from firm-level ratio data. (The market value includes the value of long-term debt.) Tables A-7 and A-8 in the Appendix provide data on the ratio by industry. The market-value-to-sales ratio is multiplied by the final year's sales to obtain an estimate of the terminal value.

The Logic behind the Market-Value-to-Sales Ratio

Using the market-value-to-sales ratio makes sense if the firms selected for inclusion in the industry average have achieved sustainable growth. For example, the biotech industry is crowded with public companies, but only a handful are self-funding.[5] Consequently, a biotech market-value-to-sales ratio must be carefully constructed.

Similarly, the market-value-to-sales ratio was widely used to value publicly traded Internet companies, and the apparent overvaluation of the dot-coms has tainted the ratio's image. But use of a market-based multiple aligns the DCF valuation result with current financial market pricing. While growth opportunities may be years away from maturity, the best estimate of the future payoff is today's market value of the same mature business model. For many Internet companies, no one knew how profits would be made, and thus the use of the market-multiple approach wasn't logically supported.

The last rows of Table 3-1 show the valuation results. The NPV is the sum of the near-term and long-term sustainable-growth components.

The Logic behind the Terminal Value

Look at the last number in Table 3-1, the percent of the NPV that comes from the terminal value. The 72 percent result is not unusually high. When DCF is used for mature businesses, the terminal value typically contributes 50 percent to 80 percent of the total value. Consequently, most of the value of a sustainable-growth business comes from the long-term component—the component we are least able to characterize.

Hence, there is a need to rigorously review the logic behind the terminal value. In practice, if the terminal value is more than 90 percent of total value, consider extending the forecast horizon. After all, if you don't know enough about the business or project to detail at least 10 percent of its value, should you be spending the investment dollars?

One rationale for sizing the terminal value is given in *Living on the Fault Line* by Geoffrey Moore, who was mentioned in Chapter 1. Moore's explanation is based on a product life cycle. Some years after its introduction, the rate of free cash flow growth from a new product slows and then declines. During the slowdown, there is a point at which the rate of cash flow growth slips below the return required by investors (the cost of capital). At this point, the present value added by an incremental year of sales is less than the year before. The rate of cash flow growth continues to fall, and eventually an additional year of product life adds no value.

In *Expectations Investing*, Mauboussin and Rappaport argue that in the long run, a company that earns more than its cost of capital will attract competition, ultimately driving down company returns. A correctly estimated terminal value, they argue, does not suggest that the company won't grow, only that it doesn't create superior shareholder returns. Empirical support for this contention is found in the book *From Good to Great,* in which the author conducted a detailed review of more than 1,400 companies and found only eleven that delivered a decade of superior shareholder returns.[6]

There's another argument for the lack of superior returns in the terminal value. If the stock market fully capitalizes available information, including the possibility for superior returns, one would expect to earn only the required return going forward. Thus the market-value-to-sales ratio method for calculating terminal value also suggests that the company grows in value, but without superior returns.

The Submarine Problem

DCF is a workhorse valuation tool, one that is used in many companies. Unfortunately, DCF fails to reliably value fast-growing business opportunities. There are two reasons: the submarine problem and omission of contingent decisions. Table 3-2 illustrates the submarine problem.

Look at the table's pattern of free cash flow. The first two years are negative. There's no way to calculate a positive terminal value from this poor near-term performance. Then like a submarine emerging out of the sea, free cash flow goes positive in the final year. The positive cash flow is needed to calculate the terminal value, and the terminal value is more than 100 percent of the NPV result. The entire valuation results rests on a single number, the existence of positive cash flow in the final year.

Is this year really indicative of long-term, sustainable growth? No, the cash flow results are precarious. A small change in assumptions dramatically changes the final year's cash flow, estimate of terminal value, and thus NPV. For example, underlying a smooth sales growth trajectory might be assumptions about the rate of market penetration for a new product. Perhaps these are based on the optimism of the project analyst. But new product sales growth is always a tricky business, and it may be difficult to achieve the breakthrough implicit in the sales forecast. Managers will be tactically responding and reacting to new sales information, possibly

Table 3-2   An Illustration of the Submarine Problem

($ millions unless noted. Totals may not add due to rounding.)

Inputs

Sales in previous year	$25	Fixed capital investment	$1.2
Sales growth rate	25%	Working capital growth rate	8%
Operating profit margin	6%	Cost of capital	10%
Cash tax rate	35%	Market value/Sales	1.5

DCF Valuation Template	2002	2003	2004	2005
CALCULATE FREE CASH FLOW				
Sales	$31.3	$39.1	$48.8	$61.0
Operating profit	$1.9	$2.3	$2.9	$3.7
less Cash taxes on operating profit	$0.7	$0.8	$1.0	$1.3
Net operating profit after tax (NOPAT)	$1.2	$1.5	$1.9	$2.4
less Fixed capital investment	$1.2	$1.2	$1.2	$1.2
less Working capital investment	$0.5	$0.6	$0.8	$1.0
Free cash flow	−$0.4	−$0.3	$0.0	$0.3
CALCULATE PRESENT VALUE OF FREE CASH FLOW				
Present value of free cash flow	−$0.4	−$0.2	$0.0	$0.2
Cumulative present value of free cash flow	−$0.4	−$0.6	−$0.6	−$0.4
CALCULATE THE TERMINAL VALUE				
Terminal value				$91.6
Present value of terminal value				**$56.8**
CALCULATE NET PRESENT VALUE				
Net present value				**$56.4**
Present value of terminal value/Net present value				101%

WRITE THE STORY

The path to sustainable growth is:	*"The project shows how it will make money in 2005. Thereafter we can expect good profits."*
A pessimist would say:	*"The entire project value rests on a small positive cash flow in 2005. This is simply not credible."*

modifying the new product investment plans. Doesn't this sound like a cash-needy growth opportunity?

DCF is the right valuation model for "business as usual." But, because of the submarine problem, it is the wrong valuation model for business opportunities based on risky fast growth. The results are quantitatively unstable. The valuation model ignores the flexibility that managers have in responding to unfolding events. The next two chapters present tools that directly address these issues.

The submarine problem also presents a serious credibility issue for the finance staff in large companies. Once or twice a year there will be an important meeting to allocate funds for new growth initiatives. The finance staff arrives with its best DCF analyses. Company executives may look at the results and sense that one push on assumptions will entirely change the results. Strategic arguments, based on concepts divorced from value creation, suddenly are stronger than any number. The choice between a logical argument and a flimsy number is clear. So, a message to the finance staff: Expand your toolkit, expand your credibility.

The Value of a Consulting Firm

In one of the largest IPOs of the year, KPMG, the consulting firm, went public in February 2001. What is a reasonable valuation of the company at the time of the IPO? How does this valuation compare with the value of other publicly traded consulting firms?

Consulting firms have a simple business model, so their valuation is quite straightforward, and the logic behind each component is unusually transparent. The industry economics also test and stretch the assumptions behind a DCF valuation in a way that is typical of many real-world applications.

Consulting firms sell the time of their employees. Growth comes from adding employees or, if employees are not fully used, selling more of their time. A nice feature of the consulting business is that capacity can be added in small increments, one employee at a time. Similarly, firms can scale back in small increments. While it is painful and costly to lose an experienced consultant, scaling down doesn't come in large lumps. The scale of a consulting firm can track market demand. In addition, the firm has virtually no fixed capital.

KPMG's revenues in 2000 were $2.7 billion, with an operating margin of 14.5 percent. The firm's revenues had grown by 27 percent in 2000 after being flat for several years. Because of the extremely weak market for consulting services in 2001, the firm expected a decrease in revenues. Table 3-3 shows a DCF valuation of KPMG at the time of its IPO. A month after its IPO, KPMG traded at about one times revenues; the DCF valuation model result was about 25 percent higher than the market value of the firm at that time.

Only a year earlier, the valuation story for consulting firms looked very different. A number of technology consulting firms including Viant, Sapient, Scient Corporation, iXL, Razorfish, and Appnet grabbed the headlines in 2000 as their market-value-to-sales ratios hit highs near 14. By mid-2001, however, their market-value-to-sales ratios had fallen to near one. How can the previous high multiples be explained? Would KPMG's stock price be expected to significantly rise from its level at the IPO?

To answer these questions, let's look at the business landscape in early 2000. All of the technology consulting firms were essentially sold out, turning away business because their employees were fully booked. The constraint on growth appeared to be how quickly each firm could attract and train employees. Viant, for example, had more than ten full-time recruiters. Other firms attempted to grow through acquisition. A consulting firm grows value by acquisition if the amount paid for the acquired firm is less than its value. This outcome is the result of either excellent negotiation (But these are all smart people, so it may be hard to gain advantage) or by operating synergy (But it's just adding bodies! How much synergy is possible?).

The terminal value of KPMG can be calculated assuming a market-value-to-sales ratio of 1.2 or by assuming a 7.5 percent annual growth rate on free cash flow *forever*.[7] At first glance, this may not seem unreasonable, but forever is a long time. The large terminal value raises the hard question about consulting firms: What makes a consulting firm's growth sustainable? What prevents early retirement by consultants? How much business can be passed on from one consultant to another? It is telling that in private market transactions, consulting firms are usually acquired for values of 1.5 to 3 times sales, with contracts that keep the acquired consultants on board and fully active for some number of years. A

Table 3-3   A DCF Valuation of KPMG at Its IPO, March 2001

($ millions unless noted. Totals may not add due to rounding.)

Inputs

Sales in previous year (adjusted)	$2,000	Fixed capital growth rate	0%
Sales growth rate	18%	Working capital growth rate	0%
Operating profit margin	14%	Cost of capital	15%
Cash tax rate	35%	Market value/Sales	1.2

DCF Valuation Template	2001	2002	2003
CALCULATE FREE CASH FLOW			
Sales	$2,360	$2,785	$3,286
Operating profit	$330	$390	$460
less Cash taxes on operating profit	$116	$136	$161
Net operating profit after tax (NOPAT)	$215	$253	$299
less Fixed capital investment	–	–	–
less Working capital investment	–	–	–
Free cash flow	$215	$253	$299
CALCULATE PRESENT VALUE OF FREE CASH FLOW			
Present value of free cash flow	$187	$192	$197
Cumulative present value of free cash flow	$187	$378	**$575**
CALCULATE TERMINAL VALUE			
Terminal value			$3,943
Present value of terminal value			**$2,255**
CALCULATE NET PRESENT VALUE			
Net present value			**$2,830**
Present value of terminal value/Net present value			80%

WRITE THE STORY

The path to sustainable growth is:	*"Consulting firms have few fixed costs and can easily adjust head count. The terminal value captures the beauty of our business model."*
A pessimist would say:	*"There is no transferable and enduring value to a consultant's business relationships; all the business disappears after the consultant leaves. The terminal value lacks a logical foundation."*

high-growth terminal value does not fit the relationship-based, human capital model of consulting.

Some might argue that the high terminal value includes some valuable real options. But as will be more clear after the next two chapters, options have a feature that consulting firms lack: the potential of a big bang for the buck. What drives option value is the chance that a future investment will pay off at 100 to 1. This happens with technology companies—think of Cisco's explosive growth from its routers. But there is no place to make this kind of bet in a consulting firm; consulting firms lack the economics to support an option premium.

In sum, a DCF valuation model fits the consulting business rather well. Consulting lacks the place to achieve a huge return from a small investment. (That's one reason why so many consulting firms have established venture capital and investment vehicles.) Finally, the assets within a consulting firm that might support a strong terminal value are fairly tenuous, so expect only a modest market-value-to-sales multiple in this industry.

Takeaways

- DCF is based on a strategy road map and is exactly the right valuation tool when planned investments are not expected to change, even if there is a bit of uncertainty.

- Terminal values often lack a strong logic, yet they contribute most of the NPV value. By definition, this is the part of the valuation story that is most unclear. A reasonable approach is to grow cash flows in the terminal value at just the rate needed to provide shareholders a competitive rate of return.

- Often DCF is misused when valuing growth opportunities because either the valuation results heavily depend on a single number—the final year's cash flow—or the analysis omits the contingent decisions common to risky, fast-growing business opportunities. The next two chapters introduce more credible valuation methods.

4

Real Options

Valuing Expansion Opportunities

Real options has attracted much interest in recent years, particularly from corporations interested in using the real options approach to identify and articulate growth opportunities. This chapter shows how the tool can be used to quantify the value of upside potential. The calculations are made easy by the use of option value lookup tables. The chapter also identifies when and where the real options tool fails to correctly value growth. An example based on Amazon.com demonstrates how to logically bound the size of an expansion option.

Recent interest in the real options approach to valuation has been sparked by the desire to logically value public Internet companies. The search for an explanation of their high value became a search for a new valuation perspective. Arriving on the scene at the same time were a slew of books and articles introducing the real options approach to managers.[1] The match was only somewhat fruitful.

Two problems surfaced:

- *Real options could not explain the difference between an Internet company's market value and its DCF value.* The Amazon.com example later in this chapter demonstrates the issues.

This chapter has benefited from collaboration with Michael Mauboussin and Al Rappaport. It contains some of the same material as Chapter 8 of their book, *Expectations Investing* (Boston: Harvard Business School Press, 2001).

- *Most growth opportunities contain private risk, but real options captures only market-priced risk.* In practice, real options analysts have tried to thoughtfully extend real options to include private risk. But this has been done in an ad hoc manner, making it difficult for others to understand the extensions and use the results.

So why a chapter on real options? First, some cash-needy growth opportunities, such as expansion options, do fit the model's assumptions. (See Figure I-1 preceding Chapter 3 for a reference regarding the key assumptions.) This chapter shows when and how the real options approach will work to value these assets. Second, many growth opportunities have a mixture of market-priced and private risk. Real options is used to address the market-priced risk in the tailored valuation templates presented in Chapters 6 to 8.

The Origins of Real Options

Real options grew out of the method to value financial option contracts. In 1973, when the breakthrough option pricing research was published, the options markets were thinly traded, in part because the traders lacked a clear valuation model.

What was so difficult? The option had an uncertain payoff that depended in some way on the stock price. But how? The answer won Robert Merton and Myron Scholes the 1997 Nobel Prize in Economics (Fisher Black, who also originated the theory, died in 1995). The exact mathematical relationship of how the value of an option contract depends on the price of the stock was captured in one formula, the Black-Scholes equation. The solution required only five inputs, four of which can be directly observed.

The transparency of logic and the simplicity of the inputs led to an explosion in the volume of traded option contracts and to the practice of financial engineering—use of the same logic to design innovative securities. Since it was developed, the Black-Scholes equation has proven to be a robust pricing model, and it is used widely.[2]

From the start, many recognized that corporate growth opportunities had the flavor of financial options. MIT professor Stewart

Myers first used the phrase *real options* in a 1984 paper to highlight corporate growth opportunities.[3] Early applications were in the oil industry, as there was a clear market-priced risk: oil prices. Since then, the real options literature has grown enormously, including applications to pollution trading allowances, technology R&D strategy, and personal finance. The Black-Scholes value of an employee stock option is now presented in many corporate filings.[4]

This book focuses on a subset of real options applications, growth opportunities, and relies on easy-to-use option pricing tools. This chapter narrows the focus further, to that of expansion options driven by market-priced risk.

The Analogy

The analogy to a financial option is the starting point for real options. This section focuses on two essential aspects of the analogy: the contingent decision and the option inputs.

The Contingent Decision

Figure 4-1 shows the typical profile of an expansion option. One type of real option, an expansion option is defined as an opportunity to expand an established line of business. The value of the expansion option (V) is shown on the left and is the output of the real options analysis. Two inputs are shown on the right: the potential investment (X) and the payoff (S). Once the investment is made, the payoff S is gained immediately, just as one would immediately acquire the stock by exercising a financial option. At time T, management decides to invest or not. If S is greater than X in T years, then the expansion investment will be made. If S is less than X in T years, then the option simply expires unused.

In Figure 4-1 S is less than X, yet V is positive. How can the option be valuable? The answer is uncertainty. Think of an option to buy a highly volatile biotech stock. S is the stock price, and X is the prespecified purchase price at time T. Today S is far less than X, but in T years, S could be significantly greater than X. The value of the option, V, captures this upside potential. Because there is some

Figure 4-1   A Typical Expansion Option

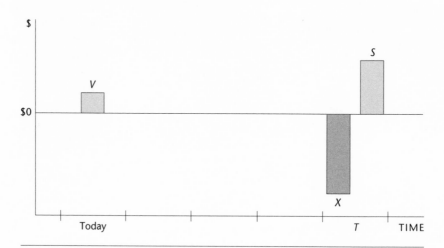

chance of a good outcome, *V* has value today. The arguments also apply to expansion options.

The magnitude of fluctuations in *S* each year is measured by σ, the volatility of the payoff value. (For a stock option σ is the volatility of the stock price.) A large value of σ indicates wider potential fluctuations of *S*. *V* can be thought of as the sum of the value of hundreds of possible outcomes for *S*: the gain from exercise at each outcome, *S* minus *X*, times the probability of that outcome.[5] When *S* minus *X* is less than zero, the outcome adds nothing to *V* as the option is left unexercised.

With both financial options and real options, the exercise decision is based on passive learning. Simply hold the financial option contract and check the stock price at time *T*. Similarly, create the expansion opportunity and check the value of its payoff at time *T*. Most problems with real options analyses arise from not recognizing that the analogy encompasses only passive learning; analysts often describe the investment decision trigger in terms of active learning. Note also that the expansion investment can be made any time before *T*, but mathematically it is straightforward to show that the value of waiting is greater than the value of early investment.

The Option Inputs

There are five inputs into the Black-Scholes equation.[6] The analogy between the financial option inputs and the expansion option counterparts is as follows:

- *Value of the payoff (S)*. The payoff in a financial option is the stock price. In an expansion option, the payoff is the value of the increased scale of the current business. The payoff value can be calculated by using valuation data on mature companies in the same industry (the market-value-to-sales ratio times projected sales) or by using a DCF analysis of the present value of free cash flows from an expansion. In a financial option, the payoff value is measured by the current stock price, so by analogy, the real option payoff is in current period dollars.

- *Cost to exercise the option (X)*. In a financial option, this is the purchase price of the stock specified in the contract. In an expansion option, this is the one-time investment in fixed and working capital required for expansion. X is in terms of dollars at time T.

- *The magnitude of uncertainty about the value of the payoff (σ)*. Volatility, or σ, measures the range of potential outcomes of S. For a traded option contract to buy a stock, the volatility of S is measured as the standard deviation of the stock's returns. Most often it is estimated from historical stock price data or by reverse-engineering the market price of a traded option contract to obtain the level of volatility consistent with the observed option price.[7]

  For an expansion option, the payoff is uncertain because of fluctuations in the market value of the established business. The volatility input for the expansion option is thus the volatility of the market value of the firm. For a firm with no debt, market value volatility is simply stock price volatility. For a firm with debt, the market value volatility is a blend of volatility from debt and equity. Debt is less volatile than equity, so market value volatility is lower than stock price volatility. Figure A-1 and Table A-6 in the Appendix show how to obtain market value volatility from stock price volatility. The tables also provide market value volatility data by industry.

- *The life of the option* (T). In a financial option, the time to expiration is stated in the option contract. In an expansion option, this input is the length of time that a company can defer the investment decision without losing the expansion opportunity.

- *The risk-free rate of return* (r). In a financial option, this input is a short-term U.S. Treasury bond rate.[8] A similar rate should be used in the expansion option valuation. One of the important features of the financial option pricing solution by Black, Merton, and Scholes is that no cost of capital calculation is required. Unfortunately, a real options valuation often requires two discount rates. While the real option valuation itself uses only the risk-free rate, frequently one input, S, must be calculated using DCF and the weighted-average cost of capital.

Valuing Expansion Options

This section shows how to value an expansion option using two calculation methods: direct application of the Black-Scholes equation and use of precalculated option value lookup tables.

Consider a company that *might* expand its distribution system in two years *if* volume continues to grow; the company has an expansion option. The company might spend $40 million to build a new distribution center ($X = \$40$), and the current estimate of the payoff to expansion is $30 million ($S = \$30$). The investment is to be made in two years ($T = 2$). The industry average market value volatility of a mature firm in the same line of business is 50 percent per year ($\sigma = 50\%$). The short-term risk-free rate of return is 5 percent per year ($r = 5\%$). Using the Black-Scholes formula, the value of the expansion option is calculated to be $6.4 million. (The formula can be found in many finance textbooks and is also posted at www.valuesweep.com.)

Table 4-1   Option Value Lookup Table

(Option values are reported as a percent of the payoff, S)

(a) Two-Year Option Life ($T=2$)

		S/X		
		0.75	1.00	1.25
Volatility (σ)	50%	21%	31%	40%
(% per year)	75%	35%	43%	50%
	100%	48%	54%	60%

(b) Three-Year Option Life ($T=3$)

		S/X		
		0.75	1.00	1.25
Volatility (σ)	50%	29%	39%	46%
(% per year)	75%	45%	52%	58%
	100%	59%	64%	68%

Corporate experience shows that direct use of the Black-Scholes equation can be problematic. First, the required math (partial differential equations) is more complex than the math required in everyday business life. Second, the equation alone provides no context or intuition about what drives option values. Precalculated lookup tables that report option values for a range of inputs, such as the one shown in Table 4-1, address these problems.

The Option Value Lookup Table

An option value lookup table precalculates the option value results. Table 4-1 is typical. The five option inputs have been reduced to two dimensions and the Black-Scholes formula has been used to obtain the results.[9] Part (a) of Table 4-1 shows the value of a two-year growth option, and part (b) shows the value of a three-year growth option. Larger option value lookup tables can be found in the Appendix.

Let's work with part (a) for a moment, which assumes T equals 2 and r equals 5 percent. The rows of the table vary by σ. For the distribution center expansion option, σ is 50 percent. The columns of the table vary by the ratio S/X. S/X is a measure of "the bang for the buck," the current value of the payoff divided by the future investment cost.[10] When S/X is below one, the investment would not be undertaken if an immediate decision had to be made. But if the decision can be delayed, the value of S/X increases because there's still time for S to evolve. For the distribution center option, S/X equals 0.75 ($30 / $40).

Table 4-1 reports the option value as a percentage of the payoff value. For example, if S is $100 and the option value factor is 95 percent, then the option value is $95. The cells of the table were populated by repeated use of the Black-Scholes formula. For the distribution center example, part (a) shows the expansion option value is 21 percent of S, or $6.4 million.

Drivers of Option Value

Option value lookup tables can be very helpful as they quickly provide intuition about the drivers of option value. A quick scan of Table 4-1 shows:

- *Option values are less than the payoff value.* An option is not a sure thing. There is usually some chance that the option will not be used, and thus its value is less than the payoff. As the S/X ratio increases to very high levels, the option value approaches 100 percent of the payoff value. Often strategists who are experiencing "options fever" fail to recognize this fact and argue strenuously for making a negative NPV investment because of its "strategic option value." Lookup tables quickly show the cap on option value.

- *Higher σ increases option value.* Looking down the rows, higher volatility causes higher option value. Volatility is an intrinsic feature of the business model, so moving down the rows is akin to moving across industries. Low values for σ are from regulated utilities and pharmaceutical companies (25 percent to 35 percent per year), while the high values are from Internet and biotech companies (80 percent to 125 percent per year).

- *Increasing T increases option value.* Suppose the distribution center expansion option had a three-year length. Moving from part (a) of Table 4-1 ($T = 2$ years) to part (b) ($T = 3$ years) shows that the option value increases from 21 to 29 percent of S. The option values in part (b) are greater because some very large payoffs are possible at the end of three years that could not be realized at the end of two years. (Figure 2-3[b] shows the same feature; notice how the potential range of outcomes for S increases with the length of time it has to evolve.)

- *Options have value even when it is unlikely they will be exercised.* For example, under the column $S/X = 0.75$ in Table 4-1, option values range from 2 percent to 59 percent of S. Particularly in low volatility industries, there is little chance that S might rise, but because it might happen, the option has value.

- *A bigger "bang for the buck" increases option value.* S/X represents the return to immediately exercising the option. In the financial markets, an option with S/X less than 1 is known as an "out-of-the-money" option. When S/X is greater than 1, the option is known as an "in-the-money" option. Finally, an "at-the-money" option has an S/X ratio equal to 1. Moving from left to right across Table 4-1, the value increases from out-of-the-money to in-the-money options.

Expansion Options at Amazon.com

Amazon.com has been the bellwether Internet stock for the past five years, as news about Amazon's revenues and working capital have moved stock prices across the Internet sector. This section values Amazon's expansion option in two ways. First, the size of the possible expansion option is inferred from the market value of the company. Second, the size of the option is inferred from Amazon's available cash, the maximum size of the expansion investment. Both approaches produce the same result: Amazon's market value in February 2000 and February 2001 was greater than can be explained by adding the value of an expansion option to the firm's DCF value.

In a thought-provoking article in the *Wall Street Journal* in February 2000, Al Rappaport divided the value of Amazon into two components: a DCF value calculated using analysts' forecasts of revenue growth and profit margin, and an inferred real option component, calculated as the difference between the market value of Amazon and its DCF value.[11] Rappaport argues that the DCF result captures the performance of Amazon's established businesses, such as books, CDs, and videos. The real option component captures value over and above the DCF result in three directions: higher sales growth and profits in the current business beyond that included in the DCF; new product offerings; and exploitation of Amazon's online leadership position in unanticipated ways.

Amazon's DCF Value

Because the expansion option component is the value of growth beyond the DCF, a closer look at the DCF is required to articulate or frame the expansion option. In February 2000, industry analysts and Amazon expected the firm's revenues to grow by 40 percent per year for the next five years and operating profits to rise to 5 percent of sales within three years.[12] By February 2001, the consensus sales growth rate had fallen to 15 percent per year, but given Amazon's focus on profitability, operating profits were expected within one year. Rappaport extended forecasts as of 2000 out to ten years, and the same is done in this chapter for forecasts as of 2001. The long near-term period most likely leads to an overestimate of DCF value, but this only strengthens the conclusions below.

The DCF analysis calls for investments of $200 million to $300 million each year for the next ten years. The funds for this investment come from the fact that Amazon is paid by customers before it pays its suppliers, and so it generates new working capital reserves as sales grow. Consequently, the DCF reflects self-funded growth.

The market value of Amazon and the DCF results are shown in Table 4-2(a).[13] The DCF value of Amazon's current business was 60 percent of the market value of the firm, and the remaining 40 percent of market value could possibly be attributed to Amazon's expansion option.

Table 4-2   The Expansion Option at Amazon.com

($ millions unless noted)

(a) Infer the Expansion from Amazon's Market Value

	February 2000	February 2001
CALCULATE MARKET VALUE OF FIRM		
Market value of common stock	$21,942	$5,343
Value of outstanding employee stock options	$6,185	$518
Book value of debt	$1,462	$643
Total market value	**$29,589**	**$6,504**
CALCULATE THE TWO COMPONENTS OF VALUE		
DCF value of current business	**$18,351**	**$3,910**
DCF value / Market value	62%	60%
Implied value of expansion option	**$11,238**	**$2,594**
DCF value / Market value	38%	40%

CALCULATE THE IMPLIED OPTION INPUTS

Input values: $S/X = 0.75$; $T = 2$;
$\sigma = 100\%$; $r = 5\%$ *(by assumption)*

	February 2000	February 2001
Option value as a percent of payoff value *(from lookup table)*	48%	48%
Implied payoff value (S)	$23,413	$5,405
Implied expansion investment (X)	$31,217	$7,206

WRITE THE STORY

The path to sustainable growth is:	*"In the past Amazon has demonstrated its ability to identify and execute on its expansion options. While from the outside we don't see the particulars, we're betting that the team can create the value shown here."*
A pessimist would say:	*"The size of the option payoff and the size of the required investment to achieve the payoff are far larger than Amazon or any firm in the retail industry has ever done. This is all a dream."*

(continued)

Table 4-2 *(continued)*

(b) Infer the Value of the Expansion Option from Amazon's Available Cash (February 2001)

ASSEMBLE THE DATA

	0.50	0.75	1.00	1.25	1.50	2.00
S/X (by assumption)						
X (available cash)	$400	$400	$400	$400	$400	$400
Implied payoff value (*S*) *(from S/X ratio)*	$200	$300	$400	$500	$600	$800
Remaining option input values: σ = 100%; *T* = 2; *r* = 5% *(by assumption)*						

CALCULATE OPTION VALUE

	0.50	0.75	1.00	1.25	1.50	2.00
Option value as a percent of payoff value *(from lookup table)*	38%	48%	54%	60%	64%	70%
Expansion option value	$76	$143	$218	$298	$382	$558
Expansion option value/Market value	1%	2%	3%	5%	6%	9%
Expansion option value/DCF value	2%	4%	6%	8%	10%	14%

WRITE THE STORY

The path to sustainable growth is:	*"Amazon has captive resources and opportunities that go beyond a simple option analysis. This company gets to see all the best deals. I'm willing to pay for that market leader position—even if it can't be quantified by a DCF or option valuation."*
A pessimist would say:	*"When the expansion option is sized to the available resources, it is simply too small to support Amazon's high market value. This company is overvalued."*

The Implied Expansion Option

If so much of Amazon's value came from an expansion option, what would the option look like? Table 4-2(a) shows the calculations for option inputs implied by the size of the expansion option value. The results for the input values are obtained by reverse-engineering an options calculation. To start, the known inputs are collected: the option value (for example, $11.2 billion in February 2000); *T* (two years); and *r* (5 percent). An assumption is that the expansion option is slightly out-of-the-money (or else it would have been started already). An initial input of 0.75 is used.

The final input required is the volatility of the payoff value. The volatility used is that of Amazon itself, 100 percent per year. This is appropriate if the expansion option simply increases Amazon's scale. (As the current market value and market value volatility include an expansion option, the precise assumption is that Amazon expands the scale of its current and future business.)

Using the option value lookup tables, the option value is found to be 48 percent of the payoff value. S can now be calculated. In February 2000, S was \$23.4 billion (\$11.2 / 0.48) and X was \$31.2 billion. In 2001, the implied values of S and X were \$5.4 billion and \$7.2 billion, respectively.

What is the business opportunity that Amazon could capture that would warrant these payoffs? Where would the firm get the money? Even at Amazon's lofty market value, it seems impossible to fund a \$15 billion or a \$7 billion investment. How would it be executed? The numbers alone don't support the existence and execution of an expansion option.

Direct Calculation of the Expansion Option Value

Another way to study Amazon's expansion option is by direct calculation. In 1999, Amazon had cash balances of \$700 million, and a reasonable assumption is that some portion of these funds could be used for an expansion investment. Let's begin with the arbitrary assumption that \$400 million is used.

Now go back to the S/X ratio. Because Amazon may not have had unique sustainable opportunities in the fast-moving Internet world, extremely high values for this ratio are questionable. A reasonable assumption is that S/X ranges from 0.50 to 2.00. With X equal to \$400 million, the range of the ratio implies that the current value of the of S ranges from \$200 million to \$800 million.

With all inputs in hand, the option value is calculated using the lookup tables in the Appendix. Table 4-2(b) shows that the expansion option value had a rather wide range, \$76 million to \$558 million in February 2001. But even the highest valued expansion option accounted for less than 10 percent of Amazon's market value. The calculations are easily repeated for an expansion investment of \$600 million and reach the same conclusions.

The Size of the Real Options Component

By February 2001, Amazon's market value had dropped to 20 percent of what it was a year earlier. The DCF value had fallen by nearly the same amount. The implied expansion option value remained about 40 percent of the market value. In 2000 and 2001, the implied values of S and X remain far out of line with the historical experience of Amazon and with the book- and CD-selling industries.

What's going on? The two snapshots of Amazon's value show that as the financial community learned more about the challenges of growing the current business, they valued it less. They also reduced the value of the expansion option component, but they didn't erase it.

Yet this analysis of Amazon suggests a problem: DCF value plus expansion option cannot explain Amazon's market value, even after a huge stock price fall. This is often the case as financial analysts tend to be overconfident of their ability to explain market values with valuation tools. As the financial markets better learn how to value companies whose main asset is growth options, the gap between model results and market value will close.

Framing the Expansion Option

The Amazon.com example demonstrates the option calculations in action, but it doesn't fully illuminate some of the issues surrounding the framing and interpretation of expansion options. Framing is the act of setting up the application, of drawing out the analogy between the expansion option and the financial option. This final section walks through a series of quick examples to illustrate the issues.

- *The value of the payoff at Yahoo!.* During the turmoil of 2000 and 2001, Yahoo! significantly revised expectations. Its advertising-based business model was not working in the downturn of 2001, and a new business model was not yet in sight. Yahoo!'s stock price fell more quickly and more deeply than did Amazon's, because without a clear business model, Yahoo! lost both its DCF value and the payoff to any expansion options.

- *The blended volatility at Omni Media.* Omni Media (Martha Stewart's company) wants to be a mature, nationwide content company. The firm creates content for Internet, print, and television. What determines the volatility of the payoff to an expansion option for Omni Media? A mix of Internet, content, and traditional publishing business models. The appropriate volatility captures the mix of risks from the online and offline worlds. Using volatility estimates from traditional publishing may omit the Internet components. Conversely, using volatility estimates from Internet-only companies neglects that a mature business will have relatively low volatility. Judgment, and a sensitivity analysis, will be required.

- *The option trigger in cable companies.* In April 1999 Laura Martin, cable and media equity analyst at Credit Suisse First Boston, issued a report using real options to value the assets of cable companies.[14] At the time, cable companies across the United States were upgrading the connection to customers' homes to a 750 MHz capacity. Only 650 MHz had identified uses, and the remainder was "dark fiber." Using a DCF model, Martin valued the projected free cash flow of the cable companies she covered. After adjusting for debt, the DCF estimate of stock price equaled the trading price.

  In a pioneering analysis, she went on to value the dark fiber as an expansion option: When the right deal came along, the cable companies would open up another channel. The expansion option simply increased the business-as-usual possibilities. The driver of the exercise decision is the arrival of an attractive deal for the channel, which is largely unrelated to the value of the payoff. The real options analogy is only an approximation.

  But when Martin's report was released, cable company stock prices increased 10 percent to 15 percent, and market values of cable companies exceeded DCF values for the remainder of 1999. As this example shows, while the analogy was not airtight, the equity report made the expansion option visible, and its value was capitalized into cable company value thereafter.

- *The value decay in online pet stores.* In 1999 venture capitalists funded six very similar companies with hundreds of millions of dollars, each racing for market share in the online pet store market.[15] The pet companies felt the pressure—it seemed that with each passing month, potential market share slipped away to competitors. Viewed from an options angle, the payoff value was decaying.

  It is straightforward to quantify the effect of value decay on the expansion option. A sixth variable, the rate of value decay, is added to the input list. (See www.valuesweep.com.) With the adjustment, the future outcome of *S* remains uncertain, but the new variable introduces a downward drift to the fluctuations, gently lowering the range of future outcomes.

  Value decay is very costly to option value. The implication was that investors grossly overestimated the value in online pet stores at the time of their funding. The implication for the management teams was that there was a reason to rush for market share. With value decay, waiting leads to a lower and lower payoff.

As these four examples illustrate, there is a bit of a craft to framing a growth option. The next chapter extends the framing discussion to private risk, which is the most frequent aspect of the growth opportunity not captured in a real option analysis.

Takeaways

- Option value lookup tables have several advantages over direct calculations for managers: They are easy to use, they help build intuition about the drivers of option value, and they contribute to transparent valuations.

- The value of a growth option is less than its payoff. The implication is that for an ongoing business, the expansion option value is typically less than the DCF value. This result creates an immediate logic check for real options results.

- The exercise decision in a real option is triggered by market-priced risk. Most growth opportunities, however, have private risk as well. Other tools are required to handle the effect of private risk on growth option value.

5

Decision Analysis

Designing Growth Opportunities

Decision analysis is a wide-ranging and long-established tool that is very useful in the design and valuation of growth projects. This chapter provides several examples of decision analysis in action and shows how it can be used to value the information gained from active learning. Decision analysis is the best tool for demonstrating the value consequences of private risk, and it completes the expanded toolkit.

Academics have long studied decision making under uncertainty. In the late 1960s, this work emerged as a separate field: decision analysis. While most of us are familiar with decision trees, the field of decision analysis is more systematic and rigorous than the simple (but very useful) decision trees suggest. How can decision analysis be used to value growth opportunities? This chapter takes a very focused approach to this question.

Decision analysis is a much-needed addition to the expanded toolkit. DCF captures mature business opportunities when it is expected that upcoming investment decisions will move forward as per plan. There's uncertainty, but managers don't anticipate changing the strategic plan in response to any of the outcomes. Real options captures the cases in which the magnitude of uncertainty is expected to change strategic plans. But in real options, the market-priced risk alone changes investment decisions.

Typically, however, the most important contingent decisions in a growth opportunity are triggered by private risk. Decision analysis addresses this feature.

As its name suggests, the purpose of decision analysis is to help managers reach a conclusion. It has been used in a wide range of significant projects—assessing nuclear power plant risk, deciding whether to seed hurricanes, selecting the optimal configuration for probes to Mars. Decision analysis has also become an industry. There are a number of consulting firms and software providers, as well as several startups, that target tailored databases and decision-analysis tools to specific industries or business problems.[1]

Growth strategy and valuation are intertwined: The value of a growth opportunity is defined as what it is worth if executed under the highest-valued strategy. Change the strategy, change the project value. To fold decision analysis into valuation, the strategic alternative is frozen, and a snapshot of value is taken.

This chapter presents three progressively more complex examples of decision analysis. The first, a common outsourcing decision, illustrates how the calculations are done. The second, an information technology (IT) investment, shows how decision analysis can be used to redesign projects, leading to a higher valued growth opportunity. The third shows how decision analysis values active learning. These examples illustrate the power of decision analysis to address private risk. The chapter's final section starts the process of narrowing the rich decision-analysis toolkit to just what is needed for valuation, a topic that is continued in Chapter 6.

Choosing between Strategic Alternatives

Most managers have some experience with decision trees, one of the central tools of decision analysis. In Figure 5-1, a decision tree is used to structure a common decision: whether to develop a new technology in-house or acquire it from an outside party. In this example, two years of in-house development leads to three possible outcomes, each with its own cost and payoff. In two of the three outcomes, the firm expects to create significant value. But there is a 20 percent chance that in-house development will fail.

Figure 5-1   A Sample Decision Tree:
Acquire New Technology or Build In-House

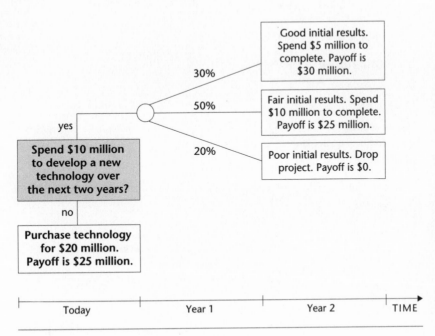

The probabilities are based on a combination of managers' experience and judgment. (Note that a common notation in decision trees is to denote the decisions by rectangles and squared corners, and the outcomes by circles and rays.)

The decision is made by calculating the value of each alternative and then picking the highest-valued alternative. For the in-house development alternative, the valuation begins by quantifying the value of each outcome—calculating the payoff and subtracting the costs. An expected value calculation is used to collapse the value of the three outcomes into a single number. (The expected value is the weighted average of the outcomes, with the probabilities used as weights.) The result is the value of the business opportunity under the in-house development strategy.

Table 5-1 records the data and calculations. A 10 percent cost of capital is used as the discount rate. As this example shows, the analysis flows from right to left in Figure 5-1, and down the rows of

Table 5-1   A Sample Decision-Analysis Calculation:
Acquire New Technology or Build In-House
($ millions unless noted)

(a) The Value of the Acquisition Alternative

CALCULATE THE VALUE OF THE ACQUISITION ALTERNATIVE

	Year	Payoff	Cost	Probability	Expected Value
Value of payoff	0	$25	$0	100%	$25.00
less Cost of acquiring the technology	0				$20.00
Value of Acquisition Alternative	0				**$5.00**

WRITE THE STORY

The advocate says: *"Acquiring technology reduces risk and gets our product to the market more quickly. The extra benefits exceed the extra cost."*

(b) The Value of the In-House Alternative

CALCULATE THE VALUE OF THE IN-HOUSE ALTERNATIVE

	Year	Payoff	Cost	Probability	Expected Value
Value of payoff					
Good outcome	2	$30	$5	30%	$7.50
Fair outcome	2	$25	$10	50%	$7.50
Bad outcome	2	$0	$0	20%	$0.00
Total	2			100%	$15.00
Present value	0				**$12.40**
less Cost of initial development	0				**$10.00**
Value of In-House Alternative	0				**$2.40**

WRITE THE STORY

The advocate says: *"Building the technology in-house is cheaper. Although it takes longer, only if we build the technology in-house do we have the opportunity to capture the full upside potential of this project."*

Table 5-1. In this way, the value of two or more alternatives can be compared at each decision point. The results show that the acquisition is the more valuable alternative.

The outsourcing example also raises the two issues that have caused decision-analysis practitioners to expand their activities beyond the use of decision trees. First, new users of decision analysis confuse decisions and outcomes. Decisions are moments of choice; outcomes are uncertain events managers can't change. Many novice users of decision analysis can't take pen to paper and construct a decision tree that correctly separates these two. Second, managerial anxieties run high when focused on risky investment decisions. Fear permeates the discussion when nothing can be done to change the future, including potentially bad outcomes. Emotions are intense when a decision must be made, particularly abandonment. To address these realities, practitioners have developed codified processes for developing alternatives and building consensus. The lesson learned in decision analysis applies to valuation as well: It takes more than math to create a successful result.

Designing the More Valuable Growth Project

Decision analysis can be a very helpful framework for organizing multistage projects that are subject to uncertainty. Once the overview is obtained, the project can be redesigned for even higher value. In practice, project design is often rushed, and significant value is lost when there is not enough time for the redesign.

Figure 5-2 illustrates a project redesign. The question in the project is how to coordinate the deployment of an information technology investment and the market test. Both have uncertain outcomes. The top portion of the figure shows the initial project design. A $10 million investment in IT is required to prepare an e-commerce infrastructure. Once the IT is successfully deployed, a $12 million market test is planned. If the market acceptance test is successful, the e-commerce offering will be launched. Assume that the value of the launch, obtained from a DCF calculation, is $72 million. The probabilities shown in the figure are based on managers' experience and expert judgment.

Figure 5-2   The Gain from Project Redesign

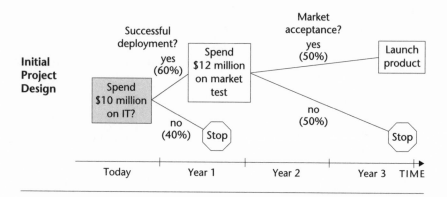

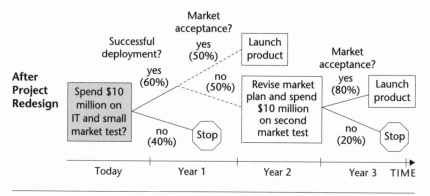

The top of Table 5-2(a) shows the calculations for the value of the project under the initial design. As before, the calculations start with the outcomes at the far right of the decision tree and move to the left. The calculations show that the project has a positive NPV of $0.28 million, so in theory, the project should begin. But the NPV seems small when compared to the $72 million payoff—one way managers gauge risk. And the NPV is small given that more than $20 million is to be invested and is at risk for a $72 million success payoff. Experienced managers will recognize that the NPV result can't really be distinguished from zero; a change in assumptions about the probabilities or payoffs will change the result.

Table 5-2   The Value of Redesigning the Growth Project

($ millions unless noted)

(a) Project Value with the Initial Design

	Year	Payoff	Probability	Expected Value
CALCULATE THE PROJECT VALUE AT THE START OF THE MARKET TEST				
Value of payoff				
Launch product outcome	3	$72	50%	$36.00
Quit outcome	3	$0	50%	$0.00
Total	3		100%	$36.00
Present value	2			$32.73
less Cost of market test	2			$12.00
Value at start of market test	2			**$20.73**
CALCULATE THE PROJECT VALUE BEFORE IT INVESTMENT				
Value of payoff				
IT success outcome	2	$20.73	60%	$12.44
Quit outcome	2	$0	40%	$0.00
Total	2		100%	$12.44
Present value	0			$10.28
less Cost of IT	0			$10.00
Value at start of IT project	0			**$0.28**

WRITE THE STORY

Start the project:	*"The project NPV is nearly zero, and that's after including a lot of risk. Chances are things will work out; after all, this is our standard new product procedure."*
Reject the project:	*"This project puts $22 million at risk yet delivers no value. Don't we have better things to do with our money?"*

(continued)

Table 5-2 *(continued)*

(b) Project Value after Redesign

	Year	Payoff	Probability	Expected Value
CALCULATE THE PROJECT VALUE BEFORE REVISED MARKET TEST				
Value of payoff				
Launch product outcome	3	$72	80%	$57.60
Quit outcome	3	$0	20%	$0.00
Total	3		100%	$57.60
Present value	2			$52.36
less Cost of revised market test	2			$13.00
Value at start of revised market test	2			**$39.36**
CALCULATE THE PAYOFF TO SUCCESSFUL IT DEPLOYMENT				
Value of the payoff				
Launch product outcome	2	$72.00	50%	$36.00
Revised market test outcome	2	$39.36	50%	$19.68
Total	2		100%	$55.68
Present value	1			**$50.62**
CALCULATE THE PROJECT VALUE BEFORE IT INVESTMENT				
Value of the payoff				
IT success outcome	1	$50.62	60%	$30.37
Quit outcome	1	$0.00	40%	$0.00
Total	1		100%	$30.37
Present value	0			$27.61
less Cost of IT	0			$15.00
Value of project before IT investment	0			**$12.61**

WRITE THE STORY

Start the project:	*"This is a great project. There is an early focus on risk reduction and there's a lot of upside potential. No wonder the project has a positive NPV."*
Reject the project:	*"Wait a minute! We could spend $28 million and still fail! This project is too expensive and too risky."*

The Redesign

So back to the drawing board. Figure 5-2 also shows a revised and higher-valued project plan. The key insight is to run a small market acceptance test while the IT infrastructure is being developed. Assuming that the smaller test provides valid results, some of the market risk can be resolved before the next decision point. If the IT is successfully deployed and the market test is successful, the project can move to product launch. This outcome saves time and money over the initial project design.

The valuation of the redesign begins by calculating the payoffs to the second market test and then moving to the left to calculate its value. This allows the value of the launch and revised marketing plan alternatives to be folded back into the IT investment decision. The result, given in Table 5-2(b), is a significant increase in value, from $0.28 million to $12.61 million. Also, under the new plan, there is only a 46 percent chance that the project will be scrapped, while under the original plan the probability of failure was 70 percent.[2]

In this simple example, the project redesign moved some of the active learning about the market to an earlier stage, creating an opportunity to modify the marketing plan and increase the chance of market success. Under the revised plan more money is spent up front ($15 million versus $10 million), and more money could be spent overall ($28 million versus $22 million). But still the project value increases. With the redesign, the follow-on investment is determined *after* some of the uncertainty is resolved.

Decision analysis is often used to increase the value of growth projects by better coordinating spending with the potential outcomes of active learning. The next example takes the use of decision analysis one step further, showing how it can be used to value the information gained from active learning.

Calculating the Value of Information

Although the phrase *active learning* comes from real options, decision analysis has a rich methodology for valuing information-gathering investment. To bring the language of the two frameworks together, an active learning investment is made only when the expected value of the information obtained exceeds the investment cost.

The example of active learning is from Pharsight, a public company that provides decision support, specialized data, tailored software tools, and consulting services to the pharmaceutical industry.[3] The key question in the example is whether to spend the time and money for a Phase II clinical trial or to proceed directly to a Phase III trial. The example is based on an actual analysis done for a drug that may reduce the risk of a fatal heart attack. The drug is to be taken on an emergency basis. Early scientific work was promising but not conclusive.

Phase II trials are also known as proof-of-concept trials because they aim to demonstrate that the scientific findings from animals also apply to humans. However, "proof" is elusive. Phase II clinical trials only imperfectly measure the effect of the drug. Even the best-designed trial does not fully resolve uncertainty. A Phase II trial has two costs: dollars and time. In this example, the Phase II trial costs $10 million and takes one year. If successful, it would be followed by a Phase III trial, which takes four years and costs $140 million. It is easy to justify spending money on Phase II if it will generate information that leads to better decisions or if it will avoid wasted spending in Phase III. The value of Phase II is in the possibility of using better information to make a different decision about continuing on to Phase III.

Figure 5-3 presents the decision tree for the active learning project. The top area lays out the timing of the first alternative, undertaking the Phase II trial. The bottom area graphs the calculations for the other alternative, skipping the trial and moving directly on to Phase III. The three Phase III outcomes are defined by how effective the drug is in reducing deaths from heart attacks. The higher payoffs reflect higher efficacy.

Conducting the Phase II trial changes three data points:

- *Costs rise.* The total trial costs increase by $10 million.

- *Phase III payoffs fall.* The trial takes one year; thus the first year of sales is lost and the drug's economic life is one year shorter. This decreases Phase III payoffs.

Figure 5-3 A Sample Decision Tree for Active Learning: Proof-of-Concept Trial in Pharmaceutical Drug Development

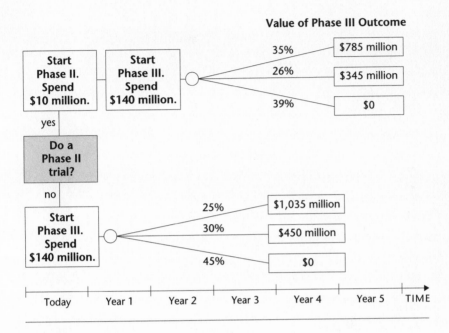

- *Phase III probabilities change.* Information from the Phase II trial is used to make a better estimate of the probability of each outcome for the Phase III trial.[4]

Table 5-3 shows the value of information calculations. Part (a) shows the value of continuing with Phase II, and part (b) shows the calculations for moving directly to Phase III. The probabilities in part (a) are from Pharsight's proprietary data set, and those in part (b) are from the firm's mathematical model of how the Phase II trial might change the information set. The results in Table 5-3 show that if Phase II is skipped, there is a 45 percent chance of losing $140 million in Phase III. Despite this risk, skipping Phase II is the highest-valued alternative.

The results in the example given in Table 5-3 illustrate the tension between the value of information and the cost of delay. In this example, the value of information is the increase in the expected

Table 5-3   The Value of Information
($ millions unless noted)

(a) Project Value with Phase II Trial

	Year	Payoff	Probability	Expected Value
CALCULATE THE PROJECT VALUE AT THE START OF PHASE III				
Value of payoff				
Good outcome	5	$941	27%	$254.05
Fair outcome	5	$409	33%	$135.00
Bad outcome	5	–	40%	$0.00
Total	5		100%	$389.05
Present value	1			$265.72
less Cost of Phase III trial	1			$140.00
Value at start of Phase III	1			**$125.72**
CALCULATE PROJECT VALUE AT THE START OF PHASE II				
Payoff to Phase II trial	0			$114.29
less Cost of Phase II trial	0			$10.00
Value at start of Phase II	0			**$104.29**
WRITE THE STORY				

Start the project:	*"This project has a positive NPV at the start of Phase II and a 60% chance of a positive payoff in Phase III."*
Reject the project:	*"The project also has a 40% chance of failure in Phase III, after spending $150 million. Too much money is at risk."*

value of Phase III from the higher probabilities of good outcomes. The cost of delay is the decrease in value of Phase III payoffs because of longer development time. (To quantify the two factors, hypothetical results are constructed. For example, the cost of delay is calculated as: [the Phase III payoff without the Phase II trial] less [the Phase III payoff with the cost of the Phase II trial but no improvement in probabilities]. Similarly, the value of information holds the Phase III payoffs constant, but allows only the probabilities to change.)[5]

Delay costs the drug development project $64 million, while the value of information gained from phase II is $27 million. Active

(b) Project Value without Phase II Trial

	Year	Payoff	Probability	Expected Value
CALCULATE PROJECT VALUE AT THE START OF PHASE III				
Value of payoff				
Good outcome	4	$1,035	25%	$258.75
Fair outcome	4	$450	30%	$135.00
Bad outcome	4	–	45%	$0.00
Total	4		100%	$393.75
Present value	1			$268.94
less cost of Phase III trial	0			$140.00
Value at start of Phase III	0			**$128.94**

WRITE THE STORY

Start the project: *"Skipping Phase II saves time and money. This is a no-brainer."*

Reject the project: *"Without Phase II there is a 45% chance of losing our $150 million investment. We need a Phase II trial to reduce our risk."*

Source: Based on data from Pharsight Inc. See www.valuesweep.com.

learning can improve the value of growth projects, but competitive forces may eat away at the success payoff while the learning takes place.

In this example only one factor (the probabilities) determined the value of information for the Phase III payoffs, while in practice the value of information would depend on many factors. Typically, value of information results are more complex and often center on the confidence interval around the probability.

Focusing Decision Analysis on Valuation

Whereas decision analysis has been used in a wonderfully rich set of applications, a focus on valuation restricts its scope. For example, a recent study used decision analysis to establish guidelines for prenatal testing to detect Down's syndrome. While the authors were able to complete a cost-benefit analysis for the test using decision analysis, they also concluded that many of the costs of a child with Down's syndrome are intangible. They urged that their quantitative results not be the only basis for decisions about testing.[6] This stark example illustrates both the wide scope for the application of decision analysis and the limits to the role of valuation in decision making.

The key to using decision analysis for valuation is in the selection of applications. The following are some guidelines:

- *Objectives are measured solely in financial terms.* It must be clear that choosing the highest-valued strategy is the optimal decision.

- *The payoffs are fully characterized by their economic value.* Issues regarding risk, follow-on opportunities, and benefits from a particular strategy must be expressed in monetary terms.

- *Market-priced risk is included in a straightforward manner.* The application frame should treat market-priced risk in a way that is consistent with financial market practices, allowing the valuation results to be compared to pricing in the public market.

These requirements restrict the scope and toolkit of decision analysis, but even within these bounds, decision analysis can play an important role in the valuation of growth opportunities.

A FAQ: Which Discount Rate?

One of the most frequently asked questions (FAQs) by managers who have tried decision analysis is about which discount rate to use in the calculations. This last section presents the theoretical arguments for the two most common choices. The takeaway—for those who would like to skip the detail—is that a risk-free rate of return should be used as the discount rate in decision-analysis applications.

To make the arguments more clear, go back to Figure 5-1 for a moment. The in-house alternative takes two years to develop.

Which discount rate should be used to calculate the present value of the payoffs? To be precise, note that the DCF payoffs at the end of each branch on the tree are calculated using the weighted-average cost of capital. The discussion is about which discount rate should be used inside the decision tree.

There are two points of view, and both are used in practice:

1. *Use the weighted-average cost of capital throughout the tree.* Some practitioners use the weighted-average cost of capital throughout a decision tree, arguing that the risk of the decision under study is captured in the depiction along the branches. For the outsourcing decision in Figure 5-1, this argument implies that it is business-as-usual risk for all risks not detailed in the decision tree branches, and that the branches completely capture the outsourcing and in-house risks. The argument does not apply branch by branch, as the risk could be quite different along any two branches.[7] The argument is based on the analysis of the entire tree, not pieces of it.

2. *Use the risk-free rate of return as the discount rate throughout the tree.* There are two theoretical arguments for using the risk-free discount rate, one from decision analysis and one from finance. The argument from decision analysis is that the risk of the opportunities is completely characterized by the payoffs and probabilities in the tree; no adjustment for risk is needed in the discount rate. (Business as usual is in one of the strategic alternatives.) In practice, it is difficult to achieve a complete description of risks through a decision tree, so some risks will be omitted. Use of the risk-free rate will underestimate risk.

   The argument from finance theory is that by definition, private risk is uncorrelated with the returns to any security or combination of securities traded in the financial markets. Investors earning a return from private risk will not require a risk premium; they expect to earn a risk-free rate of return. The finance theory perspective—which is not shared throughout the decision-analysis community—is the one used in this book.

In practice, a change in the discount rate—or the discount rate method—often does not change the investment decision. The NPV is large because even after articulating all the risks, there is still much upside potential. In some cases, however, the discount rate becomes quantitatively important. For example, capital-intensive growth projects are more sensitive to the level of the discount rate.

Sometimes emotional reactions to risk are placed into the discount rate. For example, senior managers are often considered more conservative and more risk-averse than the managers analyzing the project. Or one of the outcomes is so large, so uncertain, or so adverse that it causes executive anxiety. Corporate analysts often respond to these concerns by increasing the discount rate.

Ad hoc changes to the discount rate are inappropriate. Financial market pricing of traded assets capitalizes a wealth of information and factors, including risk aversion by financial market players, so it has "solved" the problem of how to adjust discount rates for risk. Use of the weighted-average cost of capital or the risk-free rate of return transfers financial market information to decision analysis; additional adjustments are not required.

Takeaways

- Because it directly addresses how private risk affects growth value, decision analysis is an essential tool for valuation of growth opportunities.

- The value of active learning depends on the information acquired. If the information gained can change a decision, active learning can be valuable. An example in this chapter also showed that the benefits of active learning can be offset by the time pressures of competition.

- Often decision analysis is used in an open-minded manner, with dense trees and numerous sources of uncertainty. This is an advantage in the design of growth projects, but an obstacle for transparent and valuation results. The solution is to use only a small part of the rich decision-analysis framework, keeping the focus on what is needed for valuation.

Part II

Valuing Growth

C URRENT TOOLS fail to value growth opportunities for two reasons. First, they often fail to capture the important features of growth, particularly the nature of the risk and the presence of contingent decisions. When these features are ignored by valuation tools, the results feel irrelevant. The tools of the previous chapters address this problem.

But, there's another reason valuation tools fail growth opportunities: The tools, even those in the expanded toolkit, are too dense and too confusing for regular business use. A successful valuation tool is easy to use and clearly communicates the method and results. Only then will the results be used by a wide array of professionals inside and outside the firm.

The next three chapters introduce valuation templates, a method of calculation based on tailoring the expanded toolkit to the features of the growth opportunity at hand. Built on precalculated formulas and precodified data, valuation templates are designed for ease of use and clarity. Further, because they exploit the expanded toolkit, the templates quantify the value of the important features of growth opportunities. Changing the form of the valuation tool creates an opportunity to be credible, clear, and useful to managers in everyday business life.

6

Tailored Valuation
Templates

It's time to build valuation templates, straightforward valuation tools tai-
lored to growth opportunities. This chapter develops two templates. The
first, for pharmaceutical drug development, is based on private risk alone.
The second, for oil exploration, mixes private risk and market-priced risk.
The template demonstrates how the value of growth opportunities can be
quickly updated to reflect the current pricing of market-priced risk.

The valuation templates presented in this chapter can be done on a
single screen of a spreadsheet. Imagine printing them out and lay-
ing them across the conference room table for easy comparison of
growth projects. Most important, the templates tell the story
behind each project, identifying where the risks are and articulating how sustainable growth will be achieved. Not only easy to use,
the templates are also credible. Because they are based on the
expanded toolkit, the valuation templates are grounded in rigorous
financial theory. Their design exploits data on observed transactions in the industry or sector. Making use of precalculated formulas and precodified data, templates simplify the task of valuation.

Two templates are introduced in this chapter. The first template,
for pharmaceutical drug development, shows how a simple structure can be used to capture the salient features of growth and to
provide a quick overview of an entire drug development portfolio.
The second template, for oil exploration, integrates private and

market-priced risk and demonstrates how to accomplish mark-to-market valuation of growth opportunities. The clear and simple link between the value of a private growth opportunity and public-market pricing is a powerful result and is applied in Chapter 8 to venture capital investments.

Pharmaceutical Drug Development

To my knowledge, pharmaceutical drug development is unique. Although it is a long, complex, multistaged process, there is widely available data about the average cost and length of each stage and the probability of moving on to the next stage. Tufts University, for example, publishes updated probabilities each year. There is a well-accepted method for calculating the value of a new drug once it has been launched. Thus, for this industry, it is straightforward to calculate the value of growth opportunities and to use those results to value a company's entire pipeline of growth projects.

There are seven phases of drug development:

- Discovery (R&D labs)
- Preclinical (R&D labs)
- Phase I (animal testing)
- Phase II (small-scale human trial)
- Phase III (large-scale human trial)
- NDA (New Drug Application is the final submission for approval to the U.S. Food and Drug Administration)
- Launch (sales begin)

Phases I through NDA are defined by the regulatory bodies, while the other phases are loosely defined by industry practice.

Table 6-1 shows how the value of a drug development project can be calculated for each phase of development. The calculations begin with the value of the drug at launch. As the first section of Table 6-1 shows, there are five possible payoff outcomes, which differ by the level of sales.[1] The distribution of the outcomes is skewed, with a large difference between the blockbuster outcome and the next best outcome. Consequently, although there is only a

Table 6-1   The Value of Drug Development Growth Opportunities
($ millions unless noted)

CALCULATE THE VALUE OF DRUG AT LAUNCH

Sales outcome	Value	Probability	Expected Value
Blockbuster	$1,615	10%	$162
Above average	$800	10%	$80
Average	$500	60%	$300
Below average	$350	10%	$35
Dog	$200	10%	$20
Value of launch		100%	**$597**

(continued)

Table 6-1 (continued)

CALCULATE THE VALUE OF DRUG BY PHASE

	Discovery	Preclinical	Phase I	Phase II	Phase III	NDA	Launch
Data							
Cost ($ millions)	2.2	13.8	2.8	6.4	18.1	3.3	50.0
Phase length (years)	1	3	1	2	3	3	1
Total length (years)	1	4	5	7	10	13	14
Probability of success	60%	90%	75%	50%	75%	85%	100%
Payoff at launch							$597
Calculations							
Payoff at end of phase	$11	$37	$59	$157	$311	$492	$597
Expected value	$7	$33	$44	$79	$233	$418	$597
Present value at start of phase	$6	$25	$40	$65	$175	$314	$542
less Cost of phase	$2.2	$13.8	$2.8	$6.4	$18.1	$3.3	$50.0
Value of drug by phase	**$4**	**$11**	**$37**	**$59**	**$157**	**$311**	**$492**
Value of drug by phase / Value at start of launch	1%	2%	8%	12%	32%	63%	100%
Required number of projects by phase per launch	7.7	4.6	4.2	3.1	1.6	1.2	1

Source: David Kellog and John Charnes, "Real-Options Valuation for a Biotechnology Company," Financial Analysts Journal, May–June 2000, 76–84.

small chance of a blockbuster outcome, it is a significant component of the expected value. Consistent with this skew, academic research has found that fewer than half of approved drugs earn back their cost.[2] Thus, the risk of drug development is not only in the R&D phase, but in the market launch as well.

The second section of Table 6-1 shows the calculations for the value of the drug by phase. The first few rows assemble the data, including the value of the drug at launch calculated in the first section of the table. The next rows are the valuation calculations, which begin at the right and fold back to the left. The method of valuation is as follows. For each phase, the payoff is the value of the drug at the start of the subsequent phase. The expected value is taken (value of payoff × probability of success) and the result is carried to the start of the stage by a present value calculation. The cost of the development incurred at the start of the phase is subtracted. The result is the value of the drug at the start of the phase, which is also the payoff value for the prior phase.

The results show that the value of the drug grows with each stage, as private risk is reduced. The big jumps in value come from passing through a phase with a low chance of success (survivors are valuable) and from passing through a phase with high development costs (the costs become history and don't affect value, which is forward-looking.) The value of the drug in the lab is only 1 percent of its value at launch, and the value of a drug at the NDA phase is only 63 percent of its launch value.

The results of Table 6-1 make it easy to understand why the most active market for in-licensing drug development projects is in Phase I and the early part of Phase II. These projects have some value but are not terribly expensive. In addition, there is likely to be wide divergence in information and judgment about the scientific issues that can be resolved through near-term active learning investments. There may also be significant differences in capabilities to resolve the private risk. The differences form the basis of a win-win transaction.

A High-Level Summary of Private Risk

Now let's look at Table 6-1 in terms of the structure of a valuation template. It seems that once the data are gathered, the calculations are simple. What makes this calculation so much easier than the value of information examples in Chapter 5? The answer is in the probability data.

At the end of each phase, two things happen: The regulators return with a ruling about whether the drug can continue to the next phase, and the scientific results are used to refine estimates of the chemistry, size of the target population, required dosage, form of dosage, and so on. All of this detail is captured in a single number: the probability of moving forward. Detail is crucial when making decisions about the design of an active learning investment—decisions that depend on the value of information. But too much detail destroys transparency, preventing credible comparisons of value across a number of drug prospects. In the drug development valuation template, the detail is summarized into a single probability of success. The pharmaceutical industry is unique in its widespread use and reporting of this summary data.

Table 6-1 is the first tailored valuation template in this book. It uses a specialized, yet widely available data set. Valuations are done in a transparent manner, using DCF and decision analysis. Private risk is summarized by a single probability estimate. The results, easy to understand and replicate, provide benchmarks for specialized transactions, licensing arrangements, and project management. The process of benchmarking valuations from the template creates a self-reinforcing cycle, as it also helps to refine and update the underlying data.

Using the Drug Development Valuation Template

There are two immediate applications for the valuation template: estimating the value of the drug development pipeline, and a strategic review of the number of drugs in the development pipeline.

It seems straightforward to simply use the valuation template to sum the value of all projects: Count up the number of projects by stage and sum their values. Because of the amount of disclosure required by the regulatory bodies, even external analysts can perform this calculation. The typical result is that the drug development pipeline accounts for 15 to 25 percent of the pharmaceutical firm value.

In practice, two additional issues must be addressed for reliable pipeline value results. First, the costs given in Table 6-1 are on a project-specific basis and exclude many overhead and infrastructure costs of running R&D and clinical trial programs. This is the correct approach for a project-level analysis, as overhead and infrastructure are sunk costs (precommitted expenditures), and the purpose of an NPV analysis is to quantify the incremental value of a project given its incremental expenditure. But when summing projects into a pipeline value, there should be an accounting of the other costs arising from the pipeline. Net of these costs, the value of the drugs in the development pipeline is about 8 to 14 percent of firm market value.

The second issue for pipeline value was mentioned in Chapter 2. The bottoms-up approach to valuing a pharmaceutical firm is to add the value of products in the market and the value of the products in the pipeline. This analysis is frequently undertaken by equity analysts who have found that drugs in the NDA phase and in sales account for about 50 percent of the market value of the firm.[3] The problem is that if the pipeline value is at most an additional 15 percent of market value, 35 percent of the firm value is not based on known projects.

One explanation, suggested in Chapter 2, is that the bottoms-up approach omits the value of R&D and entrenched sales capabilities. For example, one pharmaceutical company may have a well-developed sales channel for cancer drugs. Using this channel, a cancer drug's value would be far greater than industry averages. Consequently, the template underestimates the value of the company's cancer drug projects. Another explanation is that the bottoms-up approach doesn't account for the embedded options of new business opportunities—such as genomics and online connectivity to doctors—that aren't yet externally visible projects. (Genomics is the science of our common genetic makeup.)

A second use of the drug development valuation template is the strategic review of the size of the pipeline. Specifically, the question often asked is: "How many drugs are needed in each phase to create two launches per year?" (Because of the high costs, pharmaceutical firms launch only one to three drugs per year.) The size of the pipeline required is calculated one phase at a time, beginning with the launch. Using the probability of success inputs, the number of NDA applications required per launch is calculated, and then moving back in the pipeline, the number of Phase III projects per NDA application is calculated, and so on. The bottom row of Table 6-1 shows the results.

Over the past ten years, industry analysts have repeatedly found that pharmaceutical company pipelines are too small to meet the goal of one to three launches per year. The desire to increase the size of the pipeline, and to fill the holes in certain phases, has led to wide-scale licensing of drugs in development from biotech firms (known as in-licensing) and to pharmaceutical company mergers.

Other initiatives address pipeline size by changing its economics. Pharmaceutical companies have undertaken numerous programs to reduce expenses, shorten time in each phase, and increase the probability of moving forward. This type of initiative can greatly impact the value of early-stage projects. For example, suppose that the Phase III probability of success increased from 75 percent to 80 percent. Table 6-1 can be used to show that this change increases the value of a drug in discovery by 25 percent, from $4 million to $5 million. While the overall portfolio value is not much changed, early-stage projects begin to draw more resources because they are more valuable, and then the balance of the entire pipeline changes. The introduction of genomics-based projects to the drug development pipeline is expected to have this type of economic impact and is discussed in the next chapter.

A Valuation Template with Market-Priced and Private Risk

The drug development valuation template contains only private risk.[4] But now consider oil exploration. While oil exploration and drug development have important similarities—very long periods of development, sizable expenditures before revenues, fewer than one out of ten projects make it from start to finish—there is one difference that significantly changes decisions and valuation: The value of oil projects depends on oil prices, a market-priced risk. Because of this, oil exploration projects are often put on hold or canceled due to low oil prices, while drug development projects are seldom abandoned for economic reasons. The difference in strategic decisions must be captured in the valuation template.

The remainder of this section shows how to build a valuation template that incorporates the abandonment decision triggered by market-priced risk. Oil exploration is an unusually clear example, because the sources of private and market-priced risk are easily identified. While the next chapter introduces a novel and simple way to value a staged investment with market-priced risk, the focus here is on the abandonment decision alone.

Consider an oil field in the Alaskan North Slope in which exploration is complete and some test wells have been drilled. The remaining expenditure, in two investments, will complete the infrastructure needed to begin extracting the oil. The first investment is needed immediately to prepare the field. The second investment is needed in two years and covers the final equipment required to pump out the oil. Before each investment the decision to continue is made. Low oil prices could lead to abandonment or delay now (current project NPV is negative) or delay in two years (payoff is less than cost of the final investment at that time). The question is the value of the reserve, given the production decision uncertainty.

The Production Option

Part (a) of Figure 6-1 shows the components of an oil production option, while part (b) shows more detail about how market-priced risk triggers the abandonment decision. Part (a) introduces variable names that will be used throughout Part II of this book:

- *Payoff (S).* The value of continuing the project at time T. Typically S is calculated as the present value of free cash flow, using a DCF analysis. In the production example, S is based on the lifetime profile of oil to be extracted from the reserve.

- *Exercise cost (X).* The money that must be spent at time T to continue the project and obtain the payoff S. In the production option example, X might be the final infrastructure cost before production can begin.

Figure 6-1 Private and Market-Priced Risk in Oil Exploration

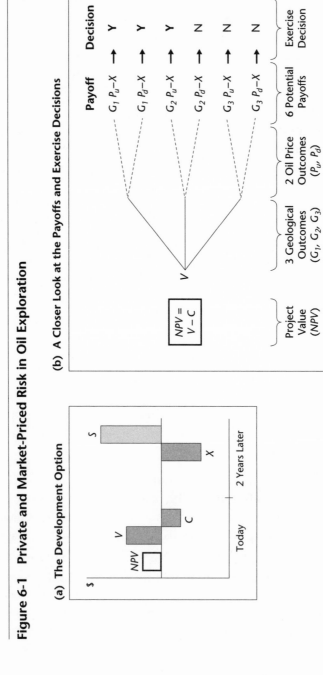

(a) The Development Option

(b) A Closer Look at the Payoffs and Exercise Decisions

- *Option value* (*V*). The value of the option to continue the project. In this book the real options approach is used to value exercise decisions triggered by market-priced risk.

- *Project cost* (*C*). The immediate cost to continue the project. In the production option example *C* might be the development investment.

- *Project NPV* (*NPV*). The current value of the project net of all costs. In the valuation templates of Chapters 6 through 8, the NPV label is used regardless of the valuation method.

Part (b) takes a closer look at the payoffs and exercise decisions, more carefully defining the conditions for continuing. If *C* is invested immediately, active learning about the geology begins. The results are known in two years. Meanwhile, oil prices fluctuate. In the simple depiction of part (b) there are three possible geological results to the active learning investment and two possible oil price outcomes, leading to six different payoffs. (In practice there may thousands of possible outcomes.)

If the geological estimate is high (G_1), production will begin for any oil price. Similarly, if the geological estimate is low (G_3), not even high oil prices can save the project. The middle outcome (G_2) is common in the industry and is an area in which oil prices swing decisions. With low oil prices (P_d), the reserve is put on hold, awaiting higher oil prices. If the oil prices are a bit higher (P_u), the decision is made to continue.

Part (b) of Figure 6-1 is both too dense and too simple. It is too dense in that the level of detail makes it difficult to quickly value a number of properties by using this detailed method. The method could be used for the North Slope example above, but the results would take many pages to summarize. The figure is unrealistically simple because actual decisions in oil exploration encompass many more outcomes and much more detail.[5] Typical complications include size of investments that depend on the geological outcome, gradations in geological outcomes that change the cost of extraction, tax rules that change the optimal extraction rate, and so on. While Figure 6-1 illustrates how active learning affects the value of the development option, the framework is not well suited to valuing growth opportunities in a transparent manner. The next section offers a valuation template that captures these same features but that is much easier to use.

A Valuation Template with Market-Priced and Private Risk

Table 6-2 shows the calculations for a growth option with private and market-priced risk. To demonstrate the role of market-priced risk, the calculations are shown for two scenarios, with oil prices at $13 and $25 per barrel. Before digging into the calculations, let's summarize the five steps shown on the table:

1. *Calculate the success payoff.* This is the value of the payoff if there is geological success.

2. *Calculate the value of the real option.* The lookup tables in the Appendix are used.

3. *Discount the value of the real option for private risk.* Table 6-2 introduces a new variable, the private risk discount (PRD), which is the decrease in the value of the real option from potential geological failure. The discounted option value is labeled V'.

4. *Calculate the project NPV.* This is the current value of the project, after accounting for market-priced risk, private risk, future investments, and current investment.

5. *Write the story.* A few choice phrases will reveal the strengths and weaknesses of the project.

The five steps reveal the key design principles of this method. The real options approach is used to quickly value the decision to abandon triggered by the market-priced risk outcome. An explicit adjustment is made for private risk with a single parameter, based on observable data. Calculating the project NPV, a point of comparison with observed asset transactions, completes the method. With this overview in hand, let's dig in to the calculations. In this example, the values of all input variables are set by assumption.

The first section of Table 6-2 calculates the success payoff. The success payoff assumes that all the private risk will resolve favorably. In this example, a forecast of geological success is made. A

Table 6-2 A Valuation Template for Private and Market-Priced Risk: The Oil Production Option Example

($ millions unless noted)

	Year	Low Prices	High Prices
CALCULATE THE SUCCESS PAYOFF			
Current estimate of future oil price *($ per barrel)*	2	$13	$25
Current estimate of geological success *(millions of barrels)*	2	12.5	12.5
DCF value of reserve with geological success	2	$12	$35
Present value of success payoff	0	**$10**	**$29**
CALCULATE THE VALUE OF THE REAL OPTION (only market-priced risk)			
S Present value of success payoff	0	$10	$29
X Cost of starting production	2	$10	$10
S/X		1.0	2.9
σ Volatility of success payoff value, annual		50%	50%
T Years		2	2
r Annual		5%	5%
Option value factor *(from Table A-1 in the Appendix)*		31%	71%
V **Real option value**	0	**$3.1**	**$20.5**
DISCOUNT THE REAL OPTION VALUE FOR PRIVATE RISK			
V Real option value	0	$3.1	$20.5
PRD Private risk discount *(external data)*		18%	18%
V' **Adjusted real option value**	0	**$2.5**	**$16.8**
CALCULATE THE PROJECT NPV			
V' Adjusted real option value	0	**$2.5**	**$16.8**
less C Immediate required investment	0	$15.0	$15.0
Project NPV	0	**$(12.5)**	**$1.8**

WRITE THE STORY

The path to sustainable growth is:	*"The project has a negative NPV because oil prices are so low. We should wait for oil prices to rise before starting this project."*
A pessimist would say:	*"I doubt that oil prices will ever rise high enough to put this option in the money."*

forecast is also made of the oil price expected in two years, based on the market expectations embedded in traded oil contracts.[6] A DCF valuation is then made of the oil reserve, as of the start of production. (Note that the oil price and estimate of the number of barrels are not direct inputs into the DCF value. They are shown for reference only.) For consistency with the analogy to a financial option, the success payoff is discounted to the current date. When the forecast is for low oil prices, the present value of the success payoff is $10 million. When high prices prevail, however, the success payoff is $29 million.

The next section of Table 6-2 calculates the value of the real option, in this case producing oil in two years. The exercise cost is $10 million. While the only input that changes between the two oil price scenarios is the value of the success payoff, this causes the S/X ratio to change and thus changes the option value factor as well. In the low-price scenario the production option is worth $3.1 million, while in the high-price scenario it is worth $20.5 million—an indication of just how sensitive oil project values are to oil prices.

Next, the real option result is discounted for private risk failure. Because the real options calculations assumed private risk success, the remaining effect of private risk is to decrease option value. For example, refer back to Figure 6-1. The real option calculation assumes geological success (G_1 and G_2), and that only low oil prices cause abandonment. The option value factor captures these abandonment decisions. The abandonment decisions caused by a bad geological outcome, G_3, have not yet been included. As abandonment decreases project value, the real option value is decreased by the adjustment for private risk failure.

The PRD is a summary measure of the value consequence of private risk failure. Details on how to calculate the PRD itself are given below. For now, assume that the input is available. Table 6-1 shows a PRD of 18 percent. The real option result is then discounted by the PRD: $V \times (1 - PRD) = V'$. As Table 6-2 shows, the resulting adjusted real option value (V') is $2.5 million for the low oil price scenario and $16.8 million for the high oil price scenario.

The last step in the calculations is to obtain the project NPV. V' is the current dollar benefit of undertaking the project, and C is the immediate cost of doing so. In Table 6-2 the low oil price scenario results in a negative project NPV. But even under the high oil price scenario, the project NPV is small, only $1.8 million on a total investment of $25 million.

Calculating the Private Risk Discount (PRD)

The PRD is a useful summary of much detail. Through simple multiplication, it adjusts a real option result for private risk failure. The quality of the PRD adjustment depends on the quality of its estimate. Importantly, the design of the valuation template allows PRD estimates to be based on observable data. In practice, the PRD estimate would be prepared in advance and would be an average of calculated values for similar growth opportunities. Sample calculations for the PRD are given in Table 6-3.

The first step in the PRD calculation is to obtain the value of the real option. C, the immediate investment cost, is subtracted, resulting in a hypothetical project NPV, one that omits private risk failure. This is noted as the hypothetical project NPV in Table 6-3. Next, the model result is compared to the actual transaction value. The difference is the private transaction market's estimate of the loss in NPV from private risk. To increase comparability across many observations, the monetary loss is converted into a percentage discount off the real option value. To summarize:

$$PRD = \frac{(\text{Hypothetical project NPV}) - (\text{Observed project NPV})}{\text{Value of the real option}}$$

To obtain a reliable estimate, a bit of matching between the model and the observation is required. For example, to estimate the PRD for use in valuing oil reserves in the Alaska North Slope, model and transactions should be matched by stage of development, geology, costs, and so on. To acquire comparability across different sized reserves, the results should be scaled, such as on a per-barrel basis. The timing of cash flows must also match.

The PRD is an extremely useful concept and is further developed in the following chapters. Chapter 7 integrates the PRD into valuation of staged growth opportunities, and Chapter 8 estimates the PRD for venture capital investments.

Table 6-3   Calculation of the Private Risk Discount (PRD): The Oil Exploration Example

CALCULATE THE PRD FROM TRANSACTION DATA

V Value of the real option	$20.50
less C Cost of phase	$15.00
Hypothetical project NPV	$5.54
less Observed project NPV	$1.84
NPV loss from private risk	$3.70
Private Risk Discount (NPV loss / *V*)	**18%**

Measuring Market-Priced Risk

Growth options in oil exploration and pharmaceutical drug development have a clear demarcation of sources of private and market-priced risk. In most growth opportunities, however, the separation is less clear. Most often, an analyst will view the growth opportunity from a scientific or technical perspective, creating a long and vivid list of private risk factors. It seems much less clear how to define the market-priced risk that drives the success payoff value.

Modern finance speaks to this issue. In his 1997 Nobel Prize speech, Robert Merton provided a precise definition of private risk and a mathematical recipe for its measure.[7] From his vantage point, private risk is what is omitted from market-priced risk.

Suppose your company creates high-performance fabrics and that one product is used for airline seat covers. Market-priced risk is clearly part of the fluctuations in the payoff, as the demand for seat covers will be correlated with the health of the airline industry. The value of the payoff could be tracked by a portfolio of traded securities. The difference between the change in the value of the growth opportunity payoff and the change in the value of the portfolio of securities is private risk. To reduce the difference, don't restrict the portfolio to those companies you think might track the project value; instead, include all the available stocks and securities (such as traded contracts for jet fuel) and use statistical tests to pick out those that best track the payoff value. The result is a data-driven measure of private and market-priced risk.

Takeaways

- This chapter developed a valuation template that captured the effects of both private and market-priced risk in an easy-to-use format. The template highlights the arguments of this book and captures the depth of the issues involved in valuing growth opportunities.

- The valuation template has been designed to exploit data from private market asset transactions, which are used to estimate the PRD. Thus, ironically, while the PRD is a measure of the value consequence of risk not priced in the financial markets, the PRD can be estimated from the value of observed transactions.

- A key requirement for valuation tools and templates is ease of use. The valuation template in this chapter requires only simple multiplication and subtraction, relying on preset formulas and data lookup tables to provide up-to-date data and intellectual rigor.

7

Valuing
Staged Growth

Staged growth opportunities require years of spending before a possible reward. Typically the stages are defined by budget cycles or when new information is revealed. Most growth opportunities have these features. This chapter shows how to build a valuation template for staged growth with private and market-priced risk. Real options is used to value the effect of market-priced risk on the decision to continue, and a new and easy approach to these calculations is introduced. The chapter closes with applications of the template to the value of Webvan and to the impact of genomics on pharmaceutical drug development.

Most growth projects are done in stages, and at the end of each stage a decision is made between continuing or abandoning the project. Typically, the calculations for valuing staged growth projects are messy and opaque. Further, these calculations seldom incorporate market-priced risk. As the last chapter showed, market-priced risk introduces an additional economic factor into the decision to continue or abandon. The presence of this factor changes project value.

This chapter lays out a straightforward method for valuing staged growth projects with market-priced and private risk. This is done in two steps. First, a valuation template for staged growth with only market-priced risk is developed. Almost no growth projects have only market-priced risk. The purpose of the template is to introduce the method of calculations in the simplest manner. The decision to continue or abandon in the presence of market-priced risk is valued using real options, and a novel way to use option value lookup tables for staged growth is presented.

The second step is to develop a valuation template for staged growth that contains both private and market-priced risk. In current practice—using decision analysis or real options—this is an amazingly dense set of calculations, requiring specialized tools and complex spreadsheets. The calculations in this chapter are a dramatic contrast to this intense effort. The templates are made simple by use of the option value lookup table and the private risk discount factor (introduced in the previous chapter.) The result is a set of calculations that can be easily completed on a single screen of a spreadsheet.

The last section of the chapter applies the staged growth valuation template to two examples. The first example is a follow-up to the Webvan example given in Chapter 1, showing how last-minute information caused the value of that firm to crumble. The second example provides some perspective on the economic implications of a genomics breakthrough. The scientific implications are breathtaking. As the example shows, so are the economic implications.

A Simple Way to Calculate
the Value of Staged Real Options

The valuation template laid out at the start of Chapter 6 for pharmaceutical drug development is at one end of the risk spectrum as it contained only private risk. This section presents a valuation template at the other end of the spectrum, one that contains only market-priced risk. In practice, growth opportunities based on real assets are almost never based on market-priced risk alone; more typically they contain mixtures of private and market-priced risk or simply private risk alone.

So the purpose of this section is not to demonstrate a valuation template with great real-world use, but to demonstrate how to calculate the value of a staged growth opportunity using real options. The next section extends the template to include private risk.

To begin, let's work through an example of a two-staged growth opportunity. Suppose the project at hand is: Start product development for a new soft drink at an immediate cost of $150 million; in two years start product testing at a cost of $200 million; in four years build out sales, marketing, and distribution at a $250 million cost. The current estimate is that the final payoff of the new soft drink product in four years, at the end of the project, is $400 million. (This is called the final payoff.) The example is typical of a sequence of growth options: spend, spend, spend, and then the payoff.

Table 7-1 shows how the value of the project can be calculated. Begin with part (a). The top section collects the data, including the current estimate of the volatility of the value of the final payoff. The next section calculates the project NPV at the start of each stage. The calculations begin at the right, at the start of the final stage. With a payoff of $400 million and a cost of $250 million, the project NPV at the start of the fourth year is $150 million.

Calculating the project value at the start of the second year is a bit more complicated because the project value is itself an option, the option to continue in the fourth year. Remember that the value of the payoff is uncertain, and while the project looks favorable currently, the option to cancel in the fourth year could be important. So before calculating the project NPV, the value of the option must be calculated. This is an option with two years to maturity and whose value is as of year 2.

The option calculations are shown below those for the project NPV. First, the payoff, $400 million, is discounted to the start of year 2 ($331) for consistency with the financial option analogy. Using the S/X ratio of 1.60, the option value is found using the look-up tables in the Appendix. The option value is $276. To indicate the timing of this result, the inputs are given in the column marked 4 Years and the result is given in the column marked 2 Years. The project NPV in year 2, $76 million, is the difference between the option value ($276) and the cost of that stage ($200). The flow of calculations repeats, leading to the calculation of the current value of the project NPV, $35 million. Repeated use of the lookup table has kept the option calculations simple.

Table 7-1   Two-Staged Growth Opportunity with Only Market-Priced Risk

($ millions unless noted)

(a) The Value by Stage, Assuming Constant Volatility

	Today	2 Years	4 Years
ASSEMBLE THE DATA			
C Cost	$150	$200	$250
S Value of final payoff			$400
σ Volatility of the final payoff			100%
CALCULATE THE PROJECT NPV			
V	$185 ◄⌐	$276 ◄⌐	$400
C	$150	$200	$250
Project NPV	**$35**	**$76**	**$150**
CALCULATE THE OPTION VALUE			
Option inputs			
S Value of the payoff *(as of start of preceding stage)*		$228	$331
X Exercise cost		$200	$250
S/X		1.14	1.32
Option results			
Option value factor *(Table A-1)*		67%	69%
V **Option value**		**$185**	**$276**

WRITE THE STORY

The path to sustainable growth is:	*"This project has a current NPV of $35 million and a potential $400 million payoff. Let's do it!"*
A pessimist would say:	*"$600 million is a lot to spend for such a risky project. More likely, the project will be halted midway and the investment lost."*

Scaling Volatility

Table 7-1(b) repeats the calculations of part (a), but with one correction, required because an option is more volatile than its underlying asset. If a payoff (S) has volatility of, say, 75 percent, an option based on that payoff will have a higher volatility, say, 110 percent. (Here's a simple example of why options have a wider range of

(b) The Value by Stage, Using Scaled Volatility

	Today	2 Years	4 Years
ASSEMBLE THE DATA			
C Cost	$150	$200	$250
S Value of final payoff			$400
σ Volatility of the final payoff			100%
CALCULATE THE PROJECT NPV			
V	$221 ◄┄┐	$276 ◄┄┐	$400
C	$150 ┊	$200 ┊	$250
Project NPV	**$71**	**$76**	**$150**
CALCULATE THE OPTION VALUE			
Option inputs			
S Value of the payoff *(as of start of preceding stage)*		$228	$331
X Exercise cost		$200	$250
S/X		1.14	1.32
σ Volatility of the payoff		134%	100%
Option results			
Option value factor *(Table A-1)*		80%	69%
V Option value		**$221**	**$276**
Volatility scaling factor *(Table A-3)*		1.18	1.34
σ' Volatility of the option		**158%**	**134%**

WRITE THE STORY

The path to sustainable growth is:	*"This project is riskier, but also more valuable than I had thought. There's no reason to delay."*
A pessimist would say:	*"Wow! 158% volatility is like holding an Internet stock at the top of the boom. What's our company doing in such a risky venture?"*

potential returns than the stocks they are written on: If you own a stock with a current price of $100 and the stock rises to $150, you get a 50 percent return. If you can buy an option for $3 that entitles you to buy the stock for $100. If the stock price increases to $150, the return to the option is \$50 / \$3 or 1,667 percent. Option volatility is measured in terms of the range of potential returns.) The size of the volatility increase will depend on all the other option inputs. Part (a) of Table 7-1 ignored this feature, so as to establish a clear framework for the calculations. Part (b) incorporates the increase in volatility that arises in each option with staged growth.

To keep the volatility calculations simple, the Appendix provides lookup tables for option volatility as well as value. For example, turn to Table A-3. If S/X is 1 and σ is 100 percent, the volatility of a two-year option with these inputs is 144 percent ($1.44 \times 100\%$). The cells of Table A-3 were populated using the Black-Scholes formula for a two-year option, and Table A-3 can be used in conjunction with Table A-1. Similarly, the volatility of a three-year option is given in Table A-4 and can be used with Table A-2.

Table 7-1(b) shows that including the scaled volatility increases the current project NPV from \$35 million to \$71 million. The increase in value arises from a higher option value factor shown under the column marked Today. In part (b), this option value factor is based on $S/X = 1.44$ and $\sigma = 134$ percent, whereas in part (a) the option value factor is based on $S/X = 1.44$ and $\sigma = 100$ percent. The higher value for the volatility input increases the option value. (The option value factor shown in the column marked 2 Years does not increase because the volatility input is that of the final payoff, which remains 100 percent.)

Part (b) shows that as the project proceeds, the volatility of the option falls from 158 percent in the current period to 134 percent in two years to 100 percent in four years. Volatility is never eliminated; it simply falls to the level of the volatility of the final payoff.

Valuing a Sequence of Real Options

The flow of calculations in Table 7-1 is remarkably simple. While a typical real options analysis of this application would use a specialized mathematical framework, the results here were obtained with only multiplication, subtraction, and two lookup tables. The lookup table approach works well because the application has been carefully selected. It is a sequence of call options, and the inputs can meaningfully be reduced to two dimensions, S/X and σ. Often real options calculations become complex when details of project-specific features are included. Frequently, the inclusion of private risk complicates the analysis, but as the following sections will show, private risk can be easily incorporated using the private risk discount factor. The straightforward calculations in Table 7-1 present a clear trade-off: Does the increased detail significantly change the results? Is it worthwhile to sacrifice the clarity and ease of calculations?

As Table 7-1 indicates, the option value and the project NPV are two distinct concepts. The option value *does not* include the cost of the current (C) phase, but it does include the contingent option exercise cost of the next phase (X). The project NPV conforms to the timing of a typical project review—the value just before the next expenditure. When one option leads to another, there's a need to be very careful and explicit about the timing of cash flows, investments, and project NPVs. Most often, this is where many errors occur in valuing a sequence of options. Usually it takes a few tries to get the correct timing of the inputs.

Lucky Over and Over Again

How does a two-stage option compare to a one-stage option? For example, suppose the soft drink product development was based on a single four-year option with $S = \$400$ million and $X = \$450$ million. The payoffs between the two-stage option and one-stage are the same, but the one-stage option has all the investment costs at the end of the four-year period.

On the surface, the two growth opportunities seem similar. Yet their valuations are quite different. The one-stage growth opportunity is worth 70 percent of the $400 million payoff, or $278 million, while the two-stage opportunity is worth only 55 percent of the $400 million payoff, or $221 million. (The value of the one-stage option was found using the Black-Scholes formula posted at www.valuesweep.com, and the value of the two-stage option is given in Table 7-1[b].) "Wait!" says the astute reader. "I thought the additional flexibility of the two-stage option would be valuable. Isn't this project feature worth something?"

First, note that flexibility is valuable. Imagine a DCF valuation of the project using the same data as in Table 7-1(b). The final cash flow is $400 million, and the costs are $150 million immediately, $200 million in two years, and $250 million in two more years. The NPV of these inputs is negative $213 million (a 10 percent discount rate is used). The difference between the negative NPV DCF result and the positive NPV options-based result demonstrates the value of flexibility. So the question is narrowed: Why does the one-stage option have a greater value?

The answer to this question is seen in Figure 7-1. The graph shows the wide range of payoff values at the end of four years. The wavy lines are two of the many possible paths for the market-priced payoff value, Project A and Project B. The horizontal dashed lines indicate the exercise cost of the options at years 2 and 4. As the figure shows, projects that survive two exercise decisions are lucky. Project A and Project B end up at nearly the same payoff value, but Project B is eliminated at the two-year decision point.

Figure 7-1 illustrates a point common to many staged growth opportunities: there is an important role for luck. Market-priced risk is beyond a manager's control. While assets can be preconfigured to be best suited for potential market-priced risk outcomes, project success remains strongly influenced by the particular path of market-priced risk. This path is purely random, and projects that survive multiple decision points are lucky over and over again. An immediate application of this insight is to the fortunes of many young public companies after the stock market fall in 2000 and 2001. While these companies may have met their objectives each quarter, the stock market has dramatically reduced their value. In many cases, this bit of bad luck may cause their demise.

This section has showed that with only market-priced risk, watching and waiting is valuable and so the one-shot project is more valuable than the two-staged project. But waiting may not be possible with private risk. The quantitative results of this section, while informative, won't apply. The structure of staged investments generally comes from private risk, through learning investments that force the end of a stage and the start of the next. This makes staged projects different from one-shot projects. Staged projects require early up-front expenditures, have a low chance of survival, and are highly volatile in their early stages.

Figure 7-1   Projects That Survive a Two-Staged Option Are Lucky

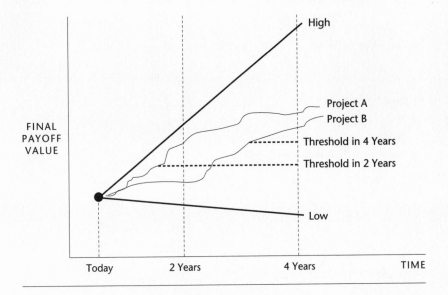

Staged Growth Opportunities
with Private and Market-Priced Risk

This section brings together two methods already presented: the private risk discount introduced in Chapter 6 and the valuation template for a sequence of real options given above. Together, the two methods form an easy and transparent way to value staged growth opportunities with market-priced and private risk—one that is much simpler than the current practice of real options and decision analysis.

Table 7-2(a) illustrates the valuation method for a two-stage growth opportunity. The flow of calculations is the same as in Table 7-1, with the addition of one row that adjusts the option value for private risk failure. The payoff variables are defined in terms of private risk success. For example, note the renaming of "final payoff" to "final success payoff."

The input data in Table 7-2(a) are the same as in Table 7-1. An estimate of the PRD is obtained from external sources. The only

Table 7-2   Two-Staged Growth Opportunity with Market-Priced and Private Risk

($ millions unless noted)

(a) The Value by Stage

	Today	2 Years	4 Years
ASSEMBLE THE DATA			
C Cost	$150	$200	$250
S Value of the final success payoff			$400
σ Volatility of the final success payoff			100%
CALCULATE THE PROJECT NPV			
V	$118 ◄⋯	$207 ◄⋯	$400
C	$150	$200	$250
Project NPV	**($32)**	**$7**	**$150**
CALCULATE THE OPTION VALUE			
Option inputs			
S Value of the success payoff *(as of start of preceding stage)*		$171	$331
X Exercise cost		$200	$250
S/X		0.86	1.32
σ Volatility of the payoff		135%	100%
Option results			
Option value factor *(Table A-1)*	76%	69%	
PRD *(external data source)*	25%	25%	
V' **Adjusted option value**	**$118** ⋯	**$207** ⋯	
Volatility scaling factor *(Table A-3)*	1.25	1.35	
σ' **Volatility of the option**	**169%**	**135%**	

WRITE THE STORY

The path to sustainable growth is:	*"The project has a negative NPV. We should wait until the the situation improves."*
A pessimist would say:	*"What are we waiting for exactly? The project remains risky and expensive."*

(b) The Value by Stage—Higher Final Payoff

	Today	2 Years	4 Years
ASSEMBLE THE DATA			
C Cost	$150	$200	$250
S Value of the final success payoff			$600
σ Volatility of the final success payoff			100%
CALCULATE THE PROJECT NPV			
V	$205◄┄┐	$342◄┄┐	$600
C	$150	$200	$250
Project NPV	**$55**	**$142**	**$350**

CALCULATE THE OPTION VALUE

Option inputs

		2 Years	4 Years
S Value of the success payoff *(as of start of preceding stage)*		$283	$496
X Exercise cost		$200	$250
S/X		1.41	1.98
σ Volatility of the payoff		129%	100%

Option results

	2 Years	4 Years
Option value factor *(Table A-1)*	80%	76%
PRD *(external data source)*	25%	25%
V' Adjusted option value	**$205**	**$342**
Volatility scaling factor *(Table A-3)*	1.22	1.29
σ' Volatility of the option	**157%**	**129%**

WRITE THE STORY

The path to sustainable growth is:	*"Now that the financial markets have increased the value of the final payoff, this looks like a great project."*
A pessimist would say:	*"How do we know that the increased payoff will last for four years? Aren't we wasting our money if the final payoff value drops before then?"*

change in the calculations between Tables 7-1 and 7-2 is that the option value obtained from the lookup tables is multiplied by (1 – PRD) to discount for private risk. The inclusion of private risk lowers the current project NPV from $71 million in Table 7-1(b) to negative $32 million in Table 7-2(a).

Note also that the S/X ratios are fairly high and the options are in the money, yet the project NPV is not positive. This is an interesting difference between real options and financial options. Real options often are well in the money, but exercise is held back or value is impaired by private risk factors. Financial options tend to be much closer to at the money, because those well in the money are exercised.[1]

The Ripple Effect

Comparison of parts (a) and (b) of Table 7-2 illustrates how a change in payoff, arising from market-priced risk, ripples through the sequence of growth options. All other inputs are the same, and the value of the final success payoff increases from $400 million in part (a) to $600 million in part (b), a 50 percent increase. As a result, the current project NPV increases from negative $32 million to positive $55 million. The current option value increases from $118 million to $205 million, an increase of 73 percent, while the volatility of the option decreases from 169 percent to 157 percent.

Table 7-2 captures the essence of how market-priced risk ripples through staged growth opportunities. While all the private risk and cost data inputs remain constant, the value and risk of the project change with the payoff value. For example, when the financial markets downgrade technology company stocks, the value of technology startups also falls. What Table 7-2 shows is that the value of the startups will fall by a greater percentage than their public market counterparts and rise by a greater percentage when the stock market improves. The table also shows that the risk of the startup increases when the value of the final payoff falls.

Table 7-2 is also unique in how it allows the user to cleanly separate the effects of private risk and market-priced risk. For example, a manager of a growth project might argue that during the previous two years much progress had been made, that the project NPV increased from $55 million to $142 million (based on part [b]). A more seasoned manager might argue that despite the progress, the value of the final payoff had fallen during those two years to such a low level that the project's mark-to-market value is only $17 million (based on part [a]). The structure of the valuation template allows this discussion—no doubt very painful to those involved in the project—to proceed based on objective data and a rational framework.

An Innovative Calculation Method

The valuation template shown in Table 7-2 is a big change from current practice. Here are some of its innovative features:

- *Tough issues, simple calculations.* The template covers private risk, market-priced risk, staged investments, and their interaction. But it does so in an easy-to-use manner.

- *Context provided.* Instead of doing black-box, one-off analyses, the valuation template allows easy comparison across growth opportunities. Using the lookup tables further increases intuition about the factors affecting option value and volatility.

- *Ready to benchmark.* In decision analysis, private risk data are based on expert judgment. The valuation template is based on the use of observed transaction data. The key is to seek data on the value consequences of private risk, not private risk itself. Only the observed value consequence of private risk is truly objective.

- *Mark-to-market.* The valuation template in Table 7-2 quantifies how market-priced risk affects the value of private growth opportunities. As the data inputs are calibrated against observed transactions, the valuation template provides an objective mark-to-market framework for growth opportunities.

- *Back of the envelope.* Ever wonder why corporate financial analysts build detailed and exhaustive spreadsheet models, while investment bankers get their valuations done on the back of the envelope? How much detail is really needed to support good decision making or to attract funding? Back-of-the-envelope calculations tell a story and highlight the story's logic. It's an illusion that more spreadsheets lead to better valuation results.

Bad News about the Final Success Payoff at Webvan

In July 2001, Webvan announced it would file for bankruptcy. The last few months of the company's life highlight the dynamics of staged growth and its value. On the surface, Webvan's bankruptcy decision seemed surprising. After all, the company had raised $850 million in funding since its inception in 1999 and announced that it needed only $25 million more to achieve profitability.[2] Webvan had tried to raise the additional funds throughout the spring of 2001 and had achieved cash flow breakeven in one market area, Fullerton, California. So why did the board of Webvan decide to close the firm?

The bankruptcy announcement was followed by a lot of expert hindsight. Many analysts focused on the $30 million to $40 million spent on specialized warehouses around the country. Others questioned the premise of Webvan, that consumers wanted to shop online to save time. In retrospect, the two points of view should have been coupled together: Demonstrate the value of the premise by growing the revenue stream in one or two markets; then expand the winning formula.

What Webvan actually did was to open several follow-on option sequences in parallel. The company opened up warehouses in new locations before becoming profitable in previous locations. The new warehouses created a sequence of options that depended on an unclear payoff value. While the warehouses reduced the private risk about the cost of delivery for online orders, they did nothing to resolve the risk about Webvan's demand.

In late June 2001 Webvan's board learned that its revenues were falling in all of its markets. The success payoff seemed more distant and more expensive than before. In parallel, the value of the option sequences in each quickly crumbled, leaving the firm with almost no value. Even $25 million would be hard to find. Bankruptcy was announced.

Valuing a Genomics Lead Stream

This last section of the chapter uses the example of genomics to illustrate some of the insights that a staged growth valuation template can provide; the template summarizes a way of thinking about the value of growth. Genomics—the science of our common genetic makeup—has the potential to radically change our health.[3] But it may also radically change the pharmaceutical industry. Working through the specifics of this potential change demonstrates some of the limitations of valuation templates. Templates are designed and calibrated against the world as it is, while disruptive change is about what might be. As the example of genomics illustrates, templates are not easily extended in this regard.

Currently, the pharmaceutical industry faces an expectations gap. To meet revenue projections made to the financial community, large pharmaceutical companies need to launch three or four innovative drugs each year, up from the current one or two. With approximately 35 percent of revenues in the top ten pharmaceutical companies from drugs licensed from external sources, the search is on for additional projects to fill the pipeline.

Many industry observers see genomics as a solution. For example, the probability of success for drugs in development shown in Table 6-1 is based on industry experience when about 500 chemical mechanisms were known. In 2000 alone, the genomics revolution created data on 10,000 mechanisms. Some experts argue that companies will use this information to better preselect drug candidates, to speed through trials, and to improve success rates. Others argue that new chemistry is accompanied by less certainty about how the mechanisms work across large groups of people and expect late-stage, expensive failures in drug development until the new chemistry is better understood.

While it is tempting to modify the current drug development valuation template with inputs based on expectations about genomics, this would be inappropriate. By design and implementation, the valuation template does not articulate a logic as to how detailed factors may change and how that feeds into value. Valuation templates are too abstract to provide the required rigor for strategy diagnostics.

To be specific, the drug development valuation template works well for current drug development methods. But the science of genomics may change the industry economics in ways not currently captured in current data:

- *Genomics may lead to small payoffs.* Pharmaceuticals is currently a hit-driven business. Only two of the five payoffs in the current valuation template generate sufficient revenue to cover costs. While genomics may enable a higher percentage of hits, the target population for each genomics-based drug is expected to be smaller. The science can be right, but the economics—size of the target market, people's willingness to pay, duration of the prescriptions, perceived effect on the symptom, and so on—can be poor.

- *Pharmaceutical companies will implement genomics, but competition may eat the gains away.* Most industry experts believe that genomics capabilities will be required to remain competitive. But it is not clear that the value of genomics will remain in the industry; consumers may benefit while drug companies compete away the profits.

- *The cost of implementing genomics may be significant.* The drug development valuation template excludes the drug company's fixed costs for R&D, clinical trials, and sales. Some estimate that R&D costs alone will rise by 50 to 100 percent with genomics.

The value consequences of genomics for large pharmaceutical firms are unclear but clearly link to broad strategic and economic forces in the industry. Valuation templates make strong assumptions about the current industry structure. To maintain its usefulness, the current valuation template for conventional drug development projects should be maintained and updated. Meanwhile, a second template should be started for genomics-based drugs. The first draft may be speculative, but over time, observed transactions and project successes can be used to update the data.

The logic behind the valuation templates is immediately useful, however, for thinking through value creation strategies. There are four publicly traded companies specializing in genomics, each with market values in the billions and revenues under $50 million.

From the staged growth vantage point, the value of a genomics company is the sum of two growth option components. First, the company holds a vast library of information about possible new drugs. The intent is to sell or license this data to others in the industry. But right now—given the speculative economics—no one can quantify the value of this data. Consequently, each genomics company has high-profile clinical trials underway to prove out the inputs into a valuation template—size of payoff, success probabilities, time in each phase, and so on. With actual experience, the price can be set for the data in the library. One immediate insight from the valuation template approach is that genomics companies will get their biggest value increase for early-stage genomics projects by demonstrating savings in the Phase III trials.

On the other hand, if the drugs fail in clinical trial, many analysts expect the "hype" about genomics to die. And if genomics companies stumble on formulating the drugs or other somewhat prosaic issues—as did the early biotech companies—their value will crumble.

If genomics succeeds, the valuation template can be used to obtain a first-order insight about the financial structure of the industry. If the early-stage projects are valuable, there will be an imbalance in many pharmaceutical firms between the plethora of genomics-based opportunities and the available capital. While in the short run capital can be moved to early-stage projects, the successful projects will require much larger amounts of capital in later stages. The need for capital will grow far beyond current industry experience.

Consequently, many experts predict the breakup of the bigger pharmaceutical companies. R&D and clinical trials could be outsourced or spun out, creating a more fragmented industry with more licensing of drugs in development. In addition, the enormous need for investment funds will put growth projects and their valuation on the front lines of transactions instead of hidden in multiproject pipelines. This will introduce market-priced risk to the industry and spur securitization of growth opportunities. The implications of genomics are indeed breathtaking, with the potential to change the size and risk profile of pharmaceutical firms.

Takeaways

- This chapter has shown how to use option value and option volatility lookup tables to quickly calculate the value of a sequence of real options. This method provides much-needed context and simplicity for managers valuing staged growth opportunities.

- The staged growth valuation template with market-priced and private risk provides a transparent and easy-to-use method to update, or mark-to-market, the values of private growth opportunities. The template cleanly separates private and market-priced risk and provides for objective estimates of both.

- The thinking behind valuation templates for staged growth also provides insight into the role of luck. Successful staged growth projects are lucky survivors of many decision points. Managers can't control market-priced risk, but it can cause failure at any stage.

8

Growth Value Benchmarks from Venture Capital

Venture capitalists—the partners in venture capital funds—routinely value and invest in cash-needy growth opportunities. This chapter captures their expertise in a template for valuing venture-funded startups. The results quantify the large amount of private risk in venture-funded growth opportunities and the significant impact of stock market fluctuations on private equity value. The venture capital template is also used to value public company startups, those companies that historically would have remained private but went public in the boom of 1999 and 2000.

Venture capital has been a glamour industry in recent years, as venture capitalists made phenomenal returns from their investments. One book's subtitle is characteristic of the glow: *The True Story of the Six Tall Men Who Backed eBay, Webvan and Other Billion-Dollar Start-ups*. The six partners at Benchmark Capital, who are the focus of the book, split a $1.5 billion gain from that firm's investment in eBay.[1] But by the end of 2001, the venture climate had chilled. Returns to previous investments appeared to be dismal—if any— and venture capitalists dramatically slowed their pace of investment in new startups. Ironically, venture capitalists were managing more money in 2001 than ever before—funds waiting to be invested in startups.

These dramatic changes are not new phenomena. Throughout its young life, the venture industry has experienced sharp swings in the funds available for investment, as well as the gains to venture investments. The dynamic nature of the industry affects not only transactions and valuations, but also the investment process itself. Consequently, some knowledge of the venture industry and its detail is needed before using venture capital valuation results.

This chapter has three parts. The first part introduces the features of venture capital funding through the experiences of Speechworks and Nuance, two companies that compete in the speech recognition technology market. Both firms were founded in 1994, had several rounds of venture funding, and went public in 2000. Their stories illuminate some of the venture industry's institutional features and highlight the challenges for a valuation model.

The second part presents a tailored valuation template and quantitative results for venture capital investments. The venture template is similar to the staged growth template with market-priced and private risk that was introduced in Chapter 7. The venture valuation template shows how changes in stock market valuations cause venture capital valuations to rise and fall more sharply than their public market counterparts. The template also identifies the stages of growth with sizable private risk.

The final part of the chapter applies the venture capital results to the valuation of public company startups. The analysis shows that of August 2001, some of these young companies traded in the public markets at lower valuations than they would have historically received from venture capitalists.

The Story of Two Venture-Funded Firms

Speechworks and Nuance are two companies that have developed speech recognition technology. Speech recognition is now used to quickly gain user information. For example, in airline travel the user might hear: "Say your departure city." The speech recognition technology translates the user's spoken reply into digital content.

Speechworks and Nuance started in the same year, 1994, and went public in the same year, 2000. In addition, they each completed a round of venture financing in May 1998. As direct competitors with similar financial histories, Speechworks and Nuance provide an interesting window on startup growth and valuation.

Speechworks began in August 1994 with a license of speech recognition technology from MIT. (The license contract is the subject of analysis in Chapter 11.) Based in Boston, Speechworks initially sold its expertise through professional (consulting) services. In 1996 the firm closed a round of angel funding and shipped its first product. Angel funding typically comes from individual investors, including family and friends, who invest alongside the entrepreneurs until the company can demonstrate the progress and plans that enable venture capital funding.[2]

Speechworks completed its first round of venture capital funding in May 1998. Although in retrospect venture funding seems like a natural step, the odds of getting a young company funded by a venture capitalist are actually quite small. One estimate is that of 300 submissions, venture capitalists will do an in-depth analysis of 45 and fund only 9.[3] Speechworks completed two rounds of venture financing in 1999 and another in May 2000. In August 2000, the company sold its stock to the public for the first time. Speechworks' revenues, losses, and funding are summarized in the top half of Table 8-1.

Nuance also started in 1994 with the license of speech recognition technology from a quasi-academic entity, SRI International. Nuance completed its first round of venture funding in January 1997, with additional rounds in 1998 and 1999. Nuance went public in April 2000, before Speechworks completed its last venture round and IPO.

There are two particularly interesting dates at which to compare the competitors' valuations. The first is May 1998 when both completed venture rounds. As Table 8-1 shows, Nuance had a valuation of $83 million for $4 million in revenue in the previous year, while Speechworks had a valuation of $20 million for $2 million in previous year's revenue. Nuance's cumulative losses were also larger, $8 million by the end of 1997, as compared to Speechworks's 1997 cumulative loss of $4 million.

Table 8-1 The History of Two Venture-Funded Startups
($ millions unless noted)

	1995	1996	1997	1998	1999	2000	2000
Speechworks							
Revenues	$0	$1	$2	$6	$14	$30	
% Professional Services	16%	20%	48%	48%	42%	37%	
Net Cash Flow	$0	–$1	–$3	–$6	–$16	–$26	
Cumulative Loss	$0	–$2	–$4	–$11	–$27	–$53	
Equity Investments	$0	$3		$7	$25	$20	$100
Postmoney Valuation		$5	$20	$111	$173	$595	
Source of Funds		Private	Venture	Venture	Venture	Corporate and IPO	
Month of Funding		December	May	January and June	May	August	
Nuance							
Revenues	$1	$1	$4	$12	$20	$52	
% Professional Services	95%	21%	37%	32%	30%	27%	
Net Cash Flow	–$1	–$3	–$4	–$7	–$19	–$23	
Cumulative Loss	–$1	–$4	–$8	–$15	–$33	–$57	
Equity Investments			$7	$15	$43	$85	
Postmoney Valuation			$28	$83	$209	$470	
Source of Funds			Venture	Venture	Venture	IPO	
Month of Funding			January	May	November	April	

Sources: Data compiled from corporate filings with the SEC and Recombinant Capital Inc. (www.recapit.com).

The valuations shown in Table 8-1 are labeled "postmoney." In the venture industry the value of the firm as it presents itself for funding is known as the "premoney" valuation, and the value of the firm including the new funds invested is known as the postmoney value. (The investment itself is the "money.") The ratio of the new investment to the postmoney valuation is the share of the firm owned by the new investment. (The new investment may not be new investors, as past investors may provide additional funds.) For example, in May 1998, Nuance's new investment took 18 percent of the equity ($15 / $83) while Speechworks's new investment took 35 percent of the equity ($7 / $20). As these calculations illustrate, the amount invested, the share of equity for that investment, and the valuation are closely related.

Now compare valuations in 2000, at the time of each company's IPO. Nuance went public in April 2000 with annual sales of $52 million and a valuation of $470 million, at a market-value-to-sales ratio of 9. In the following month, Speechworks did a venture capital financing at a similar valuation, about 9 times revenues. But four months later, Speechworks went public at a valuation of $595 million, at a market-value-to-sales ratio of 20. What happened in those few months? How can the rapid growth in value be explained?

What Determines the Value of Venture-Funded Startups?

Venture capitalists don't use formal valuation models. They rely on high-level benchmarks and rules of thumb and gauge valuations by how other deals are being priced at the time. Ideas on improving and codifying venture capital valuations have spilled out of academia and consulting firms, but none of the quantitative tools have been adopted. In practice, venture capitalists simultaneously determine the value of the startup and the amount they will invest through negotiations with the entrepreneurs. The results are determined by balancing a number of issues, many of which are not captured in formal models.

Size of investment. How much will be needed to meet the next milestone—to prove the concept, to complete the product, or to gain the first customers? The value of the firm will increase upon milestone completion, so shortly before that event the startup should be able to attract additional funding. In addition to the actual expenses, the size of the investment is influenced by a tension between entrepreneurs and venture capitalists. Entrepreneurs often want to keep the size of the investment small, so as to avoid giving the investors a large share of the firm. Venture capitalists often want to increase the size of the investment because larger investments make the best use of their limited time to search out and manage good opportunities.

Share of the firm taken by the investors. Negotiations about valuation are essentially negotiations about this term; the higher the premoney valuation, the lower the share of the firm taken by investors. Of course investors want the largest share of the firm they can negotiate, but there are bounds. Investors also fear that if they take a large share of the company, the entrepreneurs will be less motivated to work the long days required for success. (Entrepreneurs agree!) But without a large share of the firm, the venture capitalist won't get much of the final payoff.

The premoney valuation (value of the firm before investment). The irony of premoney valuations is that they don't exist until an investment is completed; a premoney valuation without an investment commitment is just an idea in the entrepreneur's mind, not a real number. The size of the investment, the percent of the equity taken, and the premoney valuation are offered at the same time. For example, in a negotiation a venture capitalist might say: "We'll take 30 percent of the firm for $10 million." The entrepreneurs then calculate that their share of the firm would be worth $23.33 million premoney (70% / 30% × $10 million), and the total firm value would be $33.33 million postmoney ($23.33 million + $10 million).

State of the IPO market and the value of high-tech companies in the public markets. Either the IPO window is open—months in which institutional investors are open to purchasing shares in an IPO; or it is closed—periods in which IPOs simply don't happen. For example, only four venture-backed companies held an IPO in the spring of 2001 and thirty-six were withdrawn because of a lack of investor interest. In contrast, there were

258 IPOs in 2000.[4] When the public markets aren't open to IPOs or when the public markets don't highly value high-tech companies, private-market valuations also fall.

The quality of the management team. Investors often read the resumes of the management team at the back of the business plan before anything else. They know that a startup will need to modify and adapt its plans as product market and financial conditions change, and only a strong team can weather the changes. Further, while it seems very creative to think up a new high-tech product, much of the product's success will come from the steady execution of the more mundane decisions that determine how the product will be sold, by whom, and how it will be priced. An experienced team can more rapidly fit the new product into the stream of high-tech commerce, placing it advantageously among the other technologies. Valuations rise when the business plan comes from a team with proven success.

The terms and conditions of the investment. The founders of the startup own the common stock, and the venture capital investors obtain preferred stock. Preferred stock contains a number of terms that put venture capital investors first in line for payments, such as preferences in the event of liquidation or rights to invest in follow-on rounds. The terms and conditions of preferred stock tend to follow industry norms and trends but are shaped a bit to the transaction at hand. Typically, the specifics don't have a strong influence on the current round of investment and valuation because in most negotiations the value of the firm is set before the terms are finalized. But the terms affect future valuations. For example, one voice technology firm, General Magic, has had difficulty in raising funds because current shareholders have strong rights and preferences that limit returns (and thus the value of the firm) to new investors.

A Look at Recent Data

The recent history of venture capital valuation results are shown in Table 8-2, which reports data for size of investment, valuation, and

Table 8-2 Venture Capital Investment and Valuations by Stage of Firm
($ millions unless noted)

Stage of Startup	1992	1993	1994	1995	1996	1997	1998	1999	2000	1992–1997	1998–2000
Median "Premoney" Valuation											
Startup	2	2	2	2	3	3	4	6	8	$3	$6
Product development	6	8	8	9	10	10	12	13	20	$9	$15
Shipping product	10	11	16	12	16	16	20	32	41	$13	$31
Profitable	16	19	20	30	20	33	24	36	39	$23	$33
IPO	NA	NA	NA	67	79	105	174	317	366	$84	$286
Median Amount Invested											
Startup	2	2	1	3	3	2	3	4	6	$2	$4
Product development	3	4	4	4	5	4	5	6	12	$4	$8
Shipping product	4	5	5	7	6	5	5	7	10	$5	$7
Profitable	5	5	6	8	10	5	9	7	12	$7	$9
IPO	39	39	50	32	33	32	44	63	77	$37	$61
Investment/"Postmoney" Valuation											
Startup	48%	45%	39%	54%	49%	43%	43%	38%	43%	46%	42%
Product development	37%	34%	31%	33%	33%	28%	31%	33%	37%	33%	33%
Shipping product	28%	29%	23%	37%	28%	22%	21%	19%	19%	28%	19%
Profitable	23%	22%	25%	20%	34%	13%	27%	17%	23%	23%	22%
IPO	NA	NA	NA	32%	29%	24%	20%	17%	17%	28%	18%

	1992	1993	1994	1995	1996	1997	1998	1999	2000
Venture Industry Data									
No. of venture investments	952	986	1036	1167	1502	1841	2046	3317	4107
No. of IPOs from venture-funded firms*	140	168	101	145	214	119	63	244	193
Median annual revenues at IPO**	NA	NA	NA	$17.4	$10.5	$10.0	$15.6	$7.6	$5.3
Median years, first VC funding to IPO	NA	NA	NA	4.2	3.1	3.1	2.7	2.8	2.9

Source: Data compiled from various publications of VentureOne Corporation (www.ventureone.com).

*IPOs of firms in the VentureOne database.

**Last full fiscal year.

share of the firm.[5] The data are given by stage of the firm. The startup stage can be fairly skeletal, with just a business plan and the founding team. For biotech firms, the development stage includes clinical trials. Not all firms are funded at each stage. For example, a startup may have an initial funding round from family and friends and then complete its first venture capital funding at the product development stage.

Venture investments tend to cluster in three large sectors: information technology, healthcare, and "other." The funding profile (size of investments, years between stages, stage at which a firm goes public) for a biotech firm in the healthcare sector will naturally be quite different from that of a computer hardware firm in the information technology sector. Consequently, venture capital data by industry is needed for accurate valuations. Table 8-2 presents industry average data to illustrate the broader issues and to provide a simple point of calibration for the venture capital valuation template developed in the next section. (See www.valuesweep.com for details on obtaining industry-level venture capital data.)

The data in Table 8-2 highlight features of the larger context in venture capital valuation:

- *There are uneven increases in value by stage of investment.* The two largest value increases are from the startup stage to product development and from the profitable stage to IPO.[6] These are also the transitions with the greatest amount of failure. Few concept plans attract the people and money needed to begin product development, and most concepts remain as visions in the minds of struggling entrepreneurs. And at the other end of staged growth, relatively few venture-backed firms complete an IPO; most are acquired for much less than an IPO-level value.

- *The largest share of the firm is taken during the first round.* Venture capitalists typically take 40 percent or more of the company during the first round of investment. In subsequent rounds, 20 percent to 30 percent is taken on average.

- *1999 and 2000 were unusual years.* The number of transactions and valuations increased significantly in 1999 and

2000. The pace of activity was high, and many characterized the period with the phrase "money was chasing deals." The share of the firm taken in exchange for a venture investment fell during these years, a reflection of the shift in negotiating power to entrepreneurs.

- *The median revenues at the time of IPO fell sharply in 1999 and 2000.* This result is largely due to a shift (perhaps one-time) in the financial markets. While in the past, the typical venture-funded startup had to show four to seven profitable quarters before it would be considered a candidate for an IPO, in 1999 and 2000 many venture-funded companies went public before becoming profitable. (The last section of this chapter discusses this phenomenon in more detail.)

Growth Value Benchmarks

Given the recent dramatic change in the venture capital environment, it's a challenge to build a credible valuation model for venture-funded startups. It's also clear that a better valuation model won't lead to better venture returns—rules of thumb work just as well given the many factors affecting value. There remains a role, however, for a more formal valuation method. The financial institutions that invest in venture capital funds (known as limited partners) and the state and regional agencies that work to foster an entrepreneurial climate all are interested in a more systematic method for valuation. Further, the template codifies the relative importance of market-priced and private risk, allowing industry participants and managers outside the venture industry to better understand this dynamic.

This section presents a tailored valuation template for valuing venture-funded startups. The template's main advantages are its ease of use, its reflection of market-priced risk, and its application of observable transaction data to estimate the private risk discount (PRD).

Table 8-3 demonstrates the valuation template for venture capital investment. Data from 1996 were used because it was a somewhat typical year for venture investing. Because the data used are based on medians and averages from different industries, the PRD

Table 8-3   Illustrative Growth Value Benchmarks from Venture Capital Investments, 1996

($ millions unless noted)

	Startup	Product Development	Shipping Product	Profitable	IPO
ASSEMBLE THE DATA					
Equity investment	$2.7	$4.9	$6.2	$10.3	$32.8
Premoney valuation	$2.8	$10.1	$15.8	$20.0	$78.7
Postmoney valuation	$5.5	$15.0	$22.0	$30.3	$111.5
Volatility of market value post-IPO					85%
CALCULATE THE OPTION VALUE					
Option Inputs					
S Value of the success payoff		$56.9 ◄┄	$67.0 ◄┄	$85.9 ◄┄	$111.5
X Exercise cost		$4.9	$6.2	$10.3	$32.8
S/X		11.62	10.80	8.34	3.40
σ Volatility of the payoff		142%	126%	105%	85%
Option Results					
Option value factor	87%	85%	78%	77%	
V Option value	**$49.5**	**$56.9** ┄	**$67.0** ┄	**$85.9** ┄	
Volatility scaling factor	1.09	1.12	1.2	1.24	
σ' Volatility of the option	154%	142%	126%	105%	
CALCULATE IMPLIED PRIVATE RISK DISCOUNT					
V Value of option	$49.5	$56.9	$67.0	$85.9	
Observed valuation (postmoney)	5.5	15	22	30.3	
Value loss from private risk	$44.02	$41.92	$44.97	$55.56	
PRD (Value loss/ Option value)	89%	74%	67%	65%	

Source: Equity investment and valuation data from VentureOne (www.ventureone.com).

estimate is illustrative but not "valuation-grade." The results will differ significantly by industry. (See www.valuesweep.com for templates by industry and for other years.)

As with the staged growth valuation templates presented in Chapter 7, the valuation analysis begins with the final stage and works back to earlier stages. To make the calculations easy to follow, it is assumed that each stage shown in Table 8-3 requires two years to complete. (The option value lookup tables in the Appendix are used for the calculations.) An IPO is the final stage shown in Table 8-3. The post-IPO company has a market value of $111 million (1996 data) and a volatility of market value of 85 percent (a typical level for high-tech and biotech firms).

Before an IPO, at the profitable stage, the startup's value is based on its option to gain the IPO payoff. The real options logic in the model is that funds raised at the IPO are the amount required to bring the firm to a mature, self-funding state. If the IPO payoff slips below the required investment, then the IPO will be delayed or abandoned. (In practice, the funds raised at the IPO and the IPO valuation are determined simultaneously. While the model does not match the real-world detail on this point, the structure of the valuation template captures the basic issues.)

Results for the PRD

The value of the real option on the IPO success payoff is $85.9 million. This hypothetical result can be compared with the postmoney valuation of a startup at the profitable stage, $30.3 million. The difference between the two is the loss in value that venture capitalists expect from private risk failure. The PRD is calculated as the value lost from private risk failure divided by the real option value. Private risk success in this template is the assumption that all technology, management, and product issues are resolved favorably—that the only remaining uncertainty is the value of the mature business in the stock market. Private risk failure can be any number of outcomes that lead to a less valuable payoff.

The hypothetical value of the startup and the estimate of the PRD for the earlier stages can be calculated in a similar manner. In each stage, there is a real option to obtain the value of the next stage. The exercise price of the option is the investment funding from the next stage. The PRD is estimated as the difference between the real option model result and the observed transaction value.[7]

The PRD results shown in Table 8-3 conform to venture industry experience. At the startup stage of venture investing, there is enormous private risk—an untested management team, no product, no market tests, and so on. Venture capitalists strongly discount value. In the middle two stages, the firm meets clear and tangible milestones, and thus the PRD is relatively small. These are years of steady development, but the big test is yet to come.

In the final years, between the profitable and IPO stages, there is again a large PRD that reflects the huge difference in value between a firm that completes an IPO and a firm that is acquired or shut down. (Recall the quote cited earlier in the book: "Most of the companies organized in Silicon Valley will become product lines of larger companies, features of product lines of larger companies, or they will fail.")[8] The large probability of a payoff less than the IPO payoff leads to a large PRD.

Venture Valuations and the Stock Market

As the high-tech sector of the stock market collapsed in value in the spring of 2001, there was a ripple-through effect on the valuations of venture-funded startups. Without an explicit model of how market-priced risk affects private valuations, entrepreneurs and venture capitalists engaged in difficult and tense negotiations, each thinking that the other side was greedy or held overinflated expectations. In particular, it was difficult for many startups to accept that new rounds of financing would be at lower valuations than previous rounds, even after all milestones had been met. These "down rounds," as they are called, are the result of market-priced risk.

The venture capital valuation template can be used to untangle the effect of market-priced risk from private risk. With the estimates of the PRD in hand, a change in the IPO payoff can be traced through to its impact on the value of venture-funded startups at each stage.

Table 8-4 demonstrates the influence of the stock market on venture capital valuations. The year 1996 is used as representative of a typical stock market. The market-value-to-sales ratio of the final success payoff is the 1996 actual level, 10.6. The "hot" stock

Table 8-4   The Temperature of the Stock Market Ripples through Venture Valuations

($ millions unless noted)

	Startup	Product Development	Shipping Product	Profitable	IPO
"Typical" stock market (1996)					
Market value/Sales					10.6
Postmoney valuations *(observed)*	$12	$17	$25	$33	$112
"Hot" stock market					
Market value/Sales					20.0
Postmoney valuations *(from template)*	$34	$39	$55	$66	$210
Hot value/Typical value	274%	225%	217%	202%	188%
"Cold" stock market					7.0
Market value/Sales					
Postmoney valuations *(from template)*	$6	$11	$17	$20	$74
Cold value/Typical value	52%	65%	67%	61%	66%

market is assumed to value venture-backed IPOs at twenty times sales while the "cold" stock market places value at seven times sales. The valuation results shown in Table 8-4 were completed using the template of Table 8-3, including the estimates of the PRD. For example, to calculate the private equity value in the hot stock market, market-value-to-sales ratio at IPO was changed to twenty. Keeping all other data inputs the same, this increased the S/X ratio and thus the real option value. The result is a hot-market value of $66 million for a startup in the profitable stage.

Table 8-4 dramatically illustrates how a change in the stock market ripples through the private equity valuations. For the hot stock market, the IPO payoff increases by 88 percent, and earlier rounds increase in value by successively larger percentages. Interestingly, a hot IPO market has the largest relative impact on early-stage financings—those furthest away from their potential IPO.

Next, consider a feature of the recent hot IPO market: the value of firms at the shipping-product stage holding an IPO. These firms got the huge IPO-driven gain in payoff value early in their corporate lives, and their subsequent fate is discussed in the next section. For venture capitalists, the potential for an early IPO payoff further increased their valuations of concept- and product development–stage companies beyond the hot-market effect alone.

Now turn to the cold-market valuations. When the market-value-to-sales ratio at IPO falls to seven, the IPO payoff falls to 66 percent of the 1996 level. Again, the venture valuations in the earlier stages fall by a larger amount. As Table 8-4 shows, a change in stock market valuations will most strongly affect early-stage firms.

Despite the sharp drop in the hypothetical startup valuations in Table 8-4 from a cold market, the template may be overvaluing startups. A cold stock market is often coupled with a very tough high-tech climate. This was certainly the case in late 2000 and in 2001. Many startups found it difficult to acquire customers, and their growth stalled. Recessionary conditions may have caused an increase in private risk that is not reflected in the valuation template.

Valuing Public Company Startups

The informal rules about the timing of an IPO changed after Netscape's IPO in 1995. Netscape was an unprofitable Internet-based company, and its IPO created huge returns for investors. Similarly, many other companies went public in the late 1990s that in other periods would have remained private and venture financed. Because these companies fit the profile of venture capital investments, the value of these public company startups can be compared to historical venture capital valuations.

Table 8-5 shows recent data on three public companies, Pharsight, Support.com, and Keynote, which are fairly typical of public company startups. Collectively the three highlight the challenges to valuing this type of firm. Pharsight is the decision-analysis software and consulting firm mentioned in Chapter 5; Support.com sells software that automates information technology support to corporations and service providers; and Keynote sells Web site performance measurement services. Keynote had its IPO in September 1999, while Pharsight and Support.com went public in the summer of 2000. None of the companies had a profitable quarter at the time of this writing in August 2001. While a detailed set of calculations can

Table 8-5   A Quick Look at Three Public-Company Startups

($ millions unless noted; all data as of August 2001)

	Pharsight (PHST)	Support.com (SPRT)	Keynote (KEYN)
Data			
Market value	$34	$116	$225
Annual revenue	$12	$19	$34
Cash	$25	$62	$269
Quarterly burn rate	($6)	($9)	($9)
Calculations			
Market value/Sales	2.83	6.24	6.62
Cash/Quarterly burn rate	4	7	30

be done for each public company startup, a broad and quick comparison to historical venture valuations highlights the key issues.

Of the three firms, Pharsight had the lowest cash reserve and the lowest market-value-to-sales ratio. The financial markets valued the company at only $9 million more than its cash. Why such a low valuation? Or is it low? At $34 million, Pharsight's market value is greater than the postmoney valuation of venture-backed firms at the shipping-product stage shown in Table 8-2, with the exception of 1999 and 2000. In addition, more than 60 percent of Pharsight's revenues came from consulting services, which don't have the high valuation multiples typically associated with high-tech companies. Until Pharsight can demonstrate strong revenue growth from software licensing, perhaps this valuation level makes some sense.

Support.com had $62 million in cash, about seven quarters worth, in August 2001. Net of cash, the financial markets are placing a value of $54 million on the company, about six times revenue. Support.com obtains more than 70 percent of its revenues from software licensing fees, a revenue mix that is in line with that of many successful software firms. Compared with historical venture results, however, the $54 million is high—higher than the postmoney valuations of firms at the same stage in any year.

In addition, the valuation template of Table 8-3 shows a large PRD as a company transitions to an IPO. The size of the PRD reflects two risks: the risk of not doing an IPO, and also the risk that a company won't make that next stage in growth—the larger scale, the more mature technology, and so on. It could be argued that Support.com has resolved the IPO risk in the PRD, but not the risk about its growth to the next stage of its corporate life. Thus, one would expect its valuation to be higher than private venture-funded firms at the same stage, but significantly less than mature companies at the same level of revenues.

Finally, consider Keynote, which has a market value less than its cash reserve. Essentially, the financial markets are signaling that they don't value the firm's business strategy or business model and that the cash is being applied to an activity that fails to earn the cost of capital. Any number of legal and governance issues may be constraining Keynote's management, keeping the firm on the value-losing strategy. (Often a large strategic change is achieved by selling the firm to another company; perhaps the constraints affect the possibility of this outcome.) Quite a few public company start-ups trade below their cash value, illustrating how issues that are difficult to directly quantify, such as governance, can affect valuation.

Takeaways

- This chapter presents a venture capital valuation template that fits the nature of startups: cash-needy growth opportunities. Valuations are completed using simple calculations on a small spreadsheet and can be followed by the many parties surrounding venture financing, including general partners, entrepreneurs, limited partners, financiers, and auditors.

- Venture capital valuations are strongly influenced by stock market valuations and IPO opportunities. The valuation template quantifies the effect of stock market fluctuations on private equity valuations and can be used for mark-to-market updates of venture investments.

- The PRD estimates show that private risk is a large factor in startup valuation, particularly at two points: the initial stages, when much about the company is uncertain, and the pre-IPO stage, when many startups simply don't achieve this valuable milestone.

9

A Close Look at
Market-Priced Risk

Much of this book was written in late 2000 and early 2001. Frankly, it is a challenge to write about the logic of valuation when the stock market plunges with each passing month. When high-flying growth companies such as Cisco, Intel, Yahoo!, and Amazon.com have market values less than 20 percent of the year before, some readers might question a basic argument in this book—that private growth-opportunity valuations should be aligned with valuations in the financial markets. This chapter takes a close look at stock market valuations and at how well the expanded toolkit explains stock prices. It also addresses how the alignment of public-market and private-market valuations can enhance the ability of growth opportunities to attract funding.

Very often managers and consultants focus on the private risk in growth opportunities, and their thinking ignores the role of market-priced risk. Managers with technical training—who are often growth project leaders—feel far removed from the financial markets. They have a lot of skepticism about the rationality of stock market pricing. Their everyday focus is on the private risk of growth opportunities.

Consultants are no different. Many decision-analysis and real options consulting firms clearly separate market prices and private risk, focusing their analysis on the latter. The result is a strategy and valuation report that has a one-off, handcrafted feel and doesn't communicate well to those who might undertake the project financing.

The purpose of this chapter is to shake up this way of thinking. Separating growth projects from market-priced risk hurts value. When the market-priced risk in a growth project is clearly understood, it is easier to finance. When managers use signals about value from the financial markets to manage their growth projects, they better understand when to proceed and when to cut their losses.

This chapter has two parts. The first part addresses how well valuation models can explain stock prices. The short answer is that much of the level of value and changes in value in public markets cannot be explained by the value of future cash flows, including options-based approaches.

This is a messy and unsatisfying conclusion for a book that attempts to break new ground in valuation methods. But it is better to be clear about this state of affairs so that we might set more reasonable expectations for the valuation of private growth opportunities. Valuation is not yet a science, and financial market valuations are not always precise.

The second part of the chapter argues that market-priced risk has a pervasive impact on the value of growth opportunities because, by definition, they are cash-needy. When public-market valuations are low, the doors to external financing are often closed, and the value of growth opportunities crumbles. Market-priced risk also opens doors. The chapter concludes with a discussion of how monetization, securitization, and insurance can increase the value of growth opportunities. These ideas are illustrated by looking at the business strategy of the Patent & License Exchange, an online intellectual property service.

Perplexed by the Stock Market

In December 2000, one of the nation's leading economists, Robert Hall of Stanford University, opened a high-profile speech with the summary statement: "Economists are as perplexed as anyone by the behavior of the stock market."[1] The puzzle he addressed in this talk, "Struggling to Understand the Stock Market," is shown in Fig-

Figure 9-1 Corporate Valuations over the Past 50 Years

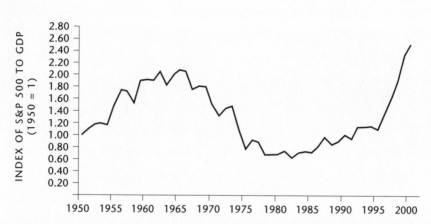

Source: Author's calculations. Data: GDP from Federal Reserve Flow of Accounts; S&P 500 index from Robert Shiller, www.econ.yale.edu/~shiller/.

ure 9-1. The graph shows that relative to the size of the economy, U.S. equity value swiftly rose to peak levels in the late 1990s. In his speech, Hall examined the key input to a DCF valuation model: corporate cash flow. He argued that in the late 1990s aggregate corporate cash flows grew rapidly. This was quickly recognized by financial market players, leading to high valuations.

There's also a second puzzle to explain, shown in Figure 9-2. The performance of two groups of stocks shown in the graph—technology and nontechnology—is dramatically different. While both sectors rose in value through the 1990s, the technology sector grew in value much more quickly and fell more sharply in 2000 and 2001. What happened to the technology sector?

Hal Varian of the University of California at Berkeley argues that in the late 1990s, the high-tech sector was hit with three waves of demand: The telecommunications sector deregulated in 1996 and began a period of heavy spending; the Y2K bug caused a wave of spending in 1998 and 1999; and the burst of Internet spending fueled high-tech demand in early 2000.[2] All have now ended, and the days of fast corporate cash flow growth in high-tech have ended as well.

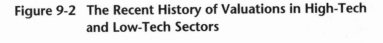

Figure 9-2 The Recent History of Valuations in High-Tech and Low-Tech Sectors

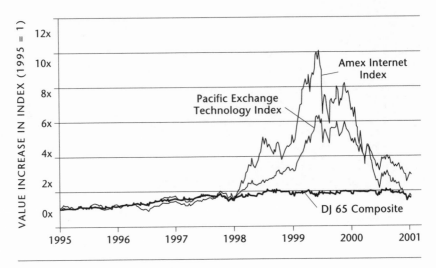

But what about the nontechnology sector shown in Figure 9-2? While lacking the drama of the two technology indices, the value of the nontechnology sector rose over 100 percent during the decade. In the spring of 1996, Federal Reserve chairman Alan Greenspan characterized the stock market valuations at that time as driven by "irrational exuberance." The phrase came from one of his advisors, Robert Shiller of Yale University, who wrote a book with the same title.[3]

DCF + Real Options . . . There's Still Irrational Exuberance

Shiller and others argue that stock market valuations in the late 1990s cannot be explained by the value of future cash flows. While the research results are based on sophisticated statistical tests of the data, the underlying arguments come from the logic behind a DCF valuation. For example, Shiller has examined whether changes in stock prices can be explained by the arrival of new information. He and other researchers have found that stock prices are far more volatile than can be explained by a DCF valuation model. In sum, the DCF valuation of future cash flows appears to only imperfectly explain the level and change in stock prices.

Could expanding the toolkit to include the real options approach strengthen the argument for rational stock price valuation? From 1995 to 2000, many young companies without profits went public. And many maintained an aggressive stance about their need to grow sales more quickly than profits. As argued in earlier chapters, DCF will incorrectly value the growth opportunities embedded in these firms. Real options advocates argued that this additional valuation tool would close the gap between the DCF value and the stock price.

My own experience, however, is that real options are typically just a fraction of the DCF value of the current business. This was demonstrated for Amazon.com in Chapter 4. Seldom do firms have access to a huge payoff, the size required to make an option more valuable than ongoing business. Public companies without profits are staged growth opportunities, and company value is but a fraction of the payoff value.

In sum, a DCF valuation of future cash flows, even adding in real options value, doesn't fully explain stock price levels or changes. Next, let's look at how well these models do at picking high-growth companies.

Results from Individual Companies

Perhaps valuation tools don't work well in the aggregate, but are best used to value individual companies, finding the discrepancies between the stock price and the true growth value. In the early 1970s, a group of fifty firms expected to grow quickly were known as the Nifty Fifty. At the time, many financial analysts argued that these were the companies to buy and hold. Consequently, their valuations were bid up to high levels. When Wharton professor Jeremy Siegel revisited the Nifty Fifty's performance twenty-five years later, he arrived at several conclusions that are of interest for valuing modern growth opportunities:[4]

- Even with hindsight, it's impossible to sort future winners from future losers in 1972. There is no clear differentiator.

- Only fifteen of the fifty stocks earned superior returns, but this was sufficient to carry the portfolio. A few hits created most of the value.

- In the long run, the firms were correctly valued. From 1972 to 1996, the average annual return to holding the entire portfolio of the Nifty Fifty was essentially the same as the return to holding the S&P 500.

- For much of the twenty-five-year period, however, the firms were significantly mispriced. The mispricing was large and persistent. (We'll revisit this issue later in the chapter.)

The analysis of the Nifty Fifty shows that standard valuation tools don't do a good job of sorting through growth opportunities on a company-by-company basis.

This conclusion is reinforced by advice given to technology investors: Don't try to pick the winners, let the stock market do it for you. When a product market is new and emerging, it can take some time for a product market winner to emerge. Some financial writers recommend that technology investors not try to sort winners from losers early on.[5] Instead, the advice goes, invest in an entire promising sector and shed companies from the stock portfolio as their losing status in the product market becomes clear. Meanwhile, the gains continue to accrue to the winners in the stock portfolio. This kind of advice reflects the difficulty of picking winning stocks in emerging and fast-moving product markets. It's not a question of a better cash flow forecast but one of making bets on product market winners.

Valuation and the Structure of the Financial Markets

To those who value private-market growth opportunities, financial market pricing appears to be clean and crisp. On closer scrutiny, however, pricing is revealed to be highly dependent on the particulars of the market structure.

Imagine, for a moment, a market with no transaction costs and many ways to arbitrage. In this setting, investors would buy underpriced stocks and sell overpriced stocks. These trades would rapidly close the mispricing gaps. Their trading activity would discipline pricing in the market.

But most financial markets have transactions costs. And most traders face liquidity constraints. The two forces work together to prevent traders from taking advantage of every last cent of mispricing. Consequently, there may be long periods in which a stock price is not explained by a valuation model, but yet, given transactions costs, there is no way to profit from the mispricing.

Mark Rubinstein of the University of California at Berkeley uses this fact to argue that the stock market was rationally valued in the late 1990s.[6] If there was substantial mispricing, he argues, then professional money managers who actively search out under- and overpriced stocks could profit handsomely. A large body of academic research shows, however, that an active investment strategy earns a lower return than passively holding a well-diversified portfolio. This conclusion prevails for the late 1990s as well, and thus, Rubinstein argues, the stock market valuations were reasonable.

In sum, given the lack of evidence on persistent profits to individual stock pickers, one could argue that companies could appear mispriced, even for long periods of time, yet no stock-picking profits could be made.

A Summary

The previous arguments suggest that it is difficult to precisely value stocks and that recent valuation levels have some reasonable foundation. While the valuation issue continues to be debated by academics, it has three immediate implications for the value of private growth opportunities:

- The discounted value of future cash flows often does not fully explain the level and changes in stock prices. Real options does not close the gap.

- There may be persistent mispricings in the stock market, in which the trading price and the price predicted by a rational model remain far apart. The structure of the market itself will determine the size and persistence of the gap.

- Public-market valuations are not scientifically precise. There is no reason to expect the precision of private-market valuations to exceed the quality of public-market results. Let's not overestimate the accuracy of valuation models.

The Pervasive Nature of Market-Priced Risk:
Part I

Investment banks routinely charge young companies 7 percent of the IPO offering as a fee for taking the firm public. If $50 million is raised, the bank takes home $3.5 million for three months of work. I once asked an entrepreneur, who had grown his company for six long and difficult years before its IPO, if he felt "ripped off" by the banks. After all, he had spent so many hours, and the banks but a few. They would profit immediately; he would still need to work hard to sustain company value. The entrepreneur was not at all bitter or cynical. He replied that the existence (but not necessarily any effort) of the investment banks greased the wheels all along the way. Without the potential of an investment bank willing to take a firm public, venture capitalists and corporations would not have invested in his startup. Long before the IPO, the growth path was smoothed and value was enhanced by the possibility of an IPO.

Part I of the pervasive nature of market-priced risk is about the correlation between stock market valuations and financing alternatives. By definition, cash-needy growth opportunities need funds. As the following example shows, decisions at even the largest companies are shaped by the current state of the financial markets.

In the fall of 1999, 3Com spun out its Palm division in a high-profile IPO. At that time, shares in Palm were worth more than shares in 3Com. The financial markets were receptive to spin-offs and put a premium on growth options. By the spring of 2001, however, things had changed. Faced with a similar opportunity to create a high-profile spin-off, bluelight.com, Kmart chose instead to fold its Internet startup into the corporate parent. The financial markets were testy, and growth options were not highly valued. Two years earlier, in another market environment, Kmart might have made a different decision.

Very generally, lower stock market values often close the door to the financing of growth. It is well documented, for example, that IPOs occur in waves.[7] For four to fifteen months, the IPO window is open, and the investment banks believe that investors will buy the shares of young companies. Then the IPO window shuts, and young firms simply can't find a bank willing to take them public.

Spin-offs are similarly thwarted. Typically higher stock values enable mergers and acquisitions, with the acquiring company offering its own stock as payment. At lower valuations, the same acquisition might require a large amount of dilution and is not contemplated.

High equity values also support the type of debt financing used to finance cash-needy growth—noninvestment grade debt or junk bonds. Junk bonds often contain equity-like components, and thus even profitless companies can issue these bonds in strong markets. For example, three profitless Internet companies—Amazon.com, Webvan, and Exodus—each issued more than $1 billion in junk bonds at the peak of the Internet boom in 1999 and 2000. In 2001, however, the markets were closed to further issues by these companies. While Amazon maintained a large cash hoard (a form of self-insurance against financial difficulties), Exodus and Webvan faced endless speculation about their demise owing to slow revenue growth and a heavy debt load.

In sum, for public- or private-market growth opportunities, lower stock market valuations hit doubly hard:

- Lower stock valuations reduce the value of the payoff to growth.

- Lower stock valuations often lead to difficulty in raising funds to support and execute cash-needy growth.

The Pervasive Nature of Market-Priced Risk: Part II

Now let's turn to the good news about market-priced risk: As more and more private risk is transformed into market-priced risk, strategic alternatives are created, and the value of the growth opportunity is increased.

A colorful example of this process is known as "Bowie bonds." In early 1997, rock star David Bowie sold a $55 million bond repayable from the future revenues of twenty-five of his albums.[8] For fifteen years, the albums are to be held by a trust that pays out royalties to bond holders. (After fifteen years the albums revert back to Bowie.) Similarly, Dreamworks, the film studio, made a deal in 1997 that enabled it to immediately start film development. The company raised $325 million based on future revenues of ten films yet to be made. In both transactions, the price of the Bowie bonds and Dreamworks securities will rise and fall with the fortunes of the artist and the studio; private risk was transformed into market-priced risk.

The monetization of entertainment-based intellectual property may feel very distant from growth opportunities inside large companies or in other industries, but in fact there are strong parallels. In a less glamorous market, a manufacturer wanted to implement a new process for assembling its product.[9] It wanted to outsource the assembly to a sequence of three companies, each a specialist in its field. Together, the assembled product would be best-in-class and cost-competitive. But financing became a problem. Banks feared the organizational links were weak and that none of the three companies would step forward in the case of a bad product.

The solution was to create a separate project management company that was able to obtain hundreds of millions of dollars worth of insurance. This "synthetic equity" would cover the lender in the case of losses, and with this change in structure, the loan was made. This example illustrates the convergence of insurance and financial markets. In some cases, insurance companies—with their large balance sheets, diversified portfolios, and need for new revenues—can step forward to catalyze the securitization process.

In sum, there are two sides to the pervasive nature of market-priced risk. Low stock valuations hurt funding opportunities and thus the value of growth opportunities. There's no insulation from this risk. At the same time, opportunities to monetize, securitize, and insure growth assets can increase the value of growth opportunities.

Pl-x: An Online Exchange to Securitize Intellectual Property

To make the arguments about market-priced risk in this chapter more concrete, let's take a brief look at a Los Angeles–based firm, the Patent and License Exchange, known as pl-x.[10] Pl-x was formed in 1999 and raised $40 million in venture capital financing in the latter part of that year. The founders, a former medical school professor and a former equity analyst, saw a business opportunity in the fragmented and opaque market for intellectual property (IP). The former professor had watched in frustration as his university's licensing office was only slowly able to search the market for a potential licensee for his patented inventions. The founders believed that IP transactions could be made much more easily and that the wide reach of the Internet could be used to make a transparent market for IP.

Pl-x is a company built around the prospect of taking the private risk of IP and making it market-priced risk. The firm has worked to assemble the infrastructure needed for a secure online IP transaction environment and to supply professional services and software to exchange member companies that encourage transactions. The pl-x offerings illustrate how the value of IP is influenced by the market infrastructure:

- *Template IP contracts.* Asset transfer is slowed when each transaction must be negotiated from the ground up. With templates, only deviations from the starting point are negotiated.

- *IP valuation methodology and services.* IP negotiations often slow or even break down entirely because of widely divergent views on valuation. Pl-x has developed a real options–based methodology for valuing IP that provides a starting point for negotiations.[11]

- *Secure transaction environment.* In many cases, IP can be easily copied or imitated, so pl-x members look for an infrastructure—both software and business processes—that restricts access to information but continues to exploit the reach of the Internet. (A tough balancing act!)

- *IP catalog.* Despite the buzz about our knowledge economy, it's often hard to find out what IP is available. An IP catalog is critically important in this fragmented but valuable market.

- *Corporate IP management software.* Similarly, many companies know they are creating IP but don't catalog it internally. The pl-x offers software that catalogs corporate IP for easy transfer to the pl-x catalog.

- *A constantly updated stream of data from the financial markets.*
  To strengthen the IP market/public market connection, pl-x
  provides a daily data sheet on the value of IP-based companies in the financial markets, as well as selected financial
  metrics for these companies.[12]

- *IP insurance.* Pl-x has arranged with a large insurance company, Swiss Re, to provide patent validity insurance for IP
  transacted through the exchange. The policy ensures that
  the claims on the patents transferred would be found valid
  in any subsequent litigation and insures the IP value against
  this risk for up to $10 million.

The array of offerings illustrates the marketplace infrastructure required to support the value of IP, and the presence of the exchange
creates value-increasing choices for those holding or searching for IP.

One might question the pl-x business model as so many other
B2Bs flounder and fail. One might also question whether IP—a
fuzzy, intangible asset often requiring much post-transaction support from the IP creator—is well suited to an online transaction
environment. But the pl-x vision should be greatly admired. If the
company succeeds, its presence will add considerable value to IP by
moving private risk to market-priced risk.

Takeaways

- It remains difficult to explain the high valuations for technology and nontechnology firms in the late 1990s. Stock
  market valuations are much higher than can be explained by
  a combination of DCF and real options.

- Identifying the market-priced risk in private growth opportunities helps to open them up to a wide range of choices for
  financing, insuring, and monetizing growth projects.

- More and more "private" risks are becoming securitized and
  traded—from the royalties of rock stars to intellectual property. Data updates for both market-priced and private risk are
  required in valuation templates. Updated data will naturally
  capture the shifting boundary between the two types of risk.

Across the Sweep of Value

W ITH THE EXPANDED TOOLKIT and tailored valuation templates in hand, Part III of this book tackles their application to the varied growth opportunities facing the modern corporation and to how these opportunities add up to sustainable business models. The span of applications in this section is wide, ranging from intellectual property to information technology investments. Each chapter answers a question about the value and management of corporate growth opportunities.

- What's needed to manage and finance a portfolio of highly risky growth projects? Chapter 10 is a case study on the value and business model of film studios.
- How can a firm sustain profits based on the selling of its ideas? The value of intellectual property, project by project and at the corporate level, is the subject of Chapter 11.
- What kind of growth opportunities can't be valued? Chapter 12 argues that information technology investments should not be selected based on their value, that the numerical results are neither well grounded nor precise.
- What are the components of a growth engine, an organization that produces valuable products and businesses from a portfolio of cash-needy growth opportunities? Chapter 13 addresses this question through a series of examples.

Together, the four chapters of Part III illustrate the important factors outside a growth project—organizational processes, financial strategy, and an understanding of the limits of valuation—that contribute to growth project value.

10

Showing Value
to Wall Street

Film Studios

For years, equity analysts have had a message to film studios: Make fewer movies. Traditional accounting and DCF measures show that films lose money on average. Yet there seems to be value in a film studio—look at Disney, MGM, and Time Warner, look at the transaction prices of film libraries. This chapter reconciles these observations, using the expanded toolkit to revisit the value of motion-picture production and the film studio business model.

Movies are fun to see, and the movie business is fun to think about. Yet it appears that this is a money-losing business. In 2000, the average cost to make and advertise a film was $78 million, while worldwide box office revenues per film were only $64 million. For years, films have lost money on average.

This chapter uses the expanded toolkit to value film studios.[1] The film studio has three assets—films in production, films recently released, and films in the library—and the analysis shows how to value each separately and how each is required for a successful studio business model. The quantitative results show that traditional valuation methods undervalue films in production and films in the library.

The results raise an important question: How should a film studio—or any other company with long-lived assets that it believes are undervalued by the financial market—communicate its value to Wall Street? Not just by showing analysts a new valuation model. This chapter argues that steady performance must be demonstrated at the corporate level to raise the external perception of value for individual film projects.

Conventional Wisdom

Revenues

Let's start with a snapshot of the industry economics and the current view from Wall Street. Perhaps the most salient feature of films is the wide dispersion of revenue outcomes. Film industry executives live on the hope of hits. But as Table 10-1 shows, these are few in number. In each year, the top film generates twice the U.S. box office revenue of the tenth film on the list. Only forty to fifty films recover their costs at the box office with revenues of more than $50 million. And in each year, more than half of the major releases return less than $14 million at the box office. While the home-country box office is but one of several revenue streams for the film producer, most other revenues are tied to box office performance, and total revenue is typically five to seven times that of the box office take.

Forecasting box office performance is difficult. As one detailed study concluded, "The individual characteristics of a movie are not sufficient to determine how it will fare in the complex dynamics of the motion picture market. [This is] not a very satisfying answer for a movie executive to hear, but one that is closer to the truth than any other answer that can be given."[2] Often a star is used to create a base level of demand, but this does not create a predictable profit stream. Think of the fees paid to Tom Hanks or Julia Roberts. The star captures the value of the increased demand through high pay and revenue-sharing agreements, leaving only the unpredictable component of the profit stream. In sum, there is much private risk attached to box office performance and ultimate revenue of a film. This risk is fully resolved on release, but the outcome cannot be predicted in advance.[3]

Table 10-1   Films: Few Hits, Lots of Dogs

U.S. Box Office Revenue ($ millions)	2000	1999	1998
	Number of Films		
Top 250 Releases			
$200+	2	4	2
$150–$200	6	5	2
$100–$149	11	8	11
$50–$99	31	30	26
$0–49	200	203	209
Releases Ranked 51–250			
$25–$49	42	35	33
$15–$24	27	28	31
$0–$14	131	139	145

Source: Data compiled from *Variety,* www.variety.com.

Costs

The cost history is not encouraging, as production and advertising costs have been rising faster than revenues. Between 1990 and 1999, costs rose an average of 9 percent per year, while box office revenues grew only 4 percent. The industry's poor economics have persisted for years. For example, one equity analyst estimates that the return on invested capital at each of the major film studios has averaged 5 percent to 7 percent each year, while the cost of capital in the industry is 10 percent.[4] Sometimes a major hit such as *Jurassic Park* or *Star Wars* will drive up the return on capital at a particular studio, but after the blockbuster the return falls back to the long-run average.

Industry accounting practices only compound the problem. Film production costs are expensed as incurred, marketing costs are immediately expensed, and abandoned films are immediately written off. Hence, while revenue streams are long-lived (seven years and more), costs are incurred and recorded up front. Without a steady stream of recent hits, it's easy for revenues to fall below costs. It is also difficult to profitably grow a film studio, as costs will increase before revenues.

The cost accounting practices also form the basis of the DCF models used by equity analysts to value film studios. Typically, these models are based on near-term (three-to-five-year) revenue and earnings forecasts. A terminal value is estimated using a P/E ratio multiplier of 13 to 14. This simple model can lead to odd results. For example, in the spring of 2001, a writer's strike threatened to halt movie production. Some equity analysts wrote that a strike would improve near-term cash flow and raised their target stock price. As later sections will show, films are the result of many decisions—none of which are captured by a DCF valuation model.

Make Fewer Films?

Given the industry economics—very small chance of a hit, each film loses money on average, studios don't return their cost of capital on average—it is not surprising that equity analysts have encouraged studios to make fewer films. Film studios have listened. In the mid-1990s, the major studios each released twenty to twenty-five films per year. By 2001, they had reduced this number to fifteen to twenty.

The reduced slate has lowered costs, but analysts also attribute the recent revenue growth at the box office to more marketing attention for each film. With fewer movies opening each year, studios spend more to advertise each film and the studios' marketing resources are spread across fewer films. These efforts increase the chance that any given film will last more than one or two weeks at the box office.

A movie's success is determined by its performance during the first two weeks at the box office. There are about 30,000 movie screens in the United States, but only 2,500 are used for box office openings.[5] Too many films simply crowd the limited screens. More advertising raises a film from the crowd. The right-sized slate for a film studio is one that is large enough to have reasonable odds for a hit, while at the same time small enough to fully exploit each film, given box office and organizational constraints.

Valuing Film Studios

The life cycle of a film is long: two years in script development, two years in production, seven years in release, and twenty or more years of economic life in the library. Library sizes range from about

1,500 films at Disney and Time Warner to 4,000 or more titles at MGM and Vivendi. One way to value a film studio is as the sum of its assets—adding up the value of films at each stage.

Valuing Films in Production and at the Box Office

Figure 10-1 shows a film's stages of development. During the first two years, the film is in script development, and here almost all films (90 percent) are abandoned.[6] It is during production the big dollars are spent, $55 million on average in 2000. Few film projects are abandoned during production because of the nature of the two important private risks, costs and box office performance. Costs accumulate day by day and receive close—daily or weekly—management scrutiny.[7] The ability to manage costs is an important factor in the studio's reputation on Wall Street, so studios will quickly cancel films with out-of-control costs. During production, no substantive information is learned about the future box office performance. This risk remains unresolved and doesn't trigger an abandonment decision.

The big moment of private-risk resolution is at the box office release. Currently, studios spend an average of $18 million in prerelease advertising. Industry wisdom is that after the first two weeks, the future revenues from the film can be accurately predicted. If the film fails to attract the required audience within two weeks, the film will be pulled from the box office. Movie theater operators are quick to abandon poorly performing films because there's a chance of better revenues from the next film on the list.

With a strong opening, the film will remain in the theaters for another two or more weeks. Studios spend $10 million to $20 million in additional advertising to support the extended stay. At box office release, a film may have three possible outcomes: "A" films make $100 million or more; "B" films, between $50 and $100 million; and "C" films, less than $50 million.

Table 10-2 shows the flow of calculations for the value of a film at the box office and in production. The top section calculates the expected value of the box office release, at the opening week and at the start of the third week if the film continues. U.S. box office revenues are extrapolated on a worldwide level by a factor of seven. The film payoff is about 30 percent of worldwide revenues, a factor

Figure 10-1　The Film Production and Release Decision Tree

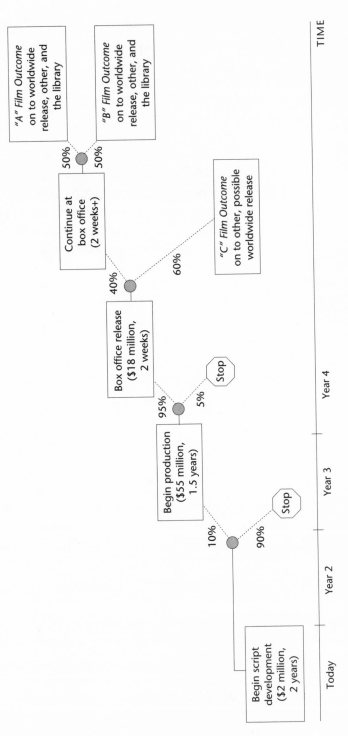

Source: Credit Suisse First Boston estimates.

Table 10-2 The Value of a Film by Stage
($ millions unless noted)

	Year	U.S. Box Office Revenue	Worldwide Revenue	Payoff Value	Additional Advertising Expense	Probability	Expected Value
CALCULATE FILM VALUE AT THE START OF BOX OFFICE RELEASE							
Value of payoff							
"A" film outcome	3.5	144	1,008	$302	20	20%	$56.5
"B" film outcome	3.5	64	448	$134	10	20%	$24.9
"C" film outcome	3.5	13	91	$27	0	60%	$16.4
Total	3.5					100%	$97.7
less Prerelease advertising expense	3.5						$18.0
Value at start of box office release	3.5						**$79.7**
Value at start of week 3 of box office release							**$203.4**
CALCULATE THE VALUE OF THE FILM AT THE START OF PRODUCTION							
Value of payoff	3.5			$80		95%	$75.8
Present value as of start of production	2						$69.1
less Cost of production	2						$55.0
Value at start of production							**$14.1**

(continued)

Table 10-2 (continued)

	Year	U.S. Box Office Revenue	Worldwide Revenue	Payoff Value	Additional Advertising Expense	Probability	Expected Value
CALCULATE THE VALUE OF THE FILM AT THE START OF SCRIPT DEVELOPMENT							
Value of payoff	2			$14		10%	$1.4
Present value as of start of script development	0						$1.2
less Expected cost of script development	0						$1.0
Value at start of script development							$0.2

WRITE THE STORY

Start the script development: *"This script is better than most. On average it is worth $400,000, but it has even greater potential to be a blockbuster. Let's proceed."*

Reject script development: *"The target audience for this script is unusually small. It can never be an 'A' film. Unless we get the script cheap, we should walk away."*

Sources: Author's calculations. Box office payoffs from *Variety;* cost data from the Motion Picture Association of America; other data from Credit Suisse First Boston.

that combines a 35 percent profit margin and discounting a seven-year, front-loaded revenue cycle to the present. At first glance, the profit margin may seem low, as there are few nonadvertising expenditures. But studios split box office revenues with exhibitors and share profits with stars, producers, directors, and others. Film accounting has been the subject of much criticism (where are the profits?); as Arnold Schwarzenegger dryly commented about the success of the film *Titanic:* "Some say its box office may grow so large that it will actually show a profit that no accountant can hide."[8]

Films Are Valuable After All

The calculations in Table 10-2 show that an "A" or "B" film is a hugely valuable property, worth $203 million on average. Two weeks earlier, at the box office opening, the film value is considerably less, just $80 million, because 60 percent of films fail at the box office.

The bottom section of Table 10-2 shows the calculations for films in production and script development. It is assumed that the $55 million production cost is fully committed up front. There are no cost savings from abandonment, an assumption consistent with out-of-control costs as the major driver of abandonment.

For script development, it is assumed that the abandonment decision is made at the end of the first year after $1 million has been spent. This assumption is consistent with viewing script development as a pay-as-you-go type of decision, not an irreversible up-front investment.

At the start of script development, the average film is worth only $200,000. Given that a film is *the* asset created by a studio, this is a fairly small number. It is also a noisy or rough estimate; after all, it is based on a fair amount of "average" data. The quantitative result suggests that films are close to zero NPV at the start. There is no sure win.

It's Tough to Value Film Libraries

Libraries are durable and rather complicated assets. Here are some factors that should be considered in valuing a library.

- *A small part of the library creates all of the revenue.* In 2000, for example, MGM made $225 million in revenues from its 4,000-film library by licensing a small number of films for television, DVD, video, and cable release. Over many years only 20 percent of films—those that reached "A" and "B" status—generate library revenue, and in any single year only a small fraction of this group creates the library revenue.

- *Successful films have very long economic lives.* Figure 10-2 shows an example of the cash flow history for a film in the MGM library, *Goldfinger.* The film was released in 1962, yet it has made more than half of its lifetime cash flow after 1980, including $6 million in recent years from DVD release. While few films reach the status of *Goldfinger,* those that do drive library value.

- *Libraries enhance the revenue from current production.* Industry practice is to bundle library films with current releases. For example, Sylvester Stallone is very popular in Italy, so the license to distribute a new Stallone film will include payment for rights to show some of his previous works on Italian television. This deal increases the value of the current release and the value of the Stallone films in the library. Balancing library revenues and current production revenues is tricky. Dreamworks, for example, is a new studio and has no library. Thus it can't increase the value of its current production in this way.[9] On the other hand, MGM has a large library, but until recently it had little production; its library value is not fully exploited.

- *New technologies create potential benefit for library value.* The history of films is characterized by a steady flow of new technologies that have increased library value. These include color films (1950s), cable television (1960s and 1970s), video (1970s), satellite delivery (1980s), and DVD (1990s).[10] Despite uncertainty about when a new technology will arrive, how it will create value, and how it will fit into the current business model, libraries stand to gain.

- *The payoff to new technology is relatively higher than in other industries.* In many industries, adoption of a new technology

Figure 10-2 The Cash Flow History of *Goldfinger*

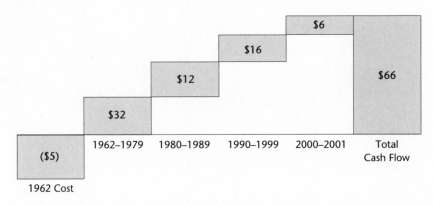

Sources: Credit Suisse First Boston; MGM; Nominal dollars.

is really a series of smaller adoptions, one for each sub-market. In contrast, a new film technology can be exploited across the entire library and film studio, making the ratio of payoff to exercise cost intrinsically higher. One example is digitization. It currently costs about $100,000 to prepare a film for DVD. Once digitized, however, the film can also be distributed over the Internet. The ability to sell to targeted audiences over the Internet may raise the value of even "C" films in the library.

- *Libraries also benefit from geographic expansion.* Since the 1960s, foreign revenues have been a constant 40 percent to 50 percent of total revenues, with the variation caused by fluctuations in foreign exchange rates.[11] But new release locations, including India and China, are opening up; these new markets offer a mix of box office, video, and television viewing.

- *It would be difficult to re-create the library.* A library of 4,000 films is the result of a huge number of small decisions about monetary expenditures, time to build, and the resolution of risk. It would take decades to create a library of this size, particularly since the size of the current release slate is only

15 to 20 films a year per studio. This creates a scarcity premium for the library—but it's a feature that is not captured in most valuation models, including the expanded toolkit.

- *A library has proven assets with extension options.* MGM, for example, has several franchises in its library: James Bond films (*Golden Eye, Tomorrow Never Dies,* and *The World Is Not Enough*), *The Thomas Crown Affair* (the original and the recent remake), and *The Birdcage* (a remake of *La Cage aux Folles*). The proven assets have created options for extensions, remakes, and character licensing over and above the average value per film in the library.

What Does Ted Turner Know That the Financial Markets Don't?

So, given the mix of factors, how much would you be willing to pay for a library? How should this asset be valued? Industry experts have noticed that private-market transactions for libraries have been priced about 15 percent higher per film than public-market valuations. What does Ted Turner—a buyer and seller of film libraries—know that the public markets don't? The following are three high-level methods to value a film library that capture some of the issues described above.

The first method to value a film library is to use a DCF analysis with a high growth rate in the terminal value. For example, in 2000, the group of "A" and "B" films in the MGM library earned $281,250 on average. The value of this annual cash flow is found by assuming a 3 percent real growth in perpetuity with a 10 percent cost of capital. The result is $4 million value per "A" or "B" film ($281,250 / (0.10 – 0.03)). With 1,600 revenue-generating films, the library value is $6.4 billion. Note that this result is highly sensitive to the assumption about the real growth rate. If a 2 percent growth rate is used, for example, the film library value is only $5.6 billion.

The second method to value film libraries is to use private-market transaction values, or comparables. For example, in late 1999, MGM received a $4 billion offer for its library, or $2.5 million per "A" and "B" title. Examination of other recently completed and proposed transactions shows a wide range of value—from $1.4 million to $4 million per "A" and "B" title.[12]

Finally, one might use the approach of Laura Martin of Credit Suisse First Boston. In her analysis, once the film's box office performance is known, the payoff is essentially that of a DCF. Before the film reaches the box office, the strongest driver is the probability of box office success, and thus the film value can be calculated using an expected value. Martin argues that the DCF value of the film in the library should be added to the expected value of the film at the start of production. With this adjustment, films are actually hugely positive NPV investments.

Using any of the three methods, film libraries, and consequently film studios, seem undervalued. But as Martin notes, with the exception of MGM, film studios are part of larger companies and are only 5 percent to 15 percent of corporate value. The undervaluation of the studios and film libraries is not enough to move entertainment company stocks.

The Film Studio Business Model

The financial market's reaction to Disney's release of *Pearl Harbor* illustrates how film success impacts the entertainment company stock price and how long-term studio value is created in other ways. Released in May 2001, *Pearl Harbor* was an expensive film: $140 million was spent on production and prerelease advertising. The film made $160 million in U.S. box offices, and Disney expects it to generate $450 million in revenues worldwide, putting it in the top twenty-five grossing films of all time.[13]

Using a DCF framework, analysts raised their projections of Disney's near-term cash flow based on the initial box office performance of *Pearl Harbor*. For example, one analyst forecasted an earnings increase of 2 to 25 cents per share in the two years following the release.[14] But a DCF-based analysis overvalues the film. In the model, the increase in near-term earnings causes the company value to rise significantly; in the terminal value the near-term increase is multiplied by a P/E ratio. Consequently, the estimate of corporate value rises far more than can be supported by a single film's success.

The correct method is to translate the payoff values in Table 10-2 directly into the stock price increase. For example, Table 10-2 shows that the value of an "A" film is $302 million. Divide this value by the number of shares outstanding to get the expected stock price increase from a hit film. An "A" film increases Disney's stock price by about $1.00 per share. Costs are already known and expensed, so stock prices move only on the news about the film's box office performance. News that film is a "C" film with no revenue should not move the stock price. News that a film is an "A" or "B" film should raise the stock price one time by a small amount.

The Value of Consistent Performance

Some investors and analysts argue that film studios should be valued based on their overall track record, not on film-by-film performance. They argue that a top management team can command a value premium if it has the know-how to exploit the opportunities in current production and the library and has a demonstrated track record of cost control. As one veteran industry observer puts it, "Not the fanciest spreadsheet analysis in the world can predict how an entertainment company will perform relative to the economy. And that's because entertainment-industry investments have instead proven over time to be far more sensitive to the deftness of a company's management in the formulation and execution of long-term growth strategies. . . . More to the point, proficiency in the care and feeding of many large (if sometimes irrationally inflated) creative egos is in and of itself a decisive management skill."[15]

MGM is a good example of the issues that arise in balancing the factors at a film studio for long-term performance. MGM's 2000 revenues were $400 million and the studio expects to release seventeen to twenty-two films annually.[16] At typical industry rates, the cost of the slate is approximately $1 billion per year (40 films in production × $25 million per year). The film library generates approximately $225 million per year, leaving most of the cost to be financed elsewhere.

Looking ahead, the studio can't expect much more in near-term revenues. Assuming an industry-average mix of "A," "B," and "C" films, a slate of twenty films generates more than $340 million in box office revenues in the year of release. But more than 50 percent of box office revenues goes to exhibitors, producers, and others, leaving a gap between current costs and current revenues.

The gap highlights the important role for financing. For example, MGM has developed joint ventures for most of its slate, so as the size of the slate doubles from ten films in 2000 to twenty films in 2001, production costs are anticipated to rise by only 30 percent.[17] The firm has also raised equity through private placements to fund previous slates. Other financing is acquired by selling foreign distribution rights in advance of production (for example, the entire production costs of *Basic Instinct II* were financed this way). These transactions create two results. First, MGM is using the proverbial Other People's Money for its own production costs. It is also using, however, Other People's Due Diligence to communicate to the financial markets that there is a credible pipeline of early-stage projects.

In sum, studio success is based on more than just a hit film. The financial markets will more highly value a studio that has a steady stream of cost-controlled production, a reasonable mix of box office performance, skills to close a wide range of financial packages, and the ingenuity to turn box office success into follow-on revenue. None of this can be measured directly, so investors look to the quality of the top management team. As one experienced entertainment industry investor summarized, "Unless the wheels are coming off year after year, I won't penalize the studio for a bad film. But when the top team leaves, such as recently happened at Warner Bros., we might want to look elsewhere."[18]

The irony is that the sophisticated valuation tools used in this chapter reinforce the conclusion that it is the fuzzy issue of people that is the primary driver of credible value in the film studio business.

Takeaways

- Traditional methods undervalue films. Growth-focused tools quantify the value of current production and libraries, showing that the industry's conventional wisdom is incorrect.

- Industry players such as Ted Turner have intuitively understood the higher valuations and acquired film properties accordingly. The valuation model is simply catching up with managerial competency. Further, studio value is a small component of corporate value, so the new valuation results cannot be used to better pick film studio stocks.

- Important factors outside the film project itself drive value. A good studio delivers cost control, a steady stream of reasonably good films, a wide range of financing, and the proven record of translating hits into long-lived revenue streams. A single hit should not move the stock price by anything but a small amount.

Valuing More than the Idea

Intellectual Property

Often described in glowing and breathless terms, intellectual property appears to be a valuable asset in our modern economy. Yet we lack a credible valuation approach for intellectual property. This slows transactions and complicates compliance with new accounting standards. Without quantitative benchmarks, intellectual property is often overvalued; it takes more than a patent to build a new business. This chapter lays out a valuation model for intellectual property and looks at the business model of two firms, MIPS Technologies and ARM Holdings, whose sole product is their intellectual property.

Intellectual property (IP) is a magical notion: Somehow we can get paid for our ideas. And in recent years this magic has gone further. Texas Instruments routinely makes $500 million a year from licensing its IP; 15 percent of IBM's profits in 2000, more than $1.7 billion, came from its IP licenses.[1]

The problem, however, is that the lack of a well-accepted valuation framework significantly slows IP-based transactions. Inventors, for example, are loath to part with "their baby" and may have unrealistically high expectations about its value. Large companies, hoping to exploit their patent portfolios, may not be able to differentiate between the IP that is valuable to business partners and the IP that is not. While the hope is that the early-stage technology, the lab discovery, or the patent will be a "Rembrandt in the attic," without a valuation model it's difficult to have a rational discussion until a buyer is found.[2] Similarly, without a shared perspective on value. IP transactions often stall, and occasionally collapse, over wildly different expectations over value.

A recent change in accounting standards is a second reason that an IP valuation model is now needed. In June 2001, the Financial Accounting Standards Board (FASB) finalized its new rulings on the accounting standards for mergers. In particular, FASB now requires that intangible assets gained through an acquisition be revalued each year. The guidelines require that IP be recorded at "fair market value," a "mark-to-market" valuation in the language of this book. Yet while the rule change requires an annual audit of intangible assets, it provides little guidance on valuation methods.[3]

IP valuation can be difficult. It requires the organization of a large number of issues, each with a fair amount of detail. Particularly to those new to the field of IP, the details can overwhelm the basic insights. To demonstrate the issues involved in IP valuation, the next section focuses on an example, an IP license for speech recognition technology from the Massachusetts Institute of Technology to Speechworks.

The middle section of the chapter lays out an innovative approach to IP valuation based on the valuation templates for staged growth introduced in Chapters 7 and 8. The IP valuation template addresses issues that are often neglected by current practice and aligns the value of IP with the value of other growth opportunities.

One of the important features of IP is that full value is obtained only when legal rights are backed by business model power. Despite the occasional story to the contrary, it is difficult for the lone inventor or the cash-starved company to enforce the value of its IP. The final section of the chapter examines the requirements and valuation of an IP-based business model.

IP valuation is a rich topic, with many details that are beyond the scope of this book. See www.valuesweep.com for further resources.

A Look at the Issues: MIT and Speechworks

In August 1994, MIT licensed some speech recognition technology to Applied Language Technologies, a company that later became Speechworks. (Speechworks's venture funding history is covered in Chapter 8.) This section introduces some of the issues affecting IP valuation by walking through the terms of this license.[4]

First, consider MIT, the licensor. MIT has an established licensing program and an interest in finding parties willing to license its IP. As a university, MIT is interested in the diffusion of knowledge, but the additional revenue generated by IP licenses is important as well. MIT's economic position as it enters negotiations is similar to that of many large companies: As long as the IP license covers its minimal ongoing IP maintenance costs, MIT is better off licensing the technology than letting it sit unused. Unless there is a bidding contest, MIT will find it difficult to get anything but a minimal value for its IP.

Next consider Speechworks, the licensee. Former MIT researchers incorporated the young company the month it completed its license, August 1994. To the founders, who wanted to build an entire company around the IP, the value of the IP was large, but as uncertain as their business prospects.

Figure 11-1 summarizes the key terms of the license. These are fairly typical terms, but there is significant variation in standard practice across industries. For example, in this license, MIT grants Speechworks all rights to its innovations, while preserving MIT's rights to the original technology. In other industries the IP creator might require rights in all future innovations as a condition of the original license. Often technologies must work together to be useful, either across generations of the same technology or across different types of technologies. Owning future innovations is important because it determines which future business relationships are possible.

Looking across Figure 11-1, what value can be placed on the license at the time of transaction in August 1994? With hindsight, it seems that MIT was lucky. Speechworks grew and thrived, so MIT's royalty stream was valuable. Between 1995 and 2000, for

---

Figure 11-1 Selected Terms of the MIT/Speechworks IP License

Term	Comment
Nonexclusive license	While this clause preserves MIT's option to license to others, the IP value declines with more licenses and with the proprietary improvements made by Speechworks.
MIT grants Speechworks the rights to all improvements	Speechworks is allowed to own all technology improvements. This will form the core of its corporate value.
MIT to be paid royalties by Speechworks	MIT takes two-thirds of the sales revenue in the early years, tapering down to 9% on average from 1995 to 2000, and 1% of product sales thereafter.
Speechworks required to meet certain business growth objectives	MIT wants the licensee to grow and flourish or to return the license. The business objectives include review of a business plan, product development date, and sales goals and dates.
Transfer of technology is restricted, but can be assigned in the event of a merger	The technology can't be transferred on its own, but transfers in the case of acquisition are allowed. MIT and Speechworks are aligned on getting the most value out of the company.

---

example, Speechworks paid MIT royalties of more than $600,000, or almost 9 percent of its product revenues. Thereafter it was required to pay 1 percent of product revenues, about $240,000 per year as of June 2001. But Speechworks's success is but one of many possible outcomes for the transaction. The more difficult question is how to value the IP at the time of the license.

Currently two IP valuation methods are used: The more traditional DCF approach and some early efforts at a real options–based approach. Accountants often use DCF to value IP, sometimes adding ad hoc adjustments to the discount rate to account for the risk of early-stage technologies. DCF-based valuation methods are used in IP litigation and for many contract negotiations.

Often based on accounting reports, DCF-based IP valuations are significantly lower than the estimate of the market value of IP inferred from high-growth companies. IP is an important component of intangible assets, which include know-how, brands, proprietary growth opportunities, and so on. Baruch Lev of New York University has addressed this issue by developing a measure for intangible asset intensity and for modifying the standard accounting-based approach by the use of equity analyst forecasts.[5] His method helps to close the gap between accounting-based and market values at an aggregate corporate level, but is not sufficiently detailed for use in the valuation of specific IP.

Some IP experts have suggested that the real options approach be used to value IP. The motivating insight is that a patent can be viewed as an option on a mature technology, with the future development costs as the exercise price. While this concept has seeped into the standard M.B.A. curriculum, the introduction has been more as a way of thinking than as a practical methodology. Too often the patent is valued as if only one stage of investment and one technology (the one covered by the patent) is required to create value.

Recently, pl-x, the online IP exchange described at the end of Chapter 9, has introduced a real options–based IP valuation method. While the method has been used in more than $1.7 billion worth of IP transactions, as of this writing it has a number of flaws. In particular, it only crudely captures the impact of the license terms and conditions on IP value.

The Hard Issues of IP Valuation

The primary reason that there is no widely adopted IP valuation methodology is that IP valuation is challenging. There are a number of rather open-ended issues that must be covered, issues that don't fit easily into a valuation methodology. Here are some of the challenges, using the MIT/Speechworks license as an example.

- *IP is often very early-stage technology.* Two consistent results emerged from the staged growth valuation templates of Chapters 7 and 8. The first is that value of early-stage technologies is small, even when the potential payoff is large. For example, while MIT has been paid over $600,000 in royalties by Speechworks, at the time of the initial IP license,

Speechworks had a low probability of achieving the success it has had to date. Based on the venture capital valuation templates, a rough approximation is that at the time of the IP license, the value of the expected royalties would have been $50,000. The second result is that early-stage valuations are highly sensitive to changes in the payoff value. With reasonable changes in the assumed payoff value, an IP value of $35,000 or $60,000 also makes sense—exactly why IP valuation can feel very imprecise.

- *Complementary assets.* An IP transaction takes place because the two parties hold complementary assets. One side holds the IP and the other holds some technology or management know-how that makes them better able to grow the IP value. In the MIT/Speechworks license MIT gains from Speechworks's focused efforts on commercialization of the technology; MIT simply doesn't have the right people or funds to complete this side of the equation. Speechworks, in turn, gains a fast start by immediately exploiting work already done at MIT. The value of the IP depends on the magnitude of the synergy of the complementary assets. Without that synergy, why transact? Hence, IP value will depend on who wants to transact. At some point, however, each party must look at the whole picture and recognize the gains from a unified view. The unified view is reflected in MIT's grant to Speechworks of the right to transfer the technology in the event of an acquisition.

- *Critical path or orphan technology?* In this license, MIT transferred the technology to Speechworks on an "as is" basis, meaning that MIT would put no further resources behind its support. That's how most companies licensing out their unwanted IP, their "orphans," would like to handle the situation. But the IP acquirer has the opposite view: the IP is an important step in the critical path to success. The IP acquirer may need specialized resources and support from the IP creator. While the orphan/critical path dichotomy forms the basis of the transaction, it also provides different perspectives on price, license terms, and support.

- *Negotiating power.* IP value is not an abstract result but an observable outcome of a negotiation. Negotiating power will strongly influence that outcome. For example, suppose Microsoft had approached MIT about the speech recognition technology instead of the group that became Speechworks. While MIT might have perceived that Microsoft had a greater ability to pay, it would also recognize that Microsoft had the resources to create a substitute technology. Hypothetically, Microsoft might have paid less than Speechworks. Financial resources and know-how will strongly influence negotiations and thus the transacted value of the IP.

- *Terms and conditions.* IP negotiations always seem backwards to those who specialize in valuation. The negotiation never starts with a high-level summary such as, "This IP is worth $25 million to us. How shall we divide costs, payments, and royalties?" Usually the opening line is something like, "We need a cost break on this term and are willing to give you a step up in royalties on the back end." Tools from financial engineering can be used to quantify the effect of alternate terms and conditions on IP value. But there are no general formulas as specific contracted restrictions will have hugely different effects by industry. For example, an exclusivity term may have no value in one industry, while in another it may be essential to the transaction.

While there is much room for improvement in the current practice of IP valuation (more on this later), the hard issues raised above demonstrate a certain fuzziness about IP value. Before wading into the valuation methodology, it is helpful to recognize this fact, to understand that there is a reasonable degree of imprecision about IP valuation.

A Method to Value IP

Figure 11-2 shows the flow of calculations for a new approach to IP valuation. Through an eight-step process, this method addresses many of the issues raised above. The eight steps fall into three main

---

Figure 11-2   IP Valuation in Eight Steps

Value the Growth Opportunity

Step 1: Create the holistic business plan based on the complementary technologies.

Step 2: Value the holistic business plan using an industry-specific staged growth valuation template.

Create an Initial Division of Value

Step 3: Create a starting point for negotiations and a schedule of costs, payments, and so on.

Step 4: Value the starting point for each party.

Step 5: Check if parts sum to holistic value.

Negotiate the Final Value

Step 6: Calculate minimum and maximum IP transaction value for each party.

Step 7: Negotiations proceed and new terms are offered.
    a) Repeat Step 6 if needed.
    b) Convert alternate terms and conditions to their value-neutral equivalent, using industry-specific information.

Step 8: Negotiations conclude; observe the transacted IP value.

This methodology is protected by a pending patent.

---

activities: value the growth opportunity, create an initial division of value between the parties, and negotiate the final value.[6]

Calculate the Value of the Growth Opportunity

The first activity establishes the value of the growth opportunity enabled by the IP. The first step is to create a single business plan that shows how the IP and the complementary assets provided by the other party fit together into a credible growth opportunity. (This step is also part of current practice. MIT, for example, wanted to immediately see a business plan from Speechworks.) While it sounds simple, this step requires a mind shift for many IP negotiators: Instead of "Beat them down to the lowest terms," it becomes "I need to understand how, where, and when the other party adds value."

The second step uses the combined asset business plan and staged growth valuation templates to value the holistic growth opportunity. The business plan is matched to a staged growth valuation template tailored by industry that has been updated with the current financial market pricing of the success payoff. The valuation templates fully capture the value consequence of the interaction of market-priced risk, private risk, and staged investment into the IP valuation. The second step is quite innovative in the IP world as it aligns IP value with that of other growth opportunities.

Create an Initial Division of Value

Steps 3 through 5 of the valuation methodology divide the value of the growth opportunity between the two parties. One side or the other will make an initial offer about terms and conditions. The starting offer divides the success payoff, defines the stages and milestones, and allocates the future costs. For example, a 10 percent royalty rate on sales over the life of the product might translate into 25 percent of the value of the payoff, and costs for the first stages of investment might be shared.

Allocating the value and costs in the joint business plan can be tricky for two reasons. First, some of the costs by the other party can be inadvertently omitted. This often happens and can lead to unintended shifts in value. For example, in one company I worked with the strategic partner ended up paying software development costs that were ten times the amount that both parties had contemplated. Disgusted with the huge expense, the partner declined to continue the IP license. Second, there is no single rule about how a given term or condition will impact value. It will vary by industry and by business model within the industry.

Step 4 values the starting offer for both parties. Each side will have a staged growth opportunity but with different payoffs and costs. Current IP valuation methods provide results for one party at a time, without a sense that the two valuations are related. The valuation is done by using the terms and conditions to shape the inputs into a staged growth valuation template.

Step 5 provides a logic check. In theory, the value to each party should sum to the holistic business plan value found in step 2. This is an important logic check and a good moment to check whether all the costs have been included. Steps 2 and 5 allow IP valuation results to be compared with those from other types of growth opportunities.

Negotiations

The last three steps use the valuation methodology to support negotiations. Step 6 calculates the minimum and maximum value to the IP for each party. Experienced negotiators understand the value of completing this step, but in practice the challenge of valuing IP often causes it to be skipped. In the MIT/Speechworks license, for example, the minimum value MIT would accept is that which would cover its administrative costs. The maximum value Speechworks would pay is the amount that causes the value of their business plan to fall to zero (the amount paid to MIT having extracted all extra value!). The final negotiated result, the IP value, will be between these two points.

It is critically important to recognize that there is a range of rational IP values, and that the observed valuation is the result of negotiations, strongly influenced by the negotiating power of each side. IP is valuable, but the allocation of value between parties is not based on a mechanistic formula.

As the negotiations proceed, new terms will be offered. As step 7 suggests, it is sometimes necessary to repeat the calculations that determine the negotiating range. In addition, alternate offers can be expressed in terms of the value for easy comparison. For example, one might be offered a floor on a royalty rate, or a higher floor accompanied by a cap. Repeating steps 3 and 4 revalues the transaction under the new alternative. Through this process, the specific terms can be found that improve the negotiated outcome for one side or the other.

In practice, industries with frequent IP transactions build template contracts, and IP valuation calculators can be easily attached. One example is a semiconductor IP exchange based in Scotland, Virtual Components Exchange (see www.vcx.org). As the offerings of this IP marketplace suggest, template contracts, exchange-based financial requirements for membership, and template valuation tools can speed transactions.

For companies out-licensing their "orphan" IP, the eight-step valuation method suggests that if there are buyers, there will be a large range in the perceived IP value. The licensing department will need to have a systematic negotiating process in place, as well as extensive data sets to support valuation during negotiations.

IP-Based Business Models

The valuation method described above is from a transaction-by-transaction perspective, as if IP were a stock, bond, or some well-defined commodity. This would be a stretch because of the many negotiable features of IP. But importantly, the value of IP must be reinforced by strong business opportunities. A look at IP-based business models illustrates the host of activities and the consistent execution of strategy required to build IP value over the long run. This last section of the chapter illustrates these issues by looking at two competitors in the semiconductor industry, MIPS Technologies and ARM Holdings.

Started in 1984, MIPS has been an innovator of a computer architecture known as RISC (Reduced Instruction Set Computer). MIPS's microprocessors are valued for their energy efficiency and computational power. MIPS does not manufacture its product; it licenses microprocessor designs to manufacturers and their customers. Customers are in the consumer electronics, electronic device, and semiconductor industries. In late 2001, about 70 percent of MIPS's revenues came from product licenses and royalties and the remainder from engineering support services. Revenues ran at about $85 million per year. The firm's chief competitor is ARM.

ARM was started in England in the early 1990s and also specialized in the RISC architecture. Between 1999 and 2001, ARM's revenues overtook those of MIPS and by late 2001 were about $140 million per year. ARM earns revenues from royalties, product licenses, development tools, sales of third-party products, and professional services. Both MIPS and ARM spend about 25 percent of their revenues on R&D.

MIPS and ARM thrive because each delivers more than just patented technology. MIPS has recently been in patent litigation, and during the proceedings one licensee commented, "MIPS is in the business of delivering a valuable product, and we licensed its technology because it is delivering something of value to us. . . . Whether the MIPS [IP] was based on a MIPS patent or an older IBM patent is not relevant."[7]

The Ecosystem

What makes the IP business model work? While patents protect their designs, customers buy from MIPS or ARM because the microprocessor designs allow them to deliver better products and to build products faster. The IP adds tangible near-term value to the customers—not potential value, demonstrable value. To deliver this type of result, MIPS and ARM have built up entire ecosystems—a network of customers, suppliers, and partners—around their products.

They, and a few other companies, compete in the world of "design starts." The goal of competition is to become the microprocessor technology specified in the definition of a new product. For example, Nintendo might be starting a design for new game hardware, and the IP companies would compete to win the microprocessor slot.

There are a limited number of potential customers for microprocessor designs and most are repeat buyers. This changes the pricing of IP from the one-off model presented in the previous section to one constrained by the nature of repeated transactions. For example, MIPS and ARM are careful to signal new product developments well in advance by providing technology road maps to the members of their ecosystem. This allows customers to anticipate the complementary investments required, and binds customer product strategy with that of MIPS or ARM. Selling development tools optimized for IP further increases customer loyalty by raising the costs of switching suppliers.

Most importantly, the ecosystem must see MIPS and ARM creating value for their customers in each purchase cycle. Failure to deliver near-term value can cause customers to flee to a competitor. This can also happen with next generation technology that is late to the market or that is not competitive. While the cost of supplying the marginal customer with an existing microprocessor design is small, and thus the profit potential large, MIPS and ARM are often at risk of losing the design win. This dampens their ability to raise prices.

For both MIPS and ARM, royalties account for about 25 percent of revenues. This revenue stream is very attractive to investors as it represents additional profits from the same R&D, but MIPS discovered corporate revenues can dramatically rise and then fall with a successful consumer product. MIPS provided the microprocessor design in one of Nintendo's hot products but failed to win the design contract for the next generation product. A successful IP-based business requires managers to place smart bets on where the next hit will be and to acquire customers in that area. Serving all possible products spreads engineering resources too thin, while focusing on too few products fails to capture the benefits of diversification.

Valuation of the IP-Based Business Model in the Financial Markets

The spring and summer of 2001 were a very tough time for technology companies. Most saw their sales fall and their valuations plunge. The financial markets, however, continue to highly value IP-based business models. MIPS, for example was trading at five times sales, and ARM was trading at twenty-eight times sales—and these were the lowest valuations of these companies in over three years. The technology sector as a whole was trading at an average of six times sales, while the computer hardware sector was trading at less than two times sales. MIPS and ARM were doing very well.

A recent quarterly report by ARM provides some clues. In June 2001, ARM announced that overall revenues had continued to grow. Royalty revenues, which depend on the economic climate, were down, but license revenues from new design starts had increased, as did revenues from professional services and development tools. New design activity is seen as countercyclical by industry observers, so in booms ARM should have high royalties and slower growth in license revenues, while in busts ARM should have low royalties and higher growth in license revenues. ARM had cash balances of more than $130 million and was profitable, with a 30 percent operating profit margin. It had a healthy financial report, particularly when compared with other technology firms.

Equity analysts see both strengths and weaknesses in IP-based business models. They point to low capital expenditures and no inventory as easy pluses. The scalability of the model is also highly regarded. Once the microprocessor design start is won, royalty revenues continue to accrue if the product takes off. Both MIPS and ARM are well poised to ride a growth wave across the entire digital consumer products sector.

To gain value from that wave, MIPS and ARM must continue producing premium IP and hold onto premium royalty rates. An industry with a few big hit products puts more pressure on their ability to target winning products and customers. If products become too specialized or targeted, MIPS and ARM lose value as a large number of products with low sales increase the cost of sales and support and lessen the chance of royalties. One equity analyst likens the stock price volatility of MIPS and ARM to that of exotic financial securities—the potential for a very high return is present, but there are large risks.[8]

Takeaways

- IP valuation requires a large amount of detail on three fronts: industry value of growth opportunities; industry norms regarding the presence and value of IP terms and conditions; and the specifics of the IP transaction at hand. These can be assembled, however, into a valuation template that not only provides a defensible IP value but that can also be benchmarked against the value of other corporate growth opportunities.

- IP valuation is inherently imprecise. The two parties will negotiate over a rational range of value. The observed IP valuation is the outcome of this negotiation and reflects financial conditions, negotiating power, and other factors.

- The key challenge for the IP-based business model is not based on the specifics of IP valuation, but the company's success in building an ecosystem around their product and their ability to deliver value to customers with each IP license. While the financial markets point to the upside potential in the business model—from licenses and royalties—analysts are also aware that IP-based business model success will rest on a few hit products.

12

Selecting the Investment

Information Technology

This chapter makes two somewhat contentious arguments. The first is about the limits to valuation methods: Growth projects based on information technology (IT) are difficult, if not impossible, to value. The second is about the Internet: While considered disruptive at the technology level, corporate initiatives based on Internet technologies often lack explosive value potential and in many cases lack sustainable competitive advantages. These points are illustrated through several topical examples including automation technology for call centers, customer relationship management software, and supply chain initiatives.

Why do valuation tools fail? Sometimes a growth opportunity can't be neatly valued—there are too many assumptions, too many poorly defined components, and lots of risk. In other cases, underneath the complexity there's just not a lot of value; there is no long-term sustainable competitive advantage. IT has both these features, making it a good example of why valuation tools fail.

The lessons from these examples apply outside the world of IT investment too. For example, the discussion continues in the next chapter by examining similar constraints that limit growth value in the chemical industry.

185

Here's the basic issue. Suppose there are several projects competing for corporate funding. One project proposes installing new software to reduce the cost of maintaining the corporate Web site. What's the value of the software? It will depend on the current technologies installed, the software deployment processes at the company, and the business importance of the Web site. In sum, the value of the software will be very specific to the company. The same software will have a different value in another company. For these and other reasons, a valuation template approach can't be applied to IT projects.

So how does one choose between IT projects, and between IT and other corporate investments? This chapter argues that the choice is made in two steps: First the valuation tool is selected, and then the decision is made between projects that appear valuable using that tool.

The choice of tool reflects the economic mood. For example, in 1999, the talk was essentially of how much business value could be created from IT spending, largely through e-commerce initiatives. Real options and decision analysis are the right kinds of valuation tool for this optimism. In 2001 the talk was largely of near-term cost savings from IT spending. Simple tools that measure cost savings such as return on investment (ROI) and payback period dominate. (These are discussed further below.) Valuation tools are not the driver of IT decisions, but they reflect the mood of the IT decision process.

There are three main topics in this chapter. The first section looks at IT valuation tools, including ROI, payback, and real options. The middle section examines the features of the IT investment that make it difficult to value and that limit the potential for value creation from large-scale IT spending. The final section examines e-commerce strategy for supply chains and suggests how each stage of investment might be valued. It identifies the limitations to a large return.

In this chapter IT spending is defined as technology acquired to improve information flow and computational power, and e-commerce spending is defined as technology that also leads to potentially value-creating business-process changes.

Two Methods to Value Growth Opportunities Based on IT Investment

IT managers have long struggled with how to value their projects, because the quantitative results communicate to the rest of the company: "Hey, look over here. You don't need to understand the technical details of this complex project: The numbers show it is really important!" This section looks at two valuation approaches for IT investments, ROI and a real options approach. As mentioned earlier, the key difference between the two methods is not in the details, but in the perspective. ROI is used when the economic mood is conservative and cautious; other methods, such as real options, are used when the mood is expansive.

ROI

Return on investment is defined several different ways in finance and accounting—book return on book capital, cash flow return on invested capital, economic rate of return on market-based valuations—and no doubt even more variations are used in practice. The mechanics are simple. Table 12-1 illustrates an ROI calculation taken from the Web site of TellMe Networks Inc. TellMe provides technology to enable automated voice interaction over the phone. For example, one of their offerings is an automated system to buy movie tickets.

Table 12-1 presents the results of an investment in technology to increase the level of automation in a call center. Live operators cost more than $1.75 per minute, while use of an automated voice system is well under $1.00 per minute. The left column of the table shows current cost of the call center, and the right column shows the cost if the automation technology is deployed. The more fully automated center saves money, as the annual cost of running the call center drops from $15.5 million to $9.9 million.

A simple DCF calculation based on annual savings for three years shows that the NPV of the automation technology is $12.55 million; it is clearly a valuable opportunity. The ROI, 809 percent, also indicates a huge benefit to the project. ROI is defined as the

Table 12-1   Sample ROI and Payback Calculations: Automated Self-Service Voice Solution

($ millions unless noted)

	Current Call Center Configuration	Front-End Automation to Call Center
Calls per year (millions)	3.1	3.1
Call length (minutes)	3	3
Automation rate	15%	50%
Annual cost of customer care	$15.5	$9.9
Annual savings		$5.6
Daily savings		$0.015
Cost of the automation investment*		$1.4
NPV (3 years)		$12.55
ROI (3 years)		809%
Payback period* (days)		90

Source: Tellme Networks Inc. (www.tellme.com).

*The example given by TellMe does not report cost of automation. This cost was inferred from the reported ROI. The payback period is also based on this cost.

gain in value from the project expressed as a percent of the investment cost and is calculated as:

(Present value of savings over three years – investment cost) – 1.

The last financial metric shown in Table 12-1 is the payback period, calculated as the investment cost divided by the daily savings. The result indicates that the project's gains offset the cost in 90 days, and thereafter the gains exceed the cost. By all three metrics, the project is stellar.

In practice, the ROI framework is not consistently applied and will vary in detail. Most often the CIO or CFO will mandate a format for calculations and a project selection hurdle such as, "Only projects demonstrating a high four-year ROI will be considered for funding." The mandate restricts the set of candidate projects to those that have the near-term, self-financed growth component of the DCF value (see Chapters 2 and 3).

It can be difficult to compare the results of two ROI analyses because of the many hidden assumptions and variations in how an ROI calculation is implemented. But frankly, this doesn't matter. The main effect of the ROI framework is not valuation but extreme narrowing of the set of acceptable projects. When the CFO says, "I'll only take projects with a demonstrated high ROI," he's asking for cost savings, not expansive and risky value creation.

Valuing Staged Growth IT Projects

During 1998 and 1999—a period of strong IT spending and high stock market valuations for technology-based companies—many looked to real options to capture the broad sweep of value creation from Internet investments. In my book on real options with Nalin Kulatilaka, we showed how to value a staged growth IT project.[1] The project was in a financial services company, and interest rate levels drove demand for the new financial products. At each stage, the decision to continue the IT deployment was determined by both market-priced and private risk. In fact, the project was halted because of an adverse interest rate move.

In practice, however, most IT analysts have not made the link between their project and market-priced risk. Consequently, a real options approach is not warranted. As was shown in Chapter 5, decision analysis may be helpful in the design of IT projects.

The specific tool aside, there is another point to be made about valuing expansive IT investment strategies. Table 12-2 provides an illustration. The table shows a staged investment for a customer relationship management (CRM) system in a service center for a computer manufacturer. The center receives 9,000 calls per day and the average sale per call is $500. Initially, the service center agents don't have access to a single structured information system. Instead, they use multiple fragmented databases and an ad hoc set of scripts.

The cost and the benefit of adopting the CRM system at each stage is shown in the left column. The middle column reports the cumulative NPV, project value upon completion of the stage. The right column reports the ROI by stage. While in practice there would be much private risk and contingent decision making, the

Table 12-2 Comparison of DCF and ROI Results: Example of Staged Installation of a Customer Relationship Management System

($ millions unless noted)

	Year	Costs and Benefits ($000)	Cumulative NPV	ROI
Current number of calls per day		9000		
Average revenue per call		$0.0005		
Initial service center revenue		$4.500		
Stage 0—Preparation				
Cost	0	$0.50		
Benefit	0	$0.00	($0.50)	
Stage 1—Integrated information system				
Cost	1	(0.50)		
Benefit—15% increase in calls handled	2	0.68	($0.40)	23%
Stage 2—Improved processes for service calls				
Cost	3	(0.30)		
Benefit—10% increase in sales	4	0.52	($0.27)	57%
Stage 3—Revenue enhancement during call				
Cost	5	(0.20)		
Benefit—15% increase in sales	6	0.85	$0.09	288%

DCF calculations most simply demonstrate how the ROI framework doesn't align with project value.

At stage 0, the company invests in an underlying technology. There are no demonstrated benefits, but this pre-work is required to begin the CRM installation. The ROI on stage 0 is meaningless. At stage 1 an integrated information system is deployed that increases the productivity of the call center agents. Revenues increase and stage 1 has a positive ROI. If the staged growth project were halted at the end of stage 1, the NPV would be negative. Continuing the deployment, stage 2 leads to an increase in sales per call as the sales process is enhanced by new information. Again the ROI is positive, but the cumulative NPV remains negative. In stage 3 revenues again increase. In this last stage the cumulative NPV is positive.

Based on the positive ROI results, it seems that each stage can be treated as a separate decision. But using NPV, the project should be undertaken only if all three stages are completed. Further, in a cautious period the CRM project would never begin because there is no ROI from stage 0. While the ROI results are misleading about the project value, they enforce a discipline based on near-term cash flow. In an expansive business climate, that constraint is relaxed and riskier multistaged IT investments are undertaken.

A Summary

In sum, this section has shown how the valuation tool sets the initial framing for a project. Only certain projects measure up under an ROI criterion, and so the main effect of this tool is to restrict the set of candidate projects. Frankly, the details of the tools don't matter too much because, as the next section argues, features of IT investments make them difficult to value in any regard. If the assumptions and constraints are well understood, using a crude valuation tool as a selection mechanism is not a bad practice.

Why Growth Opportunities Based on IT Investments Are Difficult to Value

The decision to buy a new personal computer illustrates some of the key issues for IT investment. The prices of personal computers keep falling, so we're often tempted to buy a new one. But there is a certain part of making a new computer work—software installation, learning a new setup, getting your e-mail transferred—that remains very expensive in terms of time and focus. Larger-scale IT investments have the same flavor. Here are three important reasons that even the expanded toolkit can't come up with definitive valuation results for IT projects.

It's Never Just a Technology Investment

An oft-quoted rule of thumb is that the technology is only half of the cost of a successful deployment; the other half of the cost is professional services for installation.[2] The previous chapter on intellectual property laid out a framework for valuing growth opportunities based on complementary assets. But this framework is difficult to apply to an IT investment. In the intellectual property application, the allocation of value between two assets was determined by negotiation. In an IT investment this allocation would be done by assumption. It's also difficult to allocate contributions after the project is in place.[3] The result is that we don't have a clear answer on the value of the IT alone; only the project as a whole can be valued.

Further complicating the valuation of the joint business plan for IT and non-IT investments is the changing value contribution of the complementary assets. Harvard University professor Dale Jorgenson finds that while IT investment contributed 25 percent of value growth in the U.S. economy between 1990 and 1995, it contributed 50 percent of the value growth between 1995 and 1999.[4] He found that the size of the contribution depends on the IT technologies already deployed, the specifics of the IT investment opportunity, and the overall economic growth rate.

The implication? Jorgenson's findings show that IT investment—already hard to value on a stand-alone basis—has large changes in value over time and across installations.

The Role of Market-Priced Risk in IT Valuation

Most IT managers don't see the market-priced risk in their project. But, in the past two years, the role of market-priced risk to technology value has become painfully obvious. For example, consider Kana Software, a publicly traded company that provides automated routing and responses for e-mail sent by customers to large corporations. From a revenue base of $180 million per year in 2000, the company expects revenues to grow by 6 percent to 7 percent per year.[5] As of this writing in September 2001, however, Kana is trading at a price below \$1 per share, and as a consequence it may be delisted by Nasdaq.

Despite sales growth and product credibility, corporate customers may devalue Kana's technology because they worry about the firm's survival. Young companies always face the perception that they'll close their doors and leave the customer with orphaned technology, but what's different in the current environment is that the formerly private risk of failure is now a market-priced risk. It is also a widespread concern, affecting the future and value of many young companies.

Ignoring market-priced risk misvalues projects, yet it is often difficult to link a market-priced risk directly to IT project value. In the case study given in my previous book on real options, the link was unusually clear at the conceptual level, yet the implementation was quite detailed. (The decision tree was very dense!) It is very challenging to include market-priced risk in IT project valuation.

The Role of Private Risk in IT Valuation

Private risk is also difficult to simply characterize in IT valuation. The problem is that there is a wide variation in the drivers of private risk across companies and projects. The effect of private risk on IT project value will vary significantly by project, depending on the scale of the project, the technology to be installed, the previously installed technology, and the required investments in complementary assets. It's difficult to routinize or create rules of thumb for use in valuation.

One of the most effective ways companies have found to address the private risk in IT projects is through strong processes for project selection and management. Relying on these processes, not valuation tools, is more likely to create value.

Consider, for example, Extreme Programming (XP), a method for software development conceived to "address the specific needs of software development conducted by small teams in the face of vague and changing requirements."[6] Using XP methods, software engineers have found a way to significantly reduce the private risk of late and over-budget projects, as well as the late-stage failure in which a manager says: "I never said I wanted *that!*"

A Summary

Features of IT itself make it difficult to value. These include the need for parallel investment in complementary technology, the difficulty in allocating value between IT and non-IT investment, and the characterization of market-priced and private risk. Knowing the limits of valuation tools themselves, managerial time is better spent on strong processes for IT project selection and management.

The Limited Optionality of Internet Technology

In the late 1990s the Internet emerged as a disruptive technology. The stock market also boomed. The two events intermingled through the public offerings of Internet-based companies. Consequently, a general perception has emerged that there is great value in Internet-based technologies. In the late 1990s ROI simply seemed irrelevant as Internet-based strategies touched so many areas of the company, transforming projects from IT investments to e-commerce initiatives. Most e-commerce initiatives were selected and shaped by the optimism of strategic thinking alone, without value-based decision making. In many cases there was also a staged growth mentality: "We won't make money off this investment today, but two stages down the road we'll hit the big payoff." With the collapse of the Internet sector in the stock market, much of this thinking has been discarded. So where is the value in Internet technology? It's time for a review.

My argument is that while Internet technologies have dramatically changed the costs of transactions and business connections, they lack the explosive bang first envisioned. The logic flow supporting this conclusion is as follows:

- *Internet technologies lower costs.* The implications of this cost change have been drawn out by a number of corporate strategists. The thinking runs in several directions, each a powerful vision of the future: a shift in economic power to the customer (see Patricia Seybold's *Customers.com*); a shift to strategic outsourcing (see Geoffrey Moore's *Living on the Fault*

Line); and the emergence of an information-based supply chain (see Philip Evans and Thomas Wurster's *Blown to Bits*).

- *Lowering costs is not enough.* Often, to effectively use Internet technologies companies need to invest in developing and training staff on new business logic. For example, one consulting firm reports that the majority of companies that have made CRM investments are still incapable of providing actionable advice to the customer or to sales and service agents.[7]

- *Business logic change requires organizational change, and companies have only a limited capacity for organizational change.* Changes in business logic are changes in job descriptions and organizational structure. Does more really need to be said on this topic? Anyone who has lived through a large-scale corporate reorganization or through a postmerger integration can speak to the struggle in their company about the magnitude and pace of change—as well as the anxiety and the energy drain.

- *The value of Internet technology is capped by the costs and payoffs from the business side.* Perhaps the Internet is a disruptive technology, but one never invests in the Internet alone. Investments in business logic and organizational change are people-based and can't deliver a huge "bang for your buck." There's no explosive value creation—there's no optionality—in the joint business-technology opportunity. The rapid rise and fall of business-to-business (B2B) online exchanges illustrate this point.

The next section illustrates this logic through an example of the supply chain in the electronics industry.

Valuing Supply Chain Initiatives

By one estimate, U.S. companies spent more than $2 billion on supply chain or B2B infrastructure in 2000, and this spending is projected to explode to $80.9 billion by 2005.[8] The spending covers a range of technologies, from the simple to the sophisticated. Using the electronics industry as an example, this section examines the value of each stage of evolution in the supply chain. Valuation methods play a small role in the discussion, largely because there's not much to value. Many of these projects have a distinct lack of sustainable advantage.

Moving Transactions Online

In almost all industries, the majority of supply chain transactions are currently made offline, using phone and fax to negotiate prices and confirm agreements. A typical example is Newark Electronics, which went online during 2000.[9] Newark distributes electronic components and has more than 150,000 stock-keeping units from 300 manufacturers. In March 2000, suppliers used Newark's EDI system for less than one-third of their transactions. (Electronic Data Interchange [EDI] is a private communication network used in many industries. It predates Internet technology.)

During the year, Newark invested in new Internet-based technology, and by December 2000, more than 95 percent of transactions were completed online. The transformation has saved Newark more than $1.2 million in reduced order processing and reconciliation costs, and the firm proudly notes a three-year ROI of 4,428 percent. Moving transactions online neatly fits the ROI project selection framework: The value of the project is business as usual, only cheaper.

As the Newark example shows, going online makes sense on a project-by-project basis. But it may not be a long-term source of competitive advantage. For example, the apparel industry has a strong infrastructure around EDI, and there has been is no sustainable competitive advantage from moving online. Nothing about the move is proprietary. For example, it's cheaper to process purchase orders online, but soon competitors are doing the same.

Information to Avoid Stock-Outs

The next level in supply chain evolution is driven by stock-outs, when a certain part for a product is simply not available. In the electronics industry this problem, which typically affects 10 to 20 percent of supplies, can be acute when sales momentum is strong. The existence of stock-outs has generated new business models and spurred the development of online exchanges.

One company, PartMiner, offers a solution. PartMiner hosts a large database of electronic components and runs transactions through its system. If the part is in stock, PartMiner acts as broker between the customer and supplier. Further, PartMiner carries its own inventory of parts that are in short supply; using the Internet, it's made a business out of solving the stock-out problem.

PartMiner's proprietary advantage depends on product scarcity. When there is a shortage, the customer benefits from the lower search costs on the Internet. PartMiner benefits from lower brokering costs through the Internet. But the Internet doesn't address some of the key risks. First, PartMiner holds inventory—a highly volatile asset in the electronics world. Second, companies in the electronics industry often go around PartMiner, using its posted price lists as reference points to deal with suppliers directly. Third, since PartMiner's offerings are available to all, using their system doesn't convey a proprietary advantage. It is simply an efficient way of doing business.

Information for Collaboration

The next step in supply chain sophistication is driven by the need to collaborate. For certain electronic products, more than 80 percent of the manufactured cost is established in the design phase.[10] A number of online exchanges, such as SpinCircuit or Aspect Development, bring cost information to designers and design changes to manufacturers. These exchanges act as "digital glue" for a fragmented industry.

At its best, the collaborative supply chain also speeds the design and development time of new products. Fast time to market has enormous value in the industry because electronics products have a short economic life and a well-defined sunset—would you buy a four-year-old PDA? When an electronics product is late to market, there is less time to sell, and less chance of being known in a crowded marketplace.

The very large companies, such as Cisco, Dell, and Sun Microsystems, have proprietary supply chains. The rest of the industry uses the public online supply chain sites to gain access to the same capabilities. But once again, investments tailored to the online supply chain soon become required to remain competitive; it is difficult to see sustainable competitive advantage from these activities.

Information for Production Coordination

Think of a very simple supply chain, with the product moving from manufacturer to distributor to wholesaler to end user. When each firm acts separately, changes in end-user demand are amplified as it moves down the supply chain, a phenomenon known as the bullwhip effect.[11] There is increased variation in quantity ordered from practices such as batch ordering, inflated orders (to avoid stock-outs), price fluctuations, and long lead times for manufacturing capacity.

The bullwhip effect is present even when end-user demand is stable. But it is larger when demand is highly variable, as in the electronics industry. Many electronic components go into consumer products, and there is a huge "fashion" component for demand. For example, suppose eight models of cellular phones are available, all with equivalent functionality. Because of color, interface design, or other features, one model may grab the majority of market share during their nine- to twelve-month product life. There will be a huge uptick in demand for the components of this product, and then a rapid fall—with the bullwhip effect exacerbating the magnitude of the change on the supply chain.

The industry has a number of different solutions. Supply chain software firms such i2, Manugistics, or TIBCO offer software and data feeds to coordinate electronics suppliers. Some manufacturers, such as Flextronics, Celistica, and Solectron, absorb the variability for a price. None of these solutions depends on the Internet nor is made cheaper by its technology. A third solution, described below, is to price the required flexibility into the supply chain contract.

The central issue is risk: stock-outs, excess inventory, and the wrong inventory. In practice, many firms ignore their risks in these areas. Because the benefits are diffuse and infrequent—after all, one doesn't need insurance on every product or transaction—and without adoption, there is little value in this service for suppliers.

Contracting for Risk Management

The following quote from Hewlett-Packard's 2000 Annual Report says it all: "How does someone apply their rather obscure interests in real options theory and perfect market dynamics to solving a basic business challenge at HP? Corey Billington did it. He wanted to help HP figure out a better way to manage supply chain risks inherent in volatile technology markets, so he assembled a team and built TradingHubs.com, a prototype online exchange that enables HP and its partners to buy and sell excess parts and inventory in an auction environment."[12] The annual report goes on to say that the new method saves HP 30 percent in inventory costs of certain components.

The concept is to hold auctions online to obtain up-to-date prices and market conditions for the procurement specialists at HP. Armed with data from recent auctions, the specialists then approach HP's long-term suppliers for better pricing. The team works with suppliers in one of three ways:[13]

- HP writes a traditional structured contract with the supplier. HP manages all risk.

- HP contracts for a fixed quantity that is less than anticipated needs. Then HP uses its online exchange to obtain the remainder. HP bears the risk of price spikes and stock-outs.

- HP contracts for a fixed quantity that is more than anticipated needs. Any excess supply is sold on the online exchange. HP bears the risk of not finding buyers.

What is interesting about these contractual solutions is that no HP capital is required. The key competency is in managerial perspective. Exercising this strategy requires a willingness to articulate risk, and then to develop and evaluate alternate mitigation strategies. In other industries executives are often unwilling to take the first step. For example, similar contractual opportunities exist in the electric power industry, but many executives strongly prefer the predictable nature of long-term contracts, without the flexibility of the HP process.

Closing Thoughts

Supply chain initiatives defy quick and straightforward valuation. Many times, they require significant investment in non-IT assets. A stand-alone project analysis seems to justify their adoption, but when competitive forces are factored in, the benefits erode. Many digital initiatives have the flavor of "required to compete, but no sustainable competitive advantage." There may be a window of time in which first movers gain profits, but in the long term, the advantage is eroded.

Consequently, there is only a small role for a valuation tool in the analysis of supply chain initiatives. At each stage, an investment will be made based on a near-term gain, and the valuation result simply serves as a selection mechanism among similarly beneficial projects.

Takeaways

- The most widely used IT valuation tool, ROI, selects projects based on near-term cash flow alone. However, there is only a weak link between ROI and DCF, so the ROI approach does not necessarily lead to value creation.

- Supply chain initiatives defy a quick and straightforward valuation. Much like corporate strategy, they require wide-ranging knowledge of the marketplace trends and the long-term economic forces at work. They don't fit into the valuation template approach of this book, and it is useful to understand why.

- Rather than spend time on refining valuation models for IT investment, managers might be better off strengthening processes for selecting and managing IT projects. This is perhaps an odd conclusion for a book on valuation, but it is one based on experience and a review of the challenges to valuing IT-based growth opportunities.

13

Creating the Credible Growth Engine

Here are two challenges: On paper your company appears to have lots of growth value. Yet Wall Street doesn't give you any credit. Or Wall Street did give you credit—and your stock price soared—but now you can't meet their expectations. This chapter is about the corporate growth engine, the set of activities that delivers value year after year. Examples from P&G, Anadarko Petroleum, Texaco, and Cargill Dow highlight the hard realities and the successful strategies.

This chapter is about growth value at the corporate level. Valuation templates are codified data and calculations that rest on company and industry context. The venture capital valuation template, for example, works if one follows the venture industry norms of triage. But most companies aren't that disciplined about triaging failing projects and waste corporate resources keeping them alive. For these companies, the venture capital template would overvalue projects. This short example demonstrates the reason for this chapter: It takes more than good growth projects to build corporate value.

So what does it take? There's no attempt here to unify the issues into a grand theory. To be honest, I'd look at such an effort with some skepticism. Many others have studied the issues surrounding a credible growth engine, and the problems are fairly well understood. More abstract theory won't help managers see the challenges and use the ideas. This chapter uses a series of examples to raise the key issues and to show how they were addressed by the companies profiled here.

The company examples are both focused and fragmented. But together they make the following points:

- *Increasing the scale of the corporate growth engine is difficult.* There's a pace and scale of innovation required to deliver corporate revenue growth. When the growth engine is too small, future revenues won't sustain corporate value. To fix the situation, the CEO must simultaneously address a number of very tough issues about funding, organizational change, and Wall Street's expectations. The difficulties are illustrated by the recent experience of P&G.

- *The value of growth opportunities can be seen in a company's stock price only when the company proves it has the resources and processes to exercise the options.* Most growth opportunities are follow-on options requiring a sequence of decisions and expenditures over time. As the recent experience of Anadarko Petroleum shows, when Wall Street believes that the company can identify, develop, and fund the entire option sequence, it will then "price" growth opportunities into the stock. Until then, it's a "show me, prove it to me" world, and the value of growth opportunities is steeply discounted in the financial markets.

- *Organizational issues frequently harm growth value.* Growth projects are like a slippery football that is passed around the separate parts of a large company: R&D, product development, manufacturing, marketing, and sales. The handoffs are often dropped or bungled in some way. Managers' incentives are often directed toward executing the current business, not growing future business. There's a reason some of the top strategists conclude that corporate organizations hurt value. Texaco's experience in adopting a new valuation method, real options, is used to illustrate these issues.

- *Corporate growth opportunities are fundamentally different from those funded by venture capitalists.* Venture capitalists are disciplined investors. They require the potential of a big payoff within three to five years. The value of the success payoff in most corporate growth opportunities is significantly lower than in venture-backed companies, and it takes a longer time to achieve. A joint venture between two chemical companies to create plastic from renewable resources demonstrates the issues.

Cranking Up the Engine at Procter and Gamble

Durk Jager had the shortest tenure of any CEO in P&G's history, seventeen months.[1] Promoted to the top job to kick-start the pace of innovation, his saga personifies a widely shared corporate dilemma: How do you increase the scale of the engine of growth while continuing to achieve the expected performance from the current business? Many observers empathized with his mission, his energy, his challenges . . . and ultimately the blow he took. The story has widespread appeal and penetrating lessons.

Jager became CEO in January 1999. The press release announcing his appointment stated the company's desire to accelerate growth and to leverage its global brands through "stretch, innovation, and speed." In the preceding five years, P&G's sales had grown less than 4 percent annually, and profits were flat. Since the early 1990s, there was no growth in most of P&G's product markets: Unit volumes were flat, and industry pressures prevented price increases. Many have concluded that the only way to grow revenues in the consumer goods industry is to innovate.

In recent years, P&G has spent about $2 billion annually on R&D and product development, with 90 percent of the funds going to "maintenance innovation"—product extensions and me-too catch-up products. Tide, a prominent P&G brand, gets a large part of the maintenance innovation funds. A new formulation of Tide (tablets, for example, instead of the traditional powder) can grab a fraction of a point of market share in an otherwise stagnant market. While a large R&D expenditure is required to support the current revenue stream, this spending doesn't provide significant growth. As of January 1999, P&G had not launched a successful new brand since 1961.

Table 13-1   The Value of Growth at P&G

($ millions unless noted)

Inputs

Sales in previous year (1999)	*$38,125*	Incremental fixed capital investment	*$2,000*
Sales growth rate	*4%*	Incremental working capital rate	*0%*
Operating profit margin	*12%*	Cost of capital	*10%*
Cash tax rate	*35%*	Dividends (per share)	*$1.40*

	2000	2001	2002	2003
CALCULATE FREE CASH FLOW				
Sales	$39,650	$41,236	$42,885	$44,601
Operating profit	4,758	4,948	5,146	5,352
less Cash taxes on operating profit	1,665	1,732	1,801	1,873
Net operating profit after tax (NOPAT)	3,093	3,216	3,345	3,479
less Fixed capital investment	2,000	2,000	2,000	2,000
less Working capital investment	–	–	–	–
Free cash flow	**1,093**	**1,216**	**1,345**	**1,479**
less Dividends	1,820	1,820	1,820	1,820
Free cash flow after dividends	**(727)**	**(604)**	**(475)**	**(341)**
CALCULATE PRESENT VALUE OF FREE CASH FLOW				
Present value of free cash flow	993	1,005	1,011	1,010
Cumulative present value of free cash flow	993	1,999	3,009	**4,019**
CALCULATE THE TERMINAL VALUE				
Terminal value				66,989
Present value of terminal value				45,754
CALCULATE NET PRESENT VALUE				
Net present value				**$49,773**

A DCF Valuation of P&G

Tables 13-1 and 13-2 look closely at P&G during the Jager years. Table 13-1 quantifies the growth premium Wall Street put on the company's value as of January 2000, one year after

CALCULATE THE GROWTH COMPONENT IN THE MARKET VALUE

	January 2000	March 2001
Stock price ($ per share)	$110	$55
Market value of firm, January 2000 (stock at $110 per share)	$155,600	$81,500
PV of free cash flow/Market value	1%	1%
PV of terminal value/Market value	29%	56%
Value of additional growth/Market value	70%	43%

WRITE THE STORY

The path to sustainable growth is:	"We're really shaking things up. Wall Street can expect 12–15 new product launches a year. We'll be looking to acquire products and brands that can reach our global scale. Investor confidence is warranted."
A pessimist would say:	"P&G's historical sales growth rate is 4%. Yet Wall Street has given the firm a large growth premium. This represents growth in addition to that already captured in the DCF. How will P&G grow this fast?"

Note: DCF valuation is as of January 1999. Growth component calculations for January 2000 and March 2001 are indicative, but not precise.

Jager began his tenure as CEO.[2] As the top section of the table shows, P&G pays a dividend to shareholders. Valuation, however, is based on the predividend free cash flow; ultimately, dividends are at the board's discretion. The calculations in the table are optimistic in that they assume a dividend of $1.40 per share, below P&G's recent historical average of $1.50 per share. But even with this assumption, P&G will need to obtain financing to pay its dividend.

The bottom section of Table 13-1 shows the growth expectations embedded in the P&G stock price at two points in time. The first, January 2000, is when the stock price was near its all-time high. The second, March 2001, is when the financial markets started to lose faith in P&G. As the table shows, at each point in time more than half of the company's market value came from growth beyond that accounted for in the DCF.[3]

But is there really a growth option at P&G? Given the industry's maturity, it is difficult to see a "hidden" expansion option at P&G, such as was outlined for Amazon.com in Chapter 4. There's no place to make a bet; at P&G growth comes from a portfolio of smaller opportunities. Some of the growth expectations could be met through acquisitions, and in 1999 Jager quickly acquired a water-purification firm and a pet food firm. He also made a bid for Warner Lambert, a pharmaceutical company, in early 2000.

But Wall Street and P&G's board expected most of the new growth to come from new products. In September 1999, Jager announced Reflect.com, an Internet-based beauty care company, and a new line of beauty care products. He also pushed the rapid global expansion of two new products—a dry mop and a home dry-cleaning product—and the introduction of three others. P&G told Wall Street to expect fifteen more new product launches over the next two years.

Inferring the Financial Market's Expectations about the Pace of Innovation

Table 13-2 quantifies the new product expectations implied in the financial market valuation of P&G. The table excludes acquisitions, so the number of required new products could be reduced with value-creating acquisitions. The data in Table 13-2 are from a number of sources and are rough estimates.[4] The inputs can be modified without changing the basic conclusion.

The expected level of new product introductions is calculated at two points in time: January 2000 and March 2001.[5] In January 2000, valuations across the consumer sector were high. These valuations are transformed into expectations about new revenues by the market-value-to-sales ratio. It is assumed that one-half of the growth value premium in January 2000 must be supported by revenues delivered by 2004. Working down the table, this translates into sixteen *successful* new product introductions per year. Twenty-two launches per year are required. Supporting the launch rate are fifty-six projects in development each year and 555 R&D teams. (Note that the R&D spending is already included in the P&G DCF.) The calculations show that an additional $2.8 billion must be spent

Table 13-2   The Expected Pace of Innovation at P&G
($ millions unless noted)

	January 2000	March 2001
CALCULATE REQUIRED NEW PRODUCT REVENUES		
Market value	$155,600	$81,500
Present growth value *(from Table 13-1)*	70%	43%
Size of growth component	$108,836	$34,736
Market value/Sales	3.5	2.5
Implied new revenues from new products	$31,096	$13,894
New product revenue in 2004 (50% of total)	**$15,548**	**$6,947**
CALCULATE REQUIRED NUMBER OF NEW PRODUCTS		
New product revenue *(assumption)*	$200	$200
No. of successful new products required by 2004	78	35
No. of successful new products per year, 2000–2004	**16**	**7**
CALCULATE REQUIRED ANNUAL LAUNCH AND DEVELOPMENT COSTS		
Probability of success at launch *(assumption)*	70%	70%
Cost per launch *(assumption)*	$50	$50
Required no. of launches	22	10
Total launch cost	**$1,111**	**$496**
Probability of success at development *(assumption)*	40%	40%
Cost of development *(assumption)*	$30	$30
Required no. of development projects	56	25
Total development cost	**$1,666**	**$744**
Annual R&D for new products *(included in Table 13-1)*	$200	$200
Probability of success at R&D *(assumption)*	10%	10%
No. of R&D teams	**555**	**248**
COMPARE ANNUAL REQUIRED EXPENDITURES WITH FREE CASH FLOW		
New product launch and development cost	$2,776	$1,241
Free cash flow *(from Table 13-1)*	$1,093	$1,216
Free cash flow after dividends *(from Table 13-1)*	($727)	($604)
Incremental costs/Revenue	7%	3%

WRITE THE STORY

The path to sustainable growth is:	*"Companies always have growth premiums that are greater than a valuations model can explain. We just need to put our heads down and execute."*
A pessimist would say:	*"This is a recipe for disaster. Free cash flow is negative before the costs of new products are added. This picture doesn't add up."*

each year on new product development and launches to meet the market's growth expectations.

The Hard, Hard Challenge

The numbers show just how tough Jager's job was. The high growth premium in the P&G stock implied change, but how many companies can go from a forty-year dry spell to sixteen successful new products a year? The required organizational change is almost unfathomable. Adding to Jager's pressure was the negative cash flow after dividends. The incremental growth expenditures and the cash flow shortfall would require nearly $4 billion in financing. (In fact, P&G's long-term debt increased from $6 billion to $10 billion between 1999 and 2001.) The high growth value in the stock price did not match what could be reasonably delivered.

In early 2000, P&G's stock price began to fall as the financial markets reacted negatively to P&G's proposed acquisition of Warner Lambert. The pharmaceutical company was growing at only 1 percent to 2 percent per year, and Wall Street didn't view it as a solution to increasing the scale of the growth engine. In March 2000, P&G warned that it would not meet the growth expectations it had set earlier, and the stock fell by about one-third.

In June 2000, P&G again warned of its failure to meet growth expectations, but this time it also announced a new CEO. The revenue problems arose from the lack of new products, but also from a failure to execute the established businesses. In the June 2000 conference call, P&G's CFO described spending in advance of revenues (a stretch goal problem discussed in Chapter 14) and confusion in the ranks from organizational change. A strong message could be heard from the board of P&G and from the financial markets: Innovative growth is the CEO's opportunity only if the established business is performing.

Financing Growth Options at Anadarko Petroleum

Although they seem very different, consumer goods and oil exploration share a common problem: How do you increase the scale of the growth engine, get it funded, and get credit—through a higher stock price—from Wall Street? Here's how Anadarko Petroleum solved the problem.

Anadarko is an oil exploration and production (E&P) company whose early-stage work resolves geological risk: How much oil is in the tract? What are the costs of extracting it? Oil exploration is the classic follow-on option problem and was the subject of the early academic work on real options. It takes six to fifteen years to go from the potential of oil as seen on a geological map to exploitation (the extraction of the oil). Fewer than 10 percent of projects complete all stages.

Oil Prices and Company Value

The value of E&P companies is closely tied to movements in oil prices. If oil prices are low, here's what happens:

- Current revenues fall, and the DCF component of the business (production) falls in value.

- Option sequences fall in value by an even greater percentage. This is the same result as seen in Chapter 8 for venture capital valuations. A fall in the success payoff ripples through the sequence of follow-on options.

- The fall in oil prices decreases cash flow from operations and thus reduces funds to exercise options. Consequently, many projects go into a waiting mode. This may have been anticipated in the valuation model, but more often a cash flow crunch is a further discount to value.

- The acquisition of new opportunities slows because of the lack of internal funds. Gaps appear in the project pipeline, and the value of future revenues is impaired even further.

As one Anadarko employee characterized the effect of low oil prices on the company: "We have nothing to fall back on: We can't make garbage bags and survive for two years."[6]

Because oil prices are notoriously hard to forecast and are highly volatile, financing oil exploration with straight debt is difficult. As mentioned in Chapter 9, some of the industry's innovative

Table 13-3   The Capital Spending Imbalance at Anadarko Petroleum Corp.
(in $ millions)

	Anadarko	Apache	Burlington Resources	Kerr McGee	Union Pacific Resources
Data					
Sales	701	1,297	2,313	2,696	1,728
Cash flow from operations	317	961	1,102	713	995
Capital expenditure	680	670	989	543	428
Market value of equity (March 2000)	2,100	5,998	7,448	5,200	3,237
Long-term debt	2,100	2,833	2,820	2,525	6,146
Market value (debt + equity)	4,200	8,831	10,268	7,725	9,383
Ratios					
Market value/Sales	6.0	6.8	4.4	2.9	5.4
Capital expenditure/Cash flow from operations	215%	70%	90%	76%	43%

Financial statement data for fiscal year 1999.

financing requires that the company partially hedge out oil price risk as part of its financial package.

A Firm Out of Balance

In late 1999, Anadarko was a company known to be good at exploration: It had a lot of prospects and some of the lowest finding costs in the industry. The firm was committed to scaling up its exploration efforts. From 1997 to 1999, it had cash flow from operations of $250 million to $350 million per year. Yet the company spent $600 million to $900 million a year on exploration and development, financed by a mix of debt and new equity issues. The company's long-term debt increased from $900 million to $1.4 billion over this period.

Table 13-3 compares Anadarko to four other E&P companies in 1999 by size, capital spending, and use of debt. While Anadarko's sales and market value were the smallest of the group, it had one of the highest market-value-to-sales ratios, indicating that Wall Street was capitalizing relatively more growth for Anadarko. The ratio of capital expenditures to cash flow from operations was higher than for its peers. The dollar amount of Anadarko's debt was the same as those firms with two to four times more in cash flow. Compared with the other firms, Anadarko seemed out of balance: There was too much capital spending and relatively too much debt.

Figure 13-1 shows Anadarko's stock price performance since 1997. Also plotted is a stock price index for other second-tier (nonmajor) oil companies. Oil prices were $15 per barrel at the start of this period; they rose to a high of $35 per barrel in September 2000 and fell back to $23 to $25 per barrel in early 2001. Comparing Anadarko's stock price performance with that of other companies in the industry normalizes the effect of oil price movement on corporate value. As Figure 13-1 shows, Anadarko's stock price largely tracked the comparison group index until late 1999. Then, in March 2000, Anadarko's price rose significantly when it announced its merger with Union Pacific Resources. (The combined firm continued under the Anadarko name and Anadarko management.)

Figure 13-1   Anadarko Petroleum versus Energy Industry Index

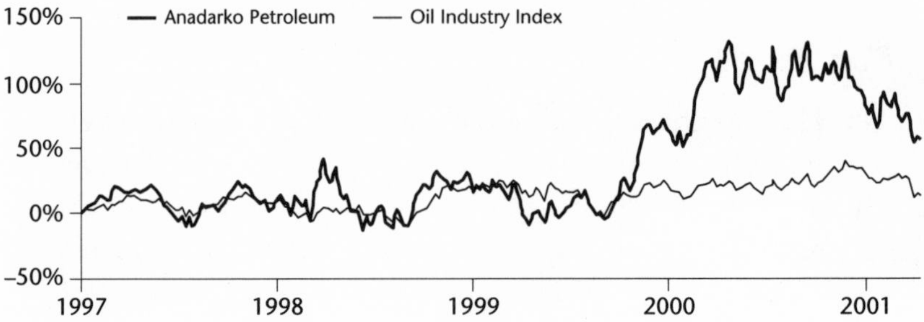

Source: www.bigcharts.com.

As Table 13-3 shows, Union Pacific Resources was the opposite of Anadarko. It had the lowest capital expenditure of the group and a cash flow from operations that was three times larger than Anadarko's. The conventional wisdom in the industry was that Union Pacific Resources held an unbalanced mix of properties: It had too many projects in production and too few in the early stages. In 2000, Union Pacific Resources anticipated raising its capital expenditures by nearly 50 percent, to $650 million. Despite this huge increase in exploration and development efforts, more than $300 million would remain in free cash flow. Union Pacific Resources also had a sizable amount of debt—an amount greater than the value of its equity.

The Financial Markets Revalue Anadarko's Early-Stage Options

As Figure 13-1 shows, Anadarko's stock price began to rise after the merger announcement, and it went higher in July 2000, after the merger closed. By the summer of 2001, Anadarko had risen 60 percent in value since March 2000, while the comparison index rose about 20 percent. (Anadarko acquired Berkeley Petroleum in January 2001 for $1 billion and GulfStream in June 2001 for $137 million.) It is always dangerous to read a stock price history and then attribute success to a single factor, but one argument is that combined cash flow from Anadarko and Union Pacific Resources provided a strong source of internal financing for Anadarko's rich stream of prospects. It removed a discount that the financial markets had placed on the value of Anadarko's early-stage options—one that arose from questions about how the follow-on sequence would be executed given Anadarko's already high debt-to-cash-flow ratio. The merger made execution of the follow-on option sequence more credible.

Anadarko's story illustrates how growth engines require a delicate balance between execution of current business, financing, and competency in the growth activity itself. While identifying growth options is a valuable skill, the value rewards come only when the execution of the option sequence is credible—when it is supported by organizational processes and dollars. Often managers tell analysts in the financial markets, "You punish us if we don't earn profits, so we can't afford to invest in growth." Anadarko's success is testimony to the pushback from the street: "Don't whine, just do it. Stock price improvements come to those who execute on the core business and deliver on growth."

Organizing for Growth Options at Texaco

Consider the following statements by three prominent strategy consultants:

- "All organizations inhibit growth. . . . Very few companies actually grow profitably and sustainably, although all plan to do so" (Chris Zook in *Profit from the Core*).[7]

- "The age of progress is over. . . . Most companies were built to do one thing exceedingly well for an exceedingly long period of time. Companies built for scale, replication, diligence, and exactitude will have to learn to change and adapt and experiment at the speed you see in the new economy" (Gary Hamel in *Leading the Revolution*).[8]

- "They led with questions, not answers" (James Collins in *Good to Great,* on how CEOs led the 11 companies, out of nearly 1,500 considered, with 15 years or more of superior stock price performance).[9]

The point? It is very difficult, and rare, to sustain growth. Companies may have a lot of good ideas and good opportunities, but the financial markets reward execution—which is particularly challenging for staged growth opportunities.

In recent years, Texaco has been a leader in the use of real options for planning and decision making. The company's head of valuation services estimates that, in the past two years, the firm has identified $3.6 billion in real options value in thirteen projects over and above a benchmark value based on their current valuation toolkit.[10] (The toolkit includes DCF, decision analysis, and simulation analysis.) Real options is viewed as uniquely capturing the effect of oil price uncertainty and better at handling the design of an option sequence. With the valuation activities complete, Texaco is now wrestling with a number of issues related to managing options-based projects. The company's experience raises three challenging questions:

How do you spread the thinking and valuation method across the company? To obtain buy-in from senior management, Texaco began its real options initiative with a series of pilot projects. Texaco found that while real options valuation results are "visibly superior to their traditional predecessors, they are limited if applied in isolation."[11] While the case for improving valuation methods is strong, there remains the issue of how to incorporate them into the day-to-day decision and evaluation processes.

How do you reward managers for growth decisions? Current performance-measurement systems translate the DCF model into observable performance criteria.[12] Most growth opportunities, however, are rich in uncertainty and contingent decisions. DCF will undervalue projects with options and lead to incorrect project decisions. Consequently, performance measures based on DCF will also destroy the value shown in the staged growth valuation model.

How do you give a manager the incentive to kill a project? How do you reward managers to make decisions made at the moment of highest value? Adam Borison, a leading real options consultant, argues that firms should be on a "diet and exercise" program for real options: the formal hierarchy and reward system, as well as the informal system for coordination of projects, should work together to encourage identification and optimal exercise of options.[13] Borison reports that failure to reward managers for growth decisions, coupled with the lack of informal and formal coordination mechanisms, led one oil company to abandon an options-based project worth $100 million.

How do you value and manage projects in a portfolio? Oil companies hold large project portfolios. A project-by-project valuation method will lead to incorrect answers for two reasons. First, all projects in the portfolio depend on the price of oil, so their values and exercise decisions are highly correlated. When oil prices rise, many projects need funds to continue exploration or development. When oil prices fall, many projects are deferred. Second, the funds available to continue exploration, development, or production are also dependent on the price of oil. Thus, management of the exercise decisions must be done at the portfolio level. If action is taken in isolation at the project level, there may not be enough cash to fund the most valuable projects.

For these reasons, the value of a project at Texaco will depend on what else is in the portfolio. Stand-alone valuation models are only the first step in the optimal deployment of resources for growth.

In sum, Texaco's experiences in changing valuation tools illustrate the challenges that prompted the stark statements by strategy gurus. Change is hard; growth is hard. What is particularly challenging is organizing large companies around the contingent decisions of growth options. These decisions are hard to time and require clear decision-making authority. Too often organizational issues impair the value of growth opportunities, project by project and at the corporate level.

The Large Company Advantage: Cargill Dow

At this point, the reader must be asking, "What possible advantage do large corporations have in identifying and managing growth opportunities?" The example in this section illustrates two large-company advantages: the ability to see new product areas that are invisible to those less involved in the product market, and the ability to back and execute very large innovative projects.

Cargill Dow started as a joint venture by Cargill Inc. and The Dow Chemical Company to create "green plastic"—plastic material based on renewable resources, such as corn.[14] Cargill Dow became a formal company in 1997. The chief technology officer of Cargill Dow did the pioneering research more than a decade ago, when he was at Cargill and charged with finding new uses for corn sugars. His breakthroughs led to a small test plant in 1994 and interest by Dow in 1995. In January 2000 the corporate parents invested $300 million. Currently, Cargill Dow maintains a small test plant, but has broken ground on a full-scale plant in Nebraska. Greenfield chemical plants typically cost $140 million to $200 million to construct.

The Risks and Scale of New Chemical Products

The market for green plastics comes from displacing incumbent petroleum-based plastics and from using the innovative physical properties of the green plastic. In the displacement market Cargill Dow must compete on cost, which is difficult to do before full-scale production. In the new products area, Cargill Dow must jointly develop the products based on green plastic with its customers. Cargill Dow has started a number of these projects, including a new film wrap for mini-disks, fabrics that are crease-resistant or that better handle moisture, synthetic yarns that are more acceptable to consumers, and packaging for golf balls. Using initial product successes from the test plant, Cargill Dow tries to pre-sell capacity in its upcoming full-scale plant. But the new product volume is unlikely to fill up the first plant.

To address the displacement market, Cargill Dow faces a problem that is common in the chemical industry: There is only limited opportunity to use the active learning strategy of "spend a little, learn a lot." Unless Cargill Dow commits to a full-scale plant that reduces costs to a competitive level, it will not be able to move into the displacement market. To open up the green plastics growth opportunity, Cargill Dow gave up its option to wait until demand emerged and instead showed a commitment to the product in advance of demand. How many startups get $300 million in backing without a solid customer base? This type of support is the domain of large corporations.

Now consider the payoff to the parent-company investors. Chemical sales have dropped nearly 4 percent a year for the past five years, and the five-year average operating margin is about 6 percent after tax. Ultimately, Cargill Dow's success comes from the displacement of petroleum-based plastics, as innovative products alone won't fill up the additional plants that the firm plans. The success payoff for Cargill Dow is not high. This growth opportunity is an entry into a commodity business, with slim margins and significant industry cycles. So why do it?

Much of the innovation in the chemicals industry is for product maintenance, as is the case at P&G. Year after year, important improvements are made in processes and products, but these are "required to compete" investments; their value is eroded by competition. In contrast, Cargill Dow has growth option potential that is scarce in the industry. The scale of the required investment creates some protection from competitors.

A historical example illustrates the investment issue. Figure 13-2 shows DuPont's spending on nylon. Although from a different era, the shape of the curve remains relevant. Notice that the largest annual spending occurred after the product was introduced in the market and supported the growth of sales. Only a small part of the spending was on the original technology. The implication for Cargill Dow is that $300 million is just a drop in the bucket. Much more will be required to grow green plastics into a successful product. Currently only large companies can fund this scale of growth opportunity.

The Advantage of Industry Insiders

A venture capitalist might argue, "If I have a dollar to invest, why would I put it into chemicals? The industry is full of low-value success payoffs, growth opportunities need lots of up-front capital, there will be need for even larger amounts of capital as sales grow, and the returns to investment take a long time. Why invest in an industry that operates on ten-year business plans? Let me go to the

Figure 13-2   The Full Cost of Developing Nylon at DuPont

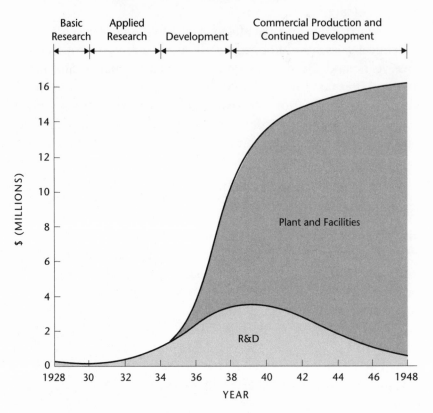

Source: F. M. Scherer, "Developing Nylon at DuPont," in *Innovation and Growth*, ed. F. M. Scherer (Cambridge, MA: MIT Press, 1986), 5.

high-tech industry, with its low up-front capital requirements, its low cost to grow sales, and its promises of a return in four to seven years." The venture capitalist's argument rings true: Chemicals is not an attractive place for venture investment.

But the venture capitalist's argument also misses an important feature of corporate growth opportunities: Outsiders, like venture capitalists, don't see the new opportunities in the corporate product space. Growth opportunities must be identified and placed on a map of the industry and its competitors. Ideas for new products and processes need to be shaped before the business model appears.

In many cases, only industry insiders have the expertise to see and shape growth. Together with their ability to marshal the required resources, large corporations will also be able to exploit growth opportunities unavailable to others.

The game large corporations play is not to return venture capital–type returns, but to do better than their peers and better than the financial markets expect. This will earn superior returns for shareholders.

Takeaways

- CEOs have two equally important objectives: to execute the current business and to undertake growth initiatives. While CEO time is largely spent on growth, the current business has significant value and a large set of resources. Failure to execute the current business is costly. Just ask Durk Jager.

- Wall Street only gives full value credit to staged growth options when it believes they can be executed. Financial resources are a huge part of the credibility. Ideas alone are not enough. A large number of early-stage prospects without resources to execute won't increase corporate value.

- Industry insiders can see into growth opportunities that are opaque to outsiders. While they may not have the fast bang for the buck that is typical of venture-backed firms in the high-tech industry, these growth opportunities are the source of proprietary and superior returns to industry insiders.

Part IV

Epilogue

I N THE THEATER, an epilogue is a short speech spoken directly to the audience at the end of the performance. The last two chapters in this book are similarly from the heart. Valuation tools and broad strategic thinking don't capture the emotions of growth. Human nature presents significant challenges for achieving the value calculated in spreadsheets or written down on paper; valuable growth opportunities are the result of attention to the human side as well.

Chapter 14 is about leading growth projects. It focuses on the leaders, how to lead the shaping of growth ideas, and how to bring a big-picture perspective into corporate processes. Each is a soft issue, yet critically important. For example, without that one person or small team, there is no sparkle, no catalyst, and no growth opportunity.

Readers are human too. In our busy world, authors can't expect readers to remember the quantitative detail and the nuances of the arguments made in previous chapters. The book concludes with Chapter 15, a short list of takeaways—a quick summary of the book's perspective.

14

Leading Growth

This chapter is about the following question: "How is the abstract value of a growth opportunity affected by the fact that it is people working in companies that give shape, form, and life to the endeavor?" While the previous thirteen chapters are about how to clearly articulate and establish authoritative, concise, and reliable valuation models, this chapter addresses how the living, human story of growth is captured in the valuation results.

Throughout this book, the drivers of growth-opportunity value have been discussed as if growth opportunities were well-defined, sharp-edged objects. But the softer, fuzzy human dimension significantly affects the value of a growth opportunity. From our psychological decision-making biases to the larger-than-life people drawn to growth projects, human traits are intertwined with the value of growth projects.

While writing this chapter, I've discarded several drafts that attempted to create a synthesis—in a somewhat dry form—of the human factor in valuation. The problem was that the drafts failed to capture the pulse, the surprises, and the zigzags of growth as I've seen it. Instead, I decided to speak personally, from my own experience.

I've been around entrepreneurs or have been involved in entrepreneurial ventures my entire adult life. Also, in my consulting work with large companies, I've experienced those gut-wrenching days when the people issues impair the value of growth. I've been there when the long-awaited IPO happens, and I've seen how dreams of success evaporate as the stock price falls below the offering price. I know the sheer exhaustion of a growth marathon punctuated by sprints. And I've benefited both financially and emotionally from taking on the challenges and achieving some success.

This chapter draws from these experiences to discuss three human dimensions of growth opportunities: the leadership; shaping the growth opportunity; and organizing companies for growth initiatives. The consequences for value and the supporting research are laid out for each topic. Other authors and academics will come up with a masterful vision. This chapter simply introduces some of the tension that is intrinsic to growth opportunities: Achieving valuable growth depends on the talents of a few key people.

It's the Guy . . . and a Village

At the heart of a growth opportunity is a person ("the Guy") who embodies the vision.[1] *Embodies* may seem like a theoretical construct, but the intent is personal: At the heart of any growth project is one person who literally breathes life into an idea. Great committees don't propel growth forward; they simply get out of its way. Similarly, a strong board of directors in a startup can't mitigate the damage to growth value caused by an ineffective CEO, despite all their worthy efforts. Their only effective course of action is to change CEOs. The Guy gives life to growth.

At the same time, the Guy needs others to make the dream a reality. After all, if there is no place for others to meaningfully contribute, the Guy is simply the lone inventor or the solo consultant. Growth leaders orchestrate the resources needed from outsiders to grow value. Recently I worked as an interim CEO in a startup. Here's who I talked to outside the firm in the first two days of the week: a corporate lawyer about employee matters; a patent attorney about ongoing filings and further IP protection; an accountant about employee matters; an immigration lawyer about a visa for a key employee; industry analysts about the direction of the product market; a business development representative from a possible competitor/collaborator; an outside consultant about working on two specific projects over the next six weeks; and investors with whom I reviewed progress toward the next milestone. All of these parties are outside the firm, but they make an important contribution. It does take a village.

The Personal Qualities

It's time to choose the leader. Here are some of the qualities I look for, each more focused by noting the offsetting tendency. For example, a vast energy reserve is focused by a tendency to procrastinate. These qualities are needed for both startups and growth projects in corporate settings.

- *The ability to visualize the future from thin air . . . and turn it into a "to do" list.* There's a magnetic energy about a person who can see and taste the future. A visionary has gravitational pull for people and dollars. But without an equally strong dose of activism, the team quietly slips away. Growth opportunities require both a vision and an action plan. The plan captures the heart of the team, propelling the group into the future.

- *An extroverted intellectual . . . and an introverted manager.* Visionary leadership requires a bit of out-of-the-box thinking, which in turn requires intellectual self-confidence. (This is not about schooling—you have to be able to deeply defend your vision. There's no right answer, and many well-educated people lack this inner quality.) Through his or her extroverted sparkle, the leader almost physically represents the idea's importance. His or her intellectualism and charisma allow others to inspect and see a diamond. At the same time, there's a pressing need to answer a ton of e-mail, see that deadlines are being met, and so on. The extrovert needs to head back to the cubicle and quietly do the work.

- *Extremely capable . . . and willing to step out of the way.* Most startups have a large capabilities gap between the CEO and the other founders. After all, as one venture capitalist summarized, if there were two people qualified and ready to be the CEO, there would be two startups. Consequently, the CEO of a startup has little backup. Yet growth requires that the leader assemble the team and grow their capabilities.

One person can't do it all. More than once a startup CEO has burned out—sometimes to the point of hospitalization—because he tried to do it all.

- *A large capacity for living with uncertainty . . . and impatience.* U.S. President Ronald Reagan was noted for his ability to sleep well at night, no matter how difficult the days. Growth leaders need to have a similar capacity of living through long periods of stress and uncertainty. Optimism is one mitigating force, and so is impatience with the status quo. The leader must supply a sense that life will be easier with major pieces of uncertainty resolved. It's hard to be always pleasant and happy about this state of affairs (no one believes you)! A sense of impatience with the status quo provides a touch of edginess that works well.

- *Courage to resolve private risk . . . and an element of immediacy.* Earlier in this list, the CEO was sent to his cubicle. Now I want him out talking to the market, working with the technical team, getting in front of real customers. Sometimes a CEO stays in the office because of a lack of courage. It's scary to test the prized idea against the real world. But as the previous chapters have demonstrated, virtually all of the value increase of a growth opportunity comes from the reduction of private risk. Startups are all about an active learning investment. Well, who's showing that they can take the news, good or bad? Who's showing what must be done right now to resolve that risk? Guy, get out of the cubicle.

- *Vast amounts of energy . . . and a bit of laziness.* Growth opportunities are marathons. They require a steady application of high energy, with spurts of work at a killer pace. Growth leaders have the capacity, but they also know how precious it is. Here's an example. If you can get your company funded with a one-page spreadsheet linked to two pages of description, do it. Why spend the time on a 250-line, 40-input spreadsheet with the latest in simulation analysis? If the first is good enough to know how to run the business and get it funded, smart managers do just that amount of work.

- *Ego invested . . . and walk-away money.* Someone has to care down at the DNA level about the vision. If no one does, nothing will ever come of the growth idea. But when the CEO merges his identity with that of the company or project—"It's my baby, and I'll run it my way"—it's a problem for everyone, and the village falls apart. Growth leaders need an insurance policy: a personal bank account that covers at least six to nine months' worth of decent living. The escape hatch creates a slight shift in attitude and opens up the work environment to more collaboration and personal investment by others. Without an escape hatch, be it money or portable skills, growth leaders fight for their way on each detail, to the detriment of value.

- *Win-win attitude . . . and the willingness to push back.* The village hangs together because the underlying exchange is win-win. The CEO keeps this focus at all times; it's the basis of durable momentum. Occasionally, however, the leader needs to defend turf. Financing, for example, is very transactional. Terms and conditions that create the best deal in a one-off mode may constrain value in the future. At these moments, it's up to the project leader to push hard, to be argumentative and somewhat inflexible—and to walk away from deals that don't work for the long run.

- *Integrity . . . without compromise.* A lack of integrity in the growth leader hurts value for all. It is truly a small world. Actions with anything less than full integrity will come back to haunt the entire venture. It's a privilege to work in a growth opportunity, to participate in the realization of new ideas. A growth leader translates that beauty and honor into everyday behavior, and the quality of his actions reflects back on the team.

So how does this list of personal qualities relate to the valuation models of earlier chapters? It does so in two ways. First, the growth projects that move forward are those that have strong growth leaders. Growth opportunities with weak leaders fall away as their projects are canceled, their doors are closed, and so on. (Note that good leadership is a necessary but not sufficient condition of growth; growth projects disappear for other reasons as well.) Valuation models are calibrated against successful ventures, and thus quantitative benchmarks assume good leadership. When using the benchmarks to evaluate a new project, there is a moment of matching: The valuation model assumes good leadership. Does the leadership of this particular project or company make the grade? If not, valuation models calibrated to observed transaction values will overestimate the value and chance of success.

Second, the leadership skills are put to the test in the early stages, in which the growth leaders shape the opportunity. The series of decisions made early on determine the size of the payoff, the nature of private risk, and the cost to exercise the follow-on options. The next section looks more closely at this process.

Shaping Fuzzy Ideas into a Growth Opportunity

One of the early leadership activities in a growth opportunity is to structure the problem that will be solved. Often the interested parties—potential employees or investors—don't have the same base of information, and often they hold vague but differing perceptions of what's important. Hence, to structure the conversation and solution, the first step is to set a common structure, a single frame of reference. This early step is critically important: The orientation opens some doors and closes others.

"Framing" is a process subtly shaped by emotions and psychological biases. Unfortunately these harm value. This section first reviews the issues that arise from the interplay between the human factor and the objective framing exercise. Then it ties the issues back to valuation and managing growth opportunities.

To begin, let's clarify why framing is so important to the value of growth opportunities. Suppose you have the idea for a very cool and innovative technology. Do you want to do it as a project under the umbrella of your current employer? As a startup with the focus on building a complete company with technology, marketing, and sales? As a startup with the focus on rapid development so as to sell the technology to a bigger company? For example, Cisco acquired twenty to thirty startups a year in 1999 and 2000. Some of these companies were formed with the almost explicit hope of being acquired by Cisco. They never intended to be a full-fledged, grown-up company, and this mental frame guides numerous growth decisions.

Anchoring the Frame

One of our human weaknesses is that we tend to anchor our thinking around a frame, updating or modifying our previous perception with great reluctance. Once a frame is established, people typically enter a problem-solving mode with it firmly in mind and filter information accordingly. Sometimes the frame should be updated, but human nature tends to continue to fit new information into the established frame. Further, most people rely on their frame when choosing the solution method. Experts advise separating the framing activity from the solution activity and checking the frame before proceeding.[2]

Risk Aversion

Research from the field of behavioral finance (the application of psychology to financial decisions) shows that our perceptions of risk and return are highly influenced by how problems are framed.[3] Recognizing a loss is very difficult. We are willing to entertain an open and wide-ranging discussion of buying or selling a stock—that is, if we don't own it. But ask us to sell a stock we own at a loss? No way. Most people have a great aversion to losses. Risk aversion makes us cautious; it stalls tough decisions and causes top management to ask for more and more spreadsheet runs on an important decision.

"Managerial exit barriers" is a good example of how loss aversion affects growth strategies. Economists and strategists use this concept to explain the delay between the date a quantitative economic model would suggest the business or plant should be closed and when managers actually close it down.[4] The delay can be quite long. For example, in my Ph.D. thesis research on declining industries, I found that in the 1920s and 1930s firms in the cotton textile industry lost money every year for more than ten years before closing.[5] Smart owners sold out or liquidated after five years, obtaining a small return on closing. Others kept their firms open until there wasn't a penny left. Other researchers have found similar results; plants often lose money for two or three years before senior managers will shut them down. The point to take forward is that, at a personal level, accepting a loss is tough. Accepting a loss is even more difficult inside organizations.

Risk aversion can cause a gap between valuation model results and intuited value. Studies show that people weigh bad outcomes roughly two and one-half times more heavily than good outcomes.[6] If the model provides a simple expected value, the research says that the value most people intuit is much lower.

The valuation templates of the previous chapters rely on observed transactions for calibration. Because these transactions are the result of a negotiation—possibly informed by valuation models—risk aversion is accounted for in the transaction value. Often in negotiations, the energetic growth leader will prepare a detailed spreadsheet justifying a high value. Negotiations will go faster if the growth leader is aware of the gap between the spreadsheet result and the intuited value on the other side of the table.

Jumping to Solutions

With the problem framed, many people jump to a solution. But this omits two important intermediate steps. The first is the generation of alternate strategies; the second is the building of a consensus around potential solutions. Practitioners of decision analysis have found that of all the steps in the analysis, the largest value gain comes from the generation of alternatives.[7] From their research on good-quality corporate decision making, Jim Matheson and David Matheson make three suggestions about generating alternatives:[8]

- *Don't kill the idea before it is fully born.* Brainstorm new alternatives without evaluating them.

- *Identify alternatives that provide a clear direction.* Sharp and credible images will survive future scrutiny and cynicism.

- *Open up the thinking.* Generate alternatives that span the space of the possible. Experience shows that the highest-valued alternative is usually somewhere in the middle of the set.

While growth leaders are pretty good at directing brainstorming sessions (remember intellectual self-confidence?), they may be less adept at pushing the group's thinking to clear images, to create credible story lines. The disciplined practice of valuation with numbers *and* words, such as those used throughout this book, helps mitigate the natural tendency toward fuzzy, optimistic thinking. Further, there needs to be a logic check on the feasibility of the suggested alternatives. Strategies that require organizational or business logic change are riskier and more expensive to implement.

An Emotional Reaction to Contingent Strategies

Growth opportunities have a clear path forward . . . for one or two steps. After that the picture clouds. Growth opportunities contain contingent strategies, in which the choice of strategy depends on the outcome: If this happens, we'll do X; if that happens, we'll do Y. Psychologists have found that while many people grasp the notion of contingent strategies, they have difficulty in planning their use. Fear prevents them from articulating the future steps.[9] Planning activities forces them to squarely face uncertainty, and that's scary.

One consequence of the lack of clarity is surprise. Recently, I heard the following from a startup CEO: "We really thought we'd finish our technology by now and have two new customers. It's quite surprising, but our tech team got off schedule and our potential customers want to wait six months because of their budget cuts. Now we're running out of money; we have only funds for two more months." How much of this status report is really a surprise? It takes time to get off schedule, and it takes time for sales cycles to stall. By failing to articulate a contingent strategy in the case of a bad outcome, the CEO has pushed his startup to the brink of failure. No funds, no customer, no technology, close the doors!

Facing up to possible bad outcomes and articulating the associated contingent strategy creates important change. First, the growth leader will try to get a bit more funding, enough to ride through a patch of bad luck. After articulating the bad news, it becomes reasonable to expect bad luck and to prepare for it. Second, a trigger point is established—one that separates temporary bad luck from permanent bad news. Permanent bad news is seldom as clear as "the market will always hate this product." More often it is in the form of "we have been trying to sell this for ten months and have no customers." Often the trigger point is a date on the calendar reserved for a cold, hard look at the business. Ironically, if investors know that the exit trigger point has been established, they are *more* willing to invest. They want the growth leader's frame to line up with investor returns.

Leading Future-Perfect Thinking

Future-perfect thinking, also called visioning, is a frame of reference that makes a future success feel very tangible. Here's a definition from an experienced software development manager: "Instead of using the simple future tense and asking 'What *should* the (software) system do?' we should use the future perfect tense and ask 'What *will* the system have done?'"[10] This shift in thinking has proven to be a very powerful form of leadership. First, clearly and specifically articulate the success outcome: When? What does it look like? How does it feel? Second, look backward and dechiper how the team got there: What were the required steps? What problems were encountered? How were the problems solved? What resources were needed and when?

There's a link between this leadership action and the valuation templates of Chapters 6 through 8. The success payoff is the value of the growth project at the end of the life of the option, if all private risk resolves successfully. Future-perfect thinking can be used to more clearly define first the success payoff, then the option to get there.

Future-Perfect Thinking at P&G

Future-perfect thinking can go awry. Chapter 13 reviewed the recent history of P&G, including the abrupt change in CEOs in June 2000. One factor that led to the departure of Durk Jager was the "surprise" that he had several quarters in a row when business units reported poor results. Jager had introduced "stretch goals"—a form of future-perfect thinking—to the firm. To shake up the old patterns, he started the practice of basing performance compensation, budget allocations, and product support spending on the stretch goals.

These actions did shake up thinking and helped P&G introduce new products and grow revenues. But they also caused the firm to spend well in advance of revenues. The mentality shifted, and managers acted as if the stretch goal had already been achieved. The moment of reconciliation came each quarter when corporate performance was reported to the world. For several quarters in a row, Jager simply didn't have the information in advance so he could gently reset equity analysts' expectations. P&G and the analysts worked off stretch goals, while actual performance was pretty good but far below these expectations. There was a surprise at each quarterly conference call—a big Wall Street no-no! This was one of the factors that led to Jager's departure. The P&G story also shows the difference in using future-perfect thinking for valuing and shaping growth opportunities and using it for corporate capital allocation and performance measurement.

Leading Growth in a Corporation

This last section looks at where in the organization growth projects might reside, and what key corporate processes will be needed to gain value from growth projects. Although this topic may sound abstract, it is accompanied by an emotional and dramatic issue for each growth project: Who is the Guy? Who will breathe fire into the idea? How does he grow value in a corporate environment? Corporate processes must make room for the growth leader.

Organizing for Growth

Here are several highly visible ways companies house their growth projects and how the personal drama of growth could unfold in each.

The corporate incubator. The corporation sets aside dollars and space for ideas that seem valuable, but don't fit elsewhere. Incubators solve the dilemma of growth projects in an operations-oriented corporate culture. The downside, however, is that when entrepreneurial talent flows to the incubator, some corporate strategists worry that the rest of the company will lose its innovative spirit.

But experience says there's another more important worry. If the corporate entrepreneur is offered a safety net, an easy return to the corporate ranks, he may never face up to the risks of the growth opportunity—and move to address them. But, if the safety net is removed entirely, why does he need the parent company?

In addition, while great growth leaders are not driven by money, they anticipate enjoying the rewards of success. How do corporate entrepreneurs earn their well-deserved reward in the incubator environment? Without resolving these issues, the probability of growing an idea into a successful business from a corporate incubator is less than for a stand-alone startup.

Corporate venture capital. In 1999 and early 2000, a large number of companies set up their own venture capital funds. Sometimes these groups have the narrow mandate of financial returns alone, in other cases they exist to identify early-stage technologies in outside startups that may benefit the corporation. In either case, the corporate venture capitalist is not the leader of growth but an enabler. This funding mechanism allows companies to invest in entrepreneurial leaders without growing their own, avoiding the incubator issues. The obvious disadvantage is that by funding outsiders, the corporation fails to develop and reward its own growth leaders.

The main problem with corporate venture capital is its size. The financial returns seem unlikely to significantly affect the corporate balance sheet, and the number of projects coming from corporate venture capital seems too small to affect the growth component of the stock price of a large company. To harvest a venture capital investment in a corporate setting, the product or technology must enable a broad-based—and thus highly valuable—change in the corporation as a whole.

Reinvent the company. Strategy consultants often promote this concept. In practice, they get the corporate entrepreneur focused and started. But reinventing the company and increasing its rate of growth depend less on a few corporate entrepreneurs than on corporate processes that stimulate and support growth while maintaining a focus on execution.

Skunk works. There are many colorful stories about how a small isolated and secret group saved the corporate day. For example, Tracy Kidder's *Soul of a New Machine* chronicles a stealth team in Boston that invented Data General's next computer product. The book depicts the careful marshaling of resources, the building of a group mentality, and the leader's sheltering of the group from corporate oversight. The act of breaking the corporate rules to foster growth can attract the hidden entrepreneurs in the company. And the legend can spread the attitude.

In sum, there's probably no superior corporate home for growth projects. A good mix might include a strong center of R&D, a smooth process of transfer of technology into product development, some urban legends about cool groups of rebels who saved the day, and a showcase incubator or corporate venture fund. With all the pieces in place, let's next turn to corporate processes.

Deciding about Growth

Much of the value of growth projects comes from making the right decisions at the right time. Can companies apply the rigor and discipline of a professional venture capitalist to internal projects? Here are some of the hard issues venture capitalists face and that corporate decision processes must also address:

- *The moment of selection.* Venture capitalists are flooded with business plans. For example, one leading early-stage venture firm receives about 12,000 business plans a year, of which it funds fifteen.[11] For a venture capitalist, the moment that has the largest effect on future returns is the moment of selection. If companies shot down as many ideas as venture capitalists did, their supply of ideas from the corporate ranks would dry up. So a key issue for internal corporate processes is how to be picky. Venture capital rates of return are obtained only if the same discriminating selection criteria are used.

- *Down rounds and going mark-to-market.* Sometimes everything goes right—the product is done, early market feedback is good, sales are picking up—but the stock market's valuation of the business opportunity is quite low. Venture capitalists will use this public-market pricing to lower the valuation of the private firm (a down round of funding) or to find an exit strategy through acquisition or liquidation. How can companies internalize and take action on the same signals? It's pretty difficult; venture capitalists are transaction-driven, while internal company processes are most often built around long-term relationships.

- *Changing horses.* While much rests on the quality of the startup's founders, it's pretty hard to find a founder who takes an idea and grows it into a real company. Usually there is a midcourse change in management. If this change is done under duress, it can get messy. If the new management can't capture the hearts of the troops, much value is lost. Sometimes the board of directors for a startup will almost surgically remove a nonperforming founder. Experience shows that this coldness is sometimes needed to preserve value. How can a corporation make the same type of change without demoralizing its corporate entrepreneurs?

- *The magnitude of private risk.* Suppose you are the division manager, and a team has approached you to internally fund their technology concept. The DCF value of the success payoff is $100 million. You consider the project to be at the start of development. First, you note that while they are asking you for $5 million, experience suggests that it will take more than $50 million to grow the concept into a mature business. Second, you note that a quick back-of-the-envelope calculation from Table 8-3 shows that a company in product development is typically worth less than 20 percent of the success payoff, and that most of the value discount comes from private risk. How can the corporation systematically manage the project to reduce this risk? Venture capitalists walk away from startups that don't meet milestones, whereas corporations most often attempt to muddle through. The magnitude of private risk in a disciplined investment environment illustrates the magnitude of the management challenge in corporations.

Takeaways

- Growth leaders are like magnets. They attract the people and resources to keep their vision alive and flourishing. Venture capitalists are known for reading the founder's resumé before looking at a business plan. That should not be surprising: It is people who make an abstract valuation result come to life.

- There are a number of psychological biases that may prevent us from rationally articulating and executing growth opportunities. A strong growth leader will help others over this hurdle and will find that by articulating a rational plan for the potentially bad outcomes, he'll more easily attract funding and employees.

- It is a challenge to find the right vehicle for large-scale growth in a large corporation. Common solutions, such as corporate venture capital, corporate incubators, and so on, simply can't create growth at a sizable scale. Growth has to come from the troops.

15

Marking a Spot
on the Map of Value

If there's one map of value, where are your growth opportunities located?
It's easy to get caught up in tools and techniques, but experience shows
that most errors in valuing growth opportunities arise when managers
lose sight of the big picture. Here are some closing thoughts that summa-
rize the insights from tools and perspectives in this book. But this is not
the last word: Check www.valuesweep.com for more ideas.

The Big Ideas

Often managers lose sight of the big picture because there's nowhere to go for a summary of the important ideas. We need a poster
on the wall. Rip out these pages and make one! This section has
three parts: calculating, communicating, and growing value.

Calculating

Think One Map. Ultimately, there's one map of value. While assets
vary in their exposure to market-priced risk, their value must still
align with the one map. Financial innovation continues to enlarge
the world of market-priced risk and open up choices. When growth
opportunities have mark-to-market valuations new and valuable
strategies will emerge. Think ahead. Think one map.

Know Your Match. Valuation templates are based on descriptions of the world as it is. If there's not a match between your project and the context that led to the numbers in the template, the results can be significantly wrong. Consider the venture capital valuation template. Those results are from professional, disciplined investors who will push out nonperforming management teams, who will find exits for companies going nowhere, and who measure results by financial return alone. If your company has broader objectives, the valuation results from this template are wrong for your growth projects. Match the template to the environment.

Value the Back-of-the-Envelope Calculation. The structure of value in growth projects is often opaque to senior management. Doing fifty different spreadsheet runs based on DCF will only further annoy top executives. Unless there's a change, the finance staff is in great danger of being shut out of the strategic decision process. Imagine that the finance types arrived at the critical meeting with a simple and compelling story of value growth, benchmarked against other opportunities, and aligned with financial market valuations. Guess what? They did it on the back of an envelope, using established valuation templates. Who is the hero now?

Think Success Payoff. Good things happen when everyone—the visionary, the team, the investors, the customers—can clearly see, almost taste, the success payoff. First, the growth opportunity can be valued; it's impossible to value the unimaginable. Second, a self-reinforcing process gets started. Everyone's actions, even the very small ones, move the project toward achieving the value shown in the numerical result.

Don't Get Creative. Your project is not that special. It won't defy the laws of economics, and it will fall into a well-known business model. We're pretty good at valuing known business models, and the growth options based on them. We even know how to discount options and mature business models for lack of resources and failure to execute. So don't get creative, get realistic.

Communicating

Tell the Story. There are a lot of "if-then" statements in a growth opportunity. Unless explained very clearly, these contingencies can be fragmented and detailed, confusing the audience (the guys with the money!). Help them out by telling the story. Make the contingencies part of a plot so that they can see how it all comes together. It's also a good way to check if the logic in the valuation model matches your own.

Draw the Pictures. Here's the formal theory: "When the principles of (information) design replicate the principles of thought, the act of arranging information becomes an act of insight."[1] Decision trees do exactly this. Timelines are also very useful in understanding the components of embedded real options. Rearranging these visual symbols sharpens the story, enables project redesign, and supports the creation of value.

The Social Life of the Number Matters. Information theory would seem to be a very abstract and dry topic. Yet as the authors of *The Social Life of Information* point out, our social communities influence how information is shaped, transmitted, and used.[2] The same is true for valuation results. Books with models, such as this one, are only the starting point. Valuation results should be communicated in a way that works for the community the managers live in. Don't stop when the calculations are done; your job continues.

Growing Value

Find Your Guy, Find Your Gal. Growth needs leaders. Growth opportunities are tricky to manage, and much of the value comes from identifying options and getting all resources together for their timely execution. There's a person out there who will bring the valuation result to life. Go find him or her!

Get the Money. Growth projects need money. If the financial markets don't think your firm has the funds to grow early-stage growth projects, value will be heavily discounted. It's quite a tricky business to increase the scale of innovation, fund new growth, and continue to execute the current business. Good financing is critical to realizing the value of growth.

Don't Whine, Just Execute. There are two reasons why a company must continue to execute its current business while investing in growth. First, the current business is a large part of corporate value. If the current business isn't humming, the CEO loses the opportunity for innovative growth. Second, the payoff to a growth option is a valuable, mature business. The more valuable the current business, the more valuable the growth option. Isn't it ironic that good advice to leaders of growth is, "Do a great job on the current business"?

The Value of a Better Number

An improved valuation model, a better number, is not the goal. The success payoff to new tools for valuing growth opportunities is to change decisions, to increase choices, and to smooth the way for faster and more valuable growth. The valuation results from improved tools are simply the means to the end.

Right now, we can't have a rational argument about the value of growth opportunities because we don't have the shared images, the common language, or the same set of valuation tools. Valuation arguments are won by the party that holds a key asset— money, an audit credential, or an important contract—not by a rational argument.

A new approach to valuation, which results in a better number, also results in a defensible location on the map of value. Let's use the tools and perspectives in this book and have a rational argument. We can refine the estimate of value through a shared understanding about the value structure of growth. We can mark the spot, and know why it is there, for all of the growth opportunities across the sweep of value.

Appendix

Growth Option Lookup Tables

- Table A-1: Option Value Factor for Two-Year Growth Option
- Table A-2: Option Value Factor for Three-Year Growth Option
- Table A-3: Volatility Scaling Factor for Two-Year Growth Option
- Table A-4: Volatility Scaling Factor for Three-Year Growth Option

Estimating Volatility

- Table A-5: Calculation of Historical Volatility for Amgen (AMGN)
- Figure A-1: Adjusting Equity Volatility to Firm Volatility
- Table A-6: Adjusting Stock Price Volatility Estimates for Debt
- Table A-7: Market-Value-to-Sales Ratio and Firm Value Volatility by Industry
- Table A-8: Market-Value-to-Sales Ratio and Firm Value Volatility by Industry, *listed in alphabetical order*

All tables in the Appendix and additional data can be downloaded at www.valuesweep.com.

Table A-1 Option Value Factor for Two-Year Growth Option

(Option values are reported as a percentage of S)

						S/X					
		0.50	0.75	1.00	1.25	1.50	2.00	3.00	5.00	7.00	10.00
	25%	1%	7%	19%	31%	41%	55%	70%	82%	87%	91%
	50%	10%	21%	31%	40%	47%	58%	71%	82%	87%	91%
	75%	24%	35%	43%	50%	55%	63%	73%	83%	87%	91%
Annual	100%	38%	48%	54%	60%	64%	70%	77%	85%	88%	92%
Volatility (σ)	125%	51%	59%	64%	68%	71%	76%	81%	87%	90%	93%
	150%	62%	68%	73%	76%	78%	81%	85%	90%	92%	94%
	175%	71%	76%	79%	82%	83%	86%	89%	92%	94%	95%
	200%	79%	83%	85%	87%	88%	90%	92%	94%	95%	96%

Option values calculated using the Black-Scholes formula. An option calculator is available at www.valuesweep.com.

Other options inputs are: $t = 2$, $r = 5\%$ per year.

Table A-2   Option Value Factor for Three-Year Growth Option

(Option values are reported as a percentage of S)

		0.50	0.75	1.00	1.25	1.50	2.00	3.00	5.00	7.00	10.00
	25%	3%	12%	24%	35%	44%	57%	71%	83%	88%	91%
	50%	17%	29%	39%	46%	52%	62%	73%	83%	88%	91%
	75%	35%	45%	52%	58%	62%	69%	77%	85%	89%	92%
Annual	**100%**	50%	59%	64%	68%	71%	76%	82%	87%	90%	93%
Volatility (σ)	**125%**	64%	70%	74%	77%	79%	82%	86%	90%	92%	94%
	150%	75%	79%	82%	84%	86%	88%	90%	93%	94%	96%
	175%	83%	86%	88%	89%	90%	92%	93%	95%	96%	97%
	200%	89%	91%	92%	93%	94%	95%	96%	97%	97%	98%

S/X

Option values calculated using the Black-Scholes formula. An option calculator is available at www.valuesweep.com

Other options inputs are: $t = 3$, $r = 5\%$ per year.

Table A-3 Volatility Scaling Factor for Two-Year Growth Option

						S/X				
	0.50	0.75	1.00	1.25	1.50	2.00	3.00	5.00	7.00	10.00
25%	7.35	4.98	3.63	2.82	2.33	1.81	1.43	1.22	1.15	1.10
50%	3.05	2.53	2.20	1.98	1.82	1.61	1.39	1.22	1.15	1.10
75%	2.05	1.83	1.69	1.59	1.52	1.42	1.30	1.19	1.14	1.10
Annual 100%	1.62	1.51	1.44	1.38	1.34	1.29	1.22	1.15	1.11	1.08
Volatility (σ) 125%	1.40	1.33	1.29	1.26	1.23	1.20	1.15	1.11	1.09	1.07
150%	1.26	1.22	1.19	1.17	1.16	1.14	1.11	1.08	1.06	1.05
175%	1.18	1.15	1.13	1.12	1.11	1.09	1.08	1.06	1.05	1.04
200%	1.12	1.10	1.09	1.08	1.07	1.06	1.05	1.04	1.03	1.03

To use the table: Suppose the volatility of the underlying asset is 75% per year and the S/X ratio is 1.5. The volatility of the option is 114% per year (1.52 × 75%).

The scaling factor is calculated using the Black-Scholes formula. An option calculator is available at www.valuesweep.com.

Other options inputs are: $t = 3$, $r = 5\%$ per year.

Table A-4 Volatility Scaling Factor for Three-Year Growth Option

Annual Volatility (σ)	S/X									
	0.50	0.75	1.00	1.25	1.50	2.00	3.00	5.00	7.00	10.00
25%	5.34	3.85	2.99	2.46	2.11	1.72	1.40	1.21	1.14	1.09
50%	2.43	2.10	1.89	1.74	1.64	1.49	1.33	1.20	1.14	1.09
75%	1.71	1.58	1.49	1.43	1.38	1.31	1.23	1.15	1.12	1.08
100%	1.41	1.34	1.29	1.26	1.24	1.20	1.16	1.11	1.09	1.07
125%	1.25	1.21	1.18	1.16	1.15	1.13	1.10	1.08	1.06	1.05
150%	1.15	1.13	1.11	1.10	1.09	1.08	1.07	1.05	1.04	1.03
175%	1.09	1.08	1.07	1.06	1.06	1.05	1.04	1.03	1.03	1.02
200%	1.06	1.05	1.04	1.04	1.04	1.03	1.03	1.02	1.02	1.01

To use the table: Suppose the volatility of the underlying asset is 75% per year and the S/X ratio is 1.5. The volatility of the option is 104% per year (1.38 × 75%).

The scaling factor is calculated using the Black-Scholes formula. An option calculator is available at www.valuesweep.com.

Other options inputs are: $t = 3$, $r = 5\%$ per year.

Estimating Historical Stock Price Volatility

Table A-5 is an example of how to estimate historical stock price volatility based on Amgen, a biotech firm. Amgen trades under the ticker symbol AMGN. The first column shows the closing stock price each month, July 1996 through June 2001. The data show that Amgen's stock price, on a split-adjusted basis, has drifted upward throughout the five-year period.

The second column reports the monthly return to the stock. A formula for the continuously compounded return should be used to maintain consistency with the assumptions in the Black-Scholes equation and other option calculators. The continuously compounded return is calculated as

$$u_t = \ln (P_t / P_{t-1})$$

where u_t is the return between $t - 1$ and t and P_t is the stock price or index value at time t (ln is the natural logarithm).

The volatility results are shown in the lower right corner of Table A-5. The monthly volatility, 12 percent, is calculated as the standard deviation of the monthly return. The annual volatility, 40 percent, is calculated as: $\sqrt{12}$ × monthly volatility.

The decision to use monthly data points is a matter of judgment. While more frequent data increase the number of data points, it often does not lead to a more precise or stable estimate of long-term volatility. The length of the historical period used is also a matter of judgment. A longer period provides more data points, but, as the true volatility may slowly change over time, the distant past might not be a good prediction of the future. At a minimum, the length of the historical period should the same as the length of time to the option's maturity. This will capture the chance of infrequent but large movements in the underlying asset, an important consideration because an option obtains a large part of its value from these outcomes.

Volatility Estimates from www.ivolatility.com

The Web site www.ivolatility.com provides two different kinds of volatility estimates for many publicly traded companies. One set of

Table A-5 Calculation of Historical Volatility for Amgen (AMGN)

Date	Stock Price at Close (P_t)	Monthly Return $ln(P_t / P_{t-1})$	Date	Stock Price at Close (P_t)	Monthly Return $ln(P_t / P_{t-1})$
Jul 96	13.7		Jan 99	32.0	0.20
Aug 96	14.6	0.06	Feb 99	31.2	−0.02
Sep 96	15.8	0.08	Mar 99	37.4	0.18
Oct 96	15.3	−0.03	Apr 99	30.7	−0.20
Nov 96	15.2	−0.01	May 99	31.6	0.03
Dec 96	13.6	−0.11	Jun 99	30.4	−0.04
Jan 97	14.1	0.04	Jul 99	38.4	0.23
Feb 97	15.3	0.08	Aug 99	41.6	0.08
Mar 97	14.0	−0.09	Sep 99	40.8	−0.02
Apr 97	14.7	0.05	Oct 99	39.9	−0.02
May 97	16.7	0.13	Nov 99	45.6	0.13
Jun 97	14.5	−0.14	Dec 99	60.1	0.28
Jul 97	14.7	0.01	Jan 00	63.7	0.06
Aug 97	12.4	−0.17	Feb 00	68.2	0.07
Sep 97	12.0	−0.03	Mar 00	61.4	−0.11
Oct 97	12.3	0.03	Apr 00	56.0	−0.09
Nov 97	12.8	0.04	May 00	63.6	0.13
Dec 97	13.5	0.06	Jun 00	70.3	0.10
Jan 98	12.5	−0.08	Jul 00	64.9	−0.08
Feb 98	13.3	0.06	Aug 00	75.8	0.15
Mar 98	15.2	0.14	Sep 00	69.8	−0.08
Apr 98	14.9	−0.02	Oct 00	57.9	−0.19
May 98	15.1	0.01	Nov 00	63.6	0.09
Jun 98	16.3	0.08	Dec 00	63.9	0.00
Jul 98	18.4	0.12	Jan 01	70.3	0.10
Aug 98	15.2	−0.19	Feb 01	72.1	0.02
Sep 98	18.9	0.22	Mar 01	60.2	−0.18
Oct 98	19.6	0.04	Apr 01	61.1	0.02
Nov 98	18.8	−0.04	May 01	66.4	0.08
Dec 98	26.1	0.33	Jun 01	60.1	−0.10
			Monthly Volatility		**12%**
			Annual Volatility		**40%**

estimates is calculated from historical stock price data, using the same method as described earlier in this Appendix. The second set of estimates is obtained by using the Black-Scholes formula to reverse-engineer the price of traded stock options, identifying the level of volatility consistent with the option price. The results of the second method are known as implied volatility estimates.

When S/X equals one—the option is at the money—the value of the option comes largely from volatility; the price of these option contracts isolates the effect of volatility on option value. Contracts at or near the money are the first choice for implied volatility estimates. An option price is forward looking and thus the implied volatility estimate is considered a forecast of volatility expected over the life of the option. Consequently, the implied volatility estimate (about the future) and the historical volatility estimate (about the past) may differ.

The volatility estimates provided at www.ivolatility.com are expressed in annual terms. Estimates for Amgen in August 2001 were a historical volatility estimate of 50 percent per year, and an implied volatility estimate of 40 percent per year.

Correcting Volatility Estimates for the Effect of Debt

Estimates of stock price volatility are fairly easy to obtain or calculate, but for most growth opportunities an adjustment is required before use as an input into the growth option formula. The payoff value of a growth option reflects gains available to the entire firm, not just the equity portion. The larger the amount of debt in the capital structure, the greater the divergence between stock price volatility and firm value volatility. The next figure and table show how to transform stock price volatility to firm value volatility.

The market value of the firm is the sum of debt and equity values. (Debt is usually taken at book value.) Firm value volatility is defined as the weighted average of the volatility of equity and the volatility of debt, after accounting for the correlation of returns between debt and equity.

The easiest way to correct stock price volatility for the effect of debt is to use Figure A-1. The figure shows the relationship

Figure A-1   Adjusting Equity Volatility to Firm Volatility

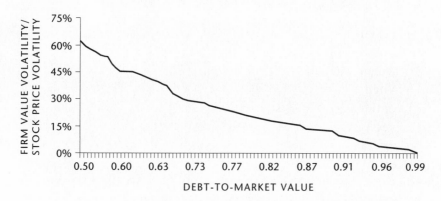

Sources: www.damadoran.com; optvar.xls; and author's calculations. Used with permission.

To estimate firm value volatility:
1. Estimate debt/market value of the firm and its stock price volatility.
2. Use the debt-to-market-value ratio to read the ratio of firm value volatility/stock price volatility from the graph.
3. Multiply the ratio by the firm's stock price volatility.

between the debt-to-market value of a firm and the ratio of the firm value volatility to the stock price volatility. For example, a firm with a debt-to-market-value ratio of 0.73 will have a firm value volatility that is 30 percent of the stock price volatility. Before using the figure, simply calculate the debt-to-market value and stock price volatility for the application at hand. Then use the figure to appropriately scale the stock price volatility. Data on debt-to-market value and stock price volatility by industry are shown in Table A-6.

Table A-7 provides a sample of reference data on the market-value-to-sales ratio and average volatility by industry.

Table A-6   Adjusting Stock Price Volatility Estimates for Debt

(Sample of 20 industries ranked by Debt/Market value)

Industry	Debt/ Market Value	Stock Price Volatility	Firm Value Volatility	Firm Value Volatility/Stock Price Volatility
Auto and truck	0.62	47%	24%	0.50
Auto parts	0.57	64%	34%	0.53
Securities brokerage	0.50	63%	36%	0.57
Cable TV	0.46	85%	51%	0.60
Steel	0.43	51%	31%	0.62
Railroad	0.41	38%	24%	0.63
Paper and forest products	0.38	41%	27%	0.66
Banking	0.30	32%	23%	0.72
Grocery	0.28	44%	32%	0.74
Natural gas	0.25	50%	38%	0.76
Furniture/Home furnishings	0.22	42%	33%	0.79
Entertainment	0.20	67%	55%	0.81
Restaurant	0.17	51%	43%	0.84
Petroleum (integrated)	0.14	42%	37%	0.87
Drugstore	0.12	58%	51%	0.88
Healthcare information systems	0.09	102%	94%	0.91
Insurance (Property/casualty)	0.07	41%	38%	0.94
Telecommunications equipment	0.05	95%	90%	0.95
Internet	0.04	139%	133%	0.96
Semiconductor	0.03	95%	92%	0.97
Market Average	**0.21**	**63%**	**50%**	**0.78**

Source: www.damadoran.com. Used with permission.

For a full listing, see www.valuesweep.com.

Table A-7 Market-Value-to-Sales Ratio and Firm Value Volatility by Industry

(Sample of 20 industries ranked by market-value-to-sales ratio)

Industry	Market Value Firm/Sales	Volatility of Firm Value
Cable TV	14.43	51%
Drug	13.62	97%
Computer software	9.27	93%
Semiconductor	7.60	92%
Banking	4.57	23%
Securities brokerage	3.96	36%
Packaging and container	3.50	24%
Electrical equipment	3.04	77%
Hotel/Gaming	2.95	31%
Beverage (soft drink)	2.83	36%
Electric utilities	2.76	16%
Household products	2.71	38%
Computer hardware	2.18	90%
Chemical	1.90	42%
Tobacco	1.54	43%
Homebuilding	1.22	29%
Petroleum (integrated)	1.21	37%
Aerospace/Defense	1.19	40%
Auto and truck	0.79	24%
Grocery	0.75	32%

Sources: Data from www.marketguide.com and www.damadoran.com; optvar.xls. Market values as of April 2001. Industry groups follow those of Marketguide.

Glossary

A Vocabulary for Growth Opportunities

Before crunching a number, before putting pen to paper, valuation requires a mental image of the growth opportunity at hand. After the calculations are complete, the analyst must communicate the numerical results and how they reflect features of the growth opportunity. Putting new quantitative tools in place is one component of change, but a new language, a larger vocabulary for shaping and describing growth opportunities, is also needed.

This glossary is a beginning. It is a set of words describing growth opportunities and aspects of their valuation. A longer version can be found at www.valuesweep.com. The first use of each phrase is indicated in parentheses.

Active learning (Chapter 2)

Investments that resolve uncertainty. A pilot project is a form of active learning. Private risk is typically resolved through investments in active learning, whereas market-priced risk is typically resolved through passive learning.

Cash-needy growth (Chapter 2)

A type of growth opportunity that requires several stages or several years of spending before a possible positive return. Traditional R&D is a typical cash-needy growth opportunity.

Contingent decision (Chapter 2)

A decision that depends on a future outcome. The timing and the set of alternatives can be specified in advance, but the actual decision taken is not known; it awaits the resolution of uncertainty.

Decision analysis (Chapter 5)

A systematic and rigorous approach to making high-quality decisions. Decision trees are a graphical tool used in decision analysis.

Discounted cash flow (DCF) (Chapter 3)

A traditional valuation method that discounts future cash flows for time and certain types of risk. DCF is the correct valuation method for sustainable growth opportunities that don't have contingent decisions.

Expansion opportunity (Chapter 4)

As narrowly defined in this book, increasing the scale of the current business. A firm with an expansion opportunity can then be valued as the sum of a DCF valuation of the current business plus the option to expand.

Expected value (Chapter 5)

The weighted average of the value of a set of uncertain outcomes. The probability of the outcome is used as the weight, and the weights must sum to 100 percent.

Framing (Chapter 14)

The act of establishing the problem to be solved. Framing includes deciding what is included and what is not, how the uncertainty is to be represented, and how decisions are contingent on uncertain future outcomes.

Growth engines (Chapter 13)

The corporate portfolio of investments and activities that lead to sales and profit growth. While the word *portfolio* sounds a bit static, the corporate growth engine has a dynamic component—the matching of the size of the engine, the funds needed to support investment, and the pace of output over time.

Growth options (Chapter 1)

Used synonymously in this book with *growth opportunities* to indicate investments that lead to significant growth. There is an option-like feature to these investments, in that today's investment creates the opportunity to invest in the future, which then creates the chance of obtaining a significant return.

Initial public offering (IPO) (Chapter 8)

The date that a company first trades its common stock in the public market. An IPO is a milestone event because the public stock price is typically much higher than the previous private equity value.

Market-priced risk (Chapter 2)

The sources of uncertainty that move stock prices. For example, airline stocks move when the jet fuel price changes, and the effect is the market-priced risk of jet fuel costs on airline company valuations.

Mark-to-market (Chapter 1)

Often financial securities trade infrequently and are carried in the accountant's books at the value of the last trade. Periodically, the value of the security will be updated to what its value would be if it were currently traded. This is known as mark-to-market. For nonfinancial assets, mark-to-market has the same implication, establishing the value of the asset if it were recently bought or sold.

Net present value (NPV) (Chapter 3)

The output of a DCF valuation, and also a valuation that includes options if they are valued explicitly. The output fully takes into account (is net of) all immediate and future investments.

Option value factor (Chapter 4)

The precalculated option value found in the lookup tables in the Appendix. To obtain the option value, multiply the option value factor by the success payoff.

Passive learning (Chapter 2)

When uncertain outcomes are revealed with no further investment. News about oil prices is obtained through passive learning (simply watching the prices move), whereas news about oil geology is obtained through active learning (investments that generated information).

Payoff (Chapter 4)

The value that might be obtained from acquiring an option. The stock price is the payoff to an equity option; a larger company is the payoff to an expansion option. See also success payoff.

Private risk (Chapter 2)

The sources of uncertainty that are not accounted for by change in the value of publicly traded securities, singly or in combination.

Technology acceptance is typically a private risk, but occasionally it is accounted for in the public-market value of a high-tech firm.

Private risk discount (PRD) (Chapter 6)

The difference between the valuation result of a real options model (which takes into account market-priced risk) and the observed transaction value of a growth opportunity. The difference between the two reflects the value consequence of private risk. The difference is expressed as a discount from the success payoff.

Public company startups (Chapter 8)

Companies that went public before obtaining cash flow breakeven. Before 1996, firms at a comparable stage of development would have been financed by venture capitalists, with a possible IPO eighteen months to two years later.

Real options (Chapter 4)

The application of financial option pricing models to real (nonfinancial) assets. Real options valuation methodology is useful for growth opportunities with contingent decisions and market-priced risk.

Staged growth opportunities (Chapter 7)

Most growth opportunities require multiple rounds of investment before a potential payoff. The timing of each stage is often discretionary. It can be determined by corporate budget cycles, but value is increased if it is coordinated with the results of active learning.

Startups (Chapter 8)

Young firms that are not yet self-funding. They often look to venture capitalists, or in some cases corporate partners, for financing. Their entire valuation rests on the value of their growth opportunities.

Success payoff (Chapter 6)

The value that might be obtained from a growth opportunity if all private risk is resolved favorably. The success payoff is the same as the payoff in a real options model, but in this book the term *success* is added for clarity about the status of private risk in valuation applications with both private and market-priced risk.

Sustainable growth (Chapter 2)

When growth can be funded by the company's own cash flow. Sustainable growth is often valued using DCF, as the size of the investment is small enough relative to the scale of the ongoing business that the investment decision is fixed, not contingent.

Terminal value (Chapter 3)

A component of value in the DCF valuation model that represents sustainable growth over a long period beginning three to five years from now. Most often the terminal value is based on a moderate rate of cash flow growth—say, at the level of GDP growth—but comprises the vast majority of value in the DCF analysis because it reflects such a long time horizon.

Valuation template (Chapter 3)

A valuation tool tailored in terms of data and methodology to value growth opportunities in a transparent and easy-to-use manner. Valuation templates can be rigorous in construction and provide strong points of comparison if constructed specifically by industry and by type of growth opportunity.

Value decay (Chapter 4)

The "leakage" or erosion of value in a potential payoff owing to competitive forces or asset decay. For example, without reinforcing advertising, brands experience value decay.

Value of information (Chapter 5)

Active learning creates information that improves estimates of the payoff and tightens the confidence interval around that estimate. The value of this type of information determines whether the investment will be taken.

Volatility (Chapter 4)

Defined in this book as the standard deviation of stock returns—a measure of the range of uncertainty about the future stock price. For example, at the time of this writing, America Online's expected stock return was approximately 17 percent per year, and its expected volatility was about 90 percent per year.

Volatility scaling factor (Chapter 7)

Used to quickly calculate the volatility of the option by multiplying the volatility of the payoff by the scaling factor (an option has higher volatility than its payoff). The use of the factor greatly simplifies the calculation of the value of a sequence of options.

Notes

Chapter 1

1. This conclusion holds for a number of variations: Try cash flow instead of earnings; include an analyst's forecasts instead of the assumption of no growth; include a long-term growth rate for the firm. Regardless, the value of known growth opportunities is typically far less than the stock price. Of course, the size of the difference varies by industry and over time, but the basic point is the same. Examples can be found in Richard Brealey and Stewart Myers, *Principles of Corporate Finance,* 5th ed. (New York: McGraw-Hill, 1996), 71, and Janice Revell, "Forget about Earnings," *Fortune,* June 11, 2001.

Chapter 2

1. Chapter 1 in Margaret Blair and Steven Wallman, *Unseen Wealth* (Washington, DC: Brookings Institution Press, 2001).

2. Geoffrey Colvin, "It's the Business Model, Stupid!" *Fortune,* January 8, 2001.

3. Michael Moritz, "A Bigger Splash," *Technology Review,* March 2001.

4. This example is unrelated to the subsequent charges of accounting fraud at Enron.

Chapter 3

1. Note that DCF is unable to value contingent decisions correctly. See pages 227 and 228 in Richard Brealey and Stewart Myers, *Principles of Corporate Finance,* 5th ed. (New York: McGraw-Hill, 1996), and Nalin

Kulatilaka and Alan Marcus, "Project Valuation under Uncertainty: When Does DCF Fail?" *Journal of Applied Corporate Finance,* Fall 1992, 92–100.

2. Good introductions to DCF are found in corporate finance textbooks and in a number of business books. See www.valuesweep.com for references.

3. Of course, there is more than one way to structure a DCF analysis and obtain essentially the same results. I'm arguing for consistency, not brainless uniformity.

4. Data in Michael Mauboussin and Al Rappaport, *Expectations Investing* (Boston: Harvard Business School Press, 2001), show the cash tax rate ranges from 27 percent to 35 percent.

5. See Cynthia Robbins-Roth, *From Alchemy to IPO* (Cambridge, MA: Perseus Publishing, 2000).

6. See Jim Collins, *Good to Great: Why Some Companies Make the Leap . . . And Others Don't* (New York: HarperCollins, 2001).

7. The formula for the present value of a cash flow will grow at rate g forever, at discount rate r: $PV = CF / (r - g)$. When r is equal to 15 percent and CF equals $299, g must equal 7.5 percent.

Chapter 4

1. See www.valuesweep.com for references and links to other Web sites.

2. Merton's Nobel Prize speech has many references, including to a paper listing the options pricing literature. See Robert Merton, "Applications of Option-Pricing Theory: Twenty-Five Years Later," *American Economic Review,* June 1998, 323–350.

3. See Stewart Myers, "Finance Theory and Financial Strategy," *Interfaces,* January–February 1984.

4. The correct valuation of employee stock options (ESOs) requires a tailored valuation model as private risk factors and legal constraints affect the exercise and value of ESOs. Consequently, the Black-Scholes formula significantly overestimates ESO value, in many cases by nearly 50 percent. A straightforward valuation model for ESOs is found in Jennifer Carpenter, "The Exercise and Valuation of Executive Stock Options," *Journal of Financial Economics,* 1998, 127–158.

5. A note to the active reader: A key point of elegance and practicality of the option pricing breakthrough is in how the probability of each outcome is defined. Read one of the many sources on financial option pricing before setting up a valuation tool.

6. A sixth input variable, the rate of dividend payout, can be included. It is discussed later in this chapter.

7. Details on how to estimate volatility are given in the Appendix. Volatility estimates can be found at www.ivolatility.com.

8. One of the most frequently asked questions about financial and real option pricing is the use of the short-term risk-free rate. It arises from a no-arbitrage condition in option pricing. During the life of the contract, the value of the option is precisely replicated by the value of a portfolio of traded securities. Over each short time interval, if no arbitrage were possible, one would earn only the short-term risk-free rate of return by selling the option and holding the portfolio. The option pricing model assumes no arbitrage and thus uses the short-term rate as an input.

9. This form of an option lookup table can also be found in standard M.B.A. finance textbooks such as Richard Brealey and Stewart Myers, *Principles of Corporate Finance,* 5th ed. (New York: McGraw-Hill, 1996), or in an article by Timothy Luehrman, "Corporate Opportunities as Real Options: Getting Started with the Numbers," *Harvard Business Review,* July–August 1998.

10. The ratio S/X mixes dollars from two periods: S is in current dollars, and X is in dollars at time T. Although in general one should avoid creating a ratio that mixes dollars from two periods, in this case the timing of the inputs maintains the analogy to the financial option.

11. Rappaport's arguments are updated in Chapter 8 of Michael Mauboussin and Al Rappaport, *Expectations Investing* (Boston: Harvard Business School Press, 2001).

12. Data and sources for the Amazon.com example are posted at www.valuesweep.com.

13. The market value of the firm is the sum of debt plus equity, where equity includes outstanding employee stock options. See Chapter 8 in Mauboussin and Rappaport, *Expectations Investing.*

14. This report can be downloaded from the Web site, www.valuesweep.com. See also Peter Tufano and Mihir Desai, "Laura Martin: Real Options and the Cable Industry," Case 201-004 (Boston: Harvard Business School, 2000).

15. "Lessons from the Dot-Com Disaster: Tale of Online Pet Stores Shows Depth of Web Delusions," *San Jose Mercury News,* May 27, 2001.

Chapter 5

1. Additional information on firms providing decision analysis through software and/or services can be found at www.valuesweep.com.

2. Under the new plan, the chance of failure is 46 percent: 40 percent chance of IT failure + 6 percent chance of market failure after IT success and a revised market plan (60% × 50% × 20%). Under the original plan,

the chance of failure was 70 percent: 40 percent chance of IT failure + 30 percent chance of market failure after IT success (60% × 50%).

3. Further details on this example can be found at www.pharsight .com and also at www.valuesweep.com. My thanks to Dr. Ron Beaver and Bill Poland of Pharsight for the use of this example, which is based on a talk given by Beaver in June 1999, "Proof of Concept: Streamlining the Value of Information."

4. The more detailed example posted at www.valuesweep.com shows how the active learning investment also reduces uncertainty about these estimates, but for simplicity of exposition, this benefit of active learning is not included here.

5. This result is obtained in two steps. First, the value of delay is calculated as the expected value of the Phase III payoffs with a Phase II trial (from Table 5-3[a]), where the weights are the probabilities of the Phase III outcomes without a Phase II trial (from Table 5-3[b].) This result, less the $140 million Phase III cost, is subtracted from the value of the Phase III project in Table 5-3(b). The difference, $64 million, is the cost of delay. Second, the value of information is calculated as the expected value of the Phase III payoffs without a Phase II trial (from Table 5-3[b]), where the weights are the probabilities of the Phase III outcomes with a Phase II trial (from Table 5-3[a]). This result, less the $140 million Phase III cost, is subtracted from the value of the Phase III project in Table 5-3(a). The difference, $27 million, is the value of information. The calculations are posted at www.valuesweep.com.

6. See Chapter 11 in Richard Zeckhauser, Ralph Keeney, and James Sebenius, *Wise Choices* (Boston: Harvard Business School Press, 1996).

7. Richard Brealey and Stewart Myers, *Principles of Corporate Finance*, 5th ed. (New York: McGraw-Hill, 1996), shows how risk changes along the branches of a decision tree.

Chapter 6

1. Data are from David Kellog and John Charnes, "Real-Options Valuation for a Biotechnology Company," *Financial Analysts Journal*, May–June 2000, 76–84. The first half of the article is similar to the discussion in this section and is a complete analysis. The second half of the article continues the analysis using real options and, in my opinion, is unnecessary.

2. See Henry Grabowski and R. Vernon, "Returns to R&D on New Drug Introductions in the 1980s," *Journal of Health Economics*, 1994, 384–406.

3. See Credit Suisse First Boston, "Listening to Market Signals," July 1999. This report shows that for all major pharmaceutical companies the

DCF value was one-half the market value in each of the previous eight years.

4. My article with Nalin Kulatilaka, "Strategy and Shareholder Value Creation: The Real Options Frontier," *Journal of Applied Corporate Finance,* Summer 2000, 8–21, provides further details on the lack of market-priced risk in pharmaceutical drug development.

5. For an example of a decision tree of oil exploration with a more typical level of detail, see Justin Claeys and Gardner Walkup, Jr., "Discovering Real Options in Oil Field Exploration and Development," Society of Petroleum Engineers, paper 52956, March 1999. The paper can be found at www.spe.org.

6. See Chapter 9 in Martha Amram and Nalin Kulatilaka, *Real Options* (Boston: Harvard Business School Press, 1999) for further details.

7. See Robert Merton, "Applications of Option-Pricing Theory: Twenty-Five Years Later," *American Economic Review,* June 1998, 323–350.

Chapter 7

1. Often financial options are kept open but are layered over through offsetting financial transactions. This form of "virtual exercise" is done to lock in gains from an in-the-money option.

2. See "WebVan Cashes Out," *San Jose Mercury News,* July 10, 2001.

3. Links to white papers on the strategic impact of genomics on the pharmaceutical industry can be found at www.valuesweep.com.

Chapter 8

1. See Randall Stross, *eBoys: The True Story of the Six Tall Men Who Backed eBay, Webvan and Other Billion-Dollar Start-Ups* (New York: Crown Business, 2000).

2. For an introduction to the venture capital industry, see Paul A. Gompers and Josh Lerner, *The Venture Capital Cycle* (Cambridge, MA: MIT Press, 2000); Paul A. Gompers, "The Rise of Venture Capital," *Business and Economic History,* Winter 1994, 1–24; and the resources provided by Josh Lerner at www.people.hbs.edu/jlerner/index.html.

3. See Greg Stevens and James Burley, "3,000 Raw Ideas = 1 Commercial Success," in *The Financial Management of R&D* (Washington, DC: Industrial Research Institute, 2001).

4. Data are from VentureOne, a private firm which collects data on the venture industry. See www.ventureone.com.

5. The data are from VentureOne. The strengths and weaknesses of this data are reviewed by Gompers and Lerner in *The Venture Capital Cycle* and discussed by Lerner at www.people.hbs.edu/jlerner/info.html.

6. The investment in an IPO is made by new shareholders who buy stock in the public market. The terms *premoney* and *postmoney* are typically used for venture capital valuations, but not IPOs. To simplify Table 8-2, this wording detail is glossed over.

7. Many venture capital firms in Silicon Valley are located on Sand Hill Road. One consulting and database provider to the industry, Sand Hill Econometrics, has built a specialized statistical model of venture capital valuations that quantifies the effect of various factors on the PRD. See www.sandhillecon.com.

8. Michael Moritz, "A Bigger Splash," *Technology Review,* March 2001, 99–101.

Chapter 9

1. Robert Hall, "Struggling to Understand the Stock Market," *American Economic Review,* June 2001, 1–11.

2. See Anna Bernasek, "Okay, Now What?" *Fortune,* June 11, 2001.

3. See Robert Shiller, *Irrational Exuberance* (Princeton, NJ: Princeton University Press, 2000).

4. See Jeremy Siegel, *Stocks for the Long Run,* 2d ed. (New York: McGraw-Hill, 2001).

5. See Geoffrey Moore, Paul Johnson, and Tom Kippola, *The Gorilla Game* (New York: HarperBusiness, 1998).

6. See Mark Rubinstein, "Rational Markets: Yes or No? The Affirmative Case," *Financial Analysts Journal,* May–June 2001, 215–230.

7. See the IPO data maintained by Professor Jay Ritter (www.bear.cba .ufl.edu/ritter/ipodata.htm) and by Professor Ivo Welch (www.ipo resources.org).

8. See Bruce Berman, ed., *Hidden Value* (London: Euromoney Publications, 1999), Chapters 10–12. See also www.ex.ac.uk/~RDavies/arian/ bowiebonds.html.

9. Martin Scherzer, "Insurance as a Financial Catalyst," *Viewpoint,* 2000 (www.mmc.com/views/00springscherzer.shtml).

10. The author is on the Board of Advisors of pl-x.

11. The pl-x methodology is trademarked as Technology Risk Reward Units or TRRU. In Chapter 11, I look more closely at IP valuation and present a different real options–based approach to IP valuation. While the details differ, TRRU and the method presented in this book attempt to align private-market IP transaction value with financial-market pricing.

12. These data can be obtained at www.dailydeal.com and at www .pl-x.com.

Chapter 10

1. Much of this chapter is the result of a collaboration with Laura Martin, formerly managing director and entertainment industry equity analyst at Credit Suisse First Boston (CSFB). Details are in her May 11, 2001, report, "Film Studio Reel Options." See www.valuesweep.com for details on obtaining the report. Much of the data in this section are from CSFB and entertainment industry sources. Complete citations are available on the Web site.

2. A. De Vany and C. Lee, "Quality Signals in Information Cascades and the Dynamics of the Distribution of Motion Picture Box Office Revenues," *Journal of Economic Dynamics & Control,* Spring 2001, 593–614.

3. Studios often recognize that certain films do better in certain seasons. For example, many recognize that action films have higher revenues in the summer. But the shared insight leads to heavy competition at the box office on key weekends and at key theaters, which negates its advantage. The result is that profits remain difficult to predict.

4. The return on invested capital is measured as EBITDA/Film Segment Assets and the cost of capital is measured by the weighted average cost of capital (WACC).

5. See Harold Vogel, *Entertainment Industry Economics,* 4th ed. (Cambridge: Cambridge University Press, 1998).

6. There is a side market known as "rework" in which half-completed scripts are bought and sold. This analysis assumes that abandoned scripts have no value.

7. See, for example, Chapters 2 and 3 in Jason Squire, ed., *The Movie Business Book,* 2d ed. (New York: Simon & Schuster, 1992).

8. Lee Berton and Roy Harris, "Reel-World Accounting," *CFO,* March 1999, 35–46.

9. Here's an example: If you rent a video of a film made by Dreamworks, the previews are for films made by other studios. The argument is that whereas Dreamworks is paid by other studios, if it had a library it could use the video time to generate even more value.

10. This point is made by many others, including Vogel, *Entertainment Industry Economics,* and Squire, *The Movie Business Book.*

11. Vogel, *Entertainment Industry Economics,* Table 2-4. Analysts expect the mix to shift to 65 percent of the international and 35 percent of the U.S. box office receipts.

12. See Vogel, *Entertainment Industry Economics,* 46, 47.

13. Headlines about the film's box office performance were dismal, largely because the chairman of Disney had inflated expectations. For example, in an e-mail to employees he announced, "There are no sure

things in the entertainment industry, but this [*Pearl Harbor*] comes close" (Russ Britt, "Disney CFO," *CBSMarketWatch.com,* June 23, 2001 [www .marketwatch.com]).

14. See John Lippman, "One Good (or Bad) Film Still Goes Straight to the Bottom Line," *Wall Street Journal,* May 24, 2001.

15. Squire, *The Movie Business Book,* 161.

16. See Laura Martin, "MGM," Credit Suisse First Boston, November 13, 2000.

17. See Brett Pulley, "The Wizard of MGM," *Forbes,* May 28, 2001.

18. See Lippman, "One Good (or Bad) Film Still Goes Straight to the Bottom Line."

Chapter 11

1. Source: www.delphion.com/about-company.

2. There is a book with this title on the importance of an intellectual property strategy. The authors' thesis is that valuable IP is often overlooked because of a lack of systematic processes to identify and prepare IP for outlicensing. See Kevin Rivette and David Kline, *Rembrandts in the Attic: Unlocking the Hidden Value of Patents* (Boston: Harvard Business School Press, 1999).

3. There are three accepted methods for determining the fair-market value of an asset: market-based comparables, DCF of future income, and replacement cost. None of these captures the full range of factors affecting IP value.

4. The complete license is contained in Speechworks's IPO prospectus (S-1/A), June 30, 2000. A copy of the license can also be found www.valuesweep.com.

5. See Baruch Lev, *Intangibles* (Washington, DC: Brookings Institution Press, 2001).

6. This figure is only a sketch of a fully developed method; see www.valuesweep.com for further details.

7. See Will Wade, "MIPS's Patent Claims in Jeopardy after Loss to Lexra," *EETimes,* June 14, 2001 (www.eetimes.com).

8. See Michael Santarini, "IP Is a Big Business but for a Few Players," *EETimes,* February 3, 2000 (www.eetimes.com).

Chapter 12

1. See Martha Amram and Nalin Kulatilaka, *Real Options* (Boston: Harvard Business School Press, 1999), Chapter 14.

2. For example, see the quote by Robert Timpson in "Gerstner's Legacy: A New Emphasis on Services at IBM," *Wall Street Journal,* June 11, 2001.

3. See Richard Brealey and Stewart Myers, *Principles of Corporate Finance*, 5th ed. (New York: McGraw-Hill, 1996), 301.

4. See Dale Jorgenson, "Information Technology and the U.S. Economy," *American Economic Review*, March 2001, 1–32.

5. See Kana Software, "KANA Announces Second Quarter 2001 Revenue" (press release, July 24, 2001).

6. See, for example, Kent Beck, *Extreme Programming Explained: Embrace Change* (Boston: Addison-Wesley, 2000).

7. See Michael Moaz, "CRM: What's Right for Customers Is the Correct Approach," Gartner Group, July 9, 2001.

8. See Richard Brown, "Many Happy Returns," *Line56*, August 31, 2001 (www.line56.com).

9. See Alorie Gilbert, "Electric Shock," *CMP Media* (www.iweek.com).

10. See Kent Shimasaki, "E-Commerce to C-Commerce and Beyond," *Electronic News*, March 19, 2001 (www.e-insite.net/electronicnews).

11. See Philip Kaminsky, David Simchi-Levi, and Edith Simchi-Levi, *Designing and Managing the Supply Chain* (Boston: McGraw-Hill, 2000), Chapter 4, for further detail and references.

12. See www.hp.com/hpinfo/investor/2000annual/everyday_acts/supply_chain_management.htm.

13. See www.hp.com/solutions1/supplychain/resources/.

Chapter 13

1. The facts and figures given about P&G are from a large number of different sources. See www.valuesweep.com for the full citations.

2. Calculations for January 1999 and January 2000 produce similar results.

3. The DCF valuation model works well for P&G because of the stability of its products and revenue streams. There is logical support for the size of the terminal value in this industry.

4. The recent new product, a dry mop, has been considered highly successful. It sold $200 million in its first six months. It is assumed that less successful new products create half that revenue annually. Data across a number of industries suggest that average launch success rates are about 60 percent, but P&G is noted for its testing expertise, and it is reasonable that their launch success rate is a bit higher. See Greg Stevens and James Burley, "3,000 Raw Ideas = 1 Commercial Success," in *The Financial Management of R&D* (Washington, DC: Industrial Research Institute, 2001).

5. F. Peter Boer creates a similar model of an R&D pipeline in Chapter 11 of *The Valuation of Technology* (New York: John Wiley & Sons, 1999). He also discusses the types of growth projects that bring financial

balance to a pipeline—a perspective that would have been appropriate for P&G.

6. Katrina Booker, "The Best Little Oil House in Texas," *Fortune,* September 3, 2001.

7. Chris Zook, *Profit from the Core* (Boston: Harvard Business School Press, 2001), 20, 149.

8. Thomas Stewart and Gary Hamel, "Today's Companies Won't Make It, and Gary Hamel Knows Why," *Fortune,* September 4, 2000.

9. Jerry Useem, "Conquering Vertical Limits," *Fortune,* February 19, 2001.

10. Soussain Faiz, manager of Global Valuation Services, Texaco, Inc., Real Options Conference, July 2001. For further details, see Faiz, "Real-Options Application: From Success in Asset Valuation to Challenges for an Enterprise Approach," Society of Petroleum Engineers, paper 68243, 2001 (www.spe.org). Texaco was acquired by Chevron in 2000. These comments reflect Texaco before the merger.

11. See Faiz, "Real-Options Application."

12. These performance-measurement systems include economic value added (EVA), economic profit, and cash flow ROI.

13. Adam Borison, ROV Group partner and leader, "Diet and Exercise," draft working paper, Applied Decision Analysis LLC/Pricewaterhousecoopers LLP, August 2001. Borison is now affiliated with SDG (www.sdg.com).

14. See www.cargilldow.com. Information for this section taken from Cargill Dow press releases and a March 2001 interview with the CEO; see www.greenatworkmag.com.

Chapter 14

1. Why not "the Gal"? That is definitely a road less traveled, but it can be done. I use the male reference in this book because that is most often the way the world is right now.

2. See, for example, Donald Gause and Gerald Weinberg, *Are Your Lights On?* (New York: Dover House Publishing, 1990).

3. Two accessible introductions to the results of behavioral finance are Robert Shiller, *Irrational Exuberance* (Princeton, NJ: Princeton University Press, 2000), and Hersh Shefrin, *Beyond Greed and Fear* (Boston: Harvard Business School Press, 1999).

4. See Kathryn Harrigan, "Strategy Formulation in Declining Industries," *Academy of Management Review,* October 1980, 509–604. In Martha Schary, "Exit from a Declining Industry" (Ph.D. diss., MIT, 1987), I show that a real options perspective can explain some of the "delay." Typi-

cally, the delay is defined as the difference between the shutdown date that arises from a DCF valuation model and actual behavior. When the model includes uncertainty the gap between model and actual behavior is reduced.

5. Ibid.

6. See Shefrin, *Beyond Greed and Fear.*

7. See David Skinner, *Introduction to Decision Analysis,* 2d ed. (Gainesville, FL: Probabilistic Publishing, 1999), Chapter 4.

8. See David Matheson and Jim Matheson, *The Smart Organization* (Boston: Harvard Business School Press, 1998).

9. See Jonathan Baron, *Thinking and Deciding,* 2d ed. (Cambridge: Cambridge University Press, 1994).

10. See Luke Hohmann, *Journey of the Software Professional* (Upper Saddle River, NJ: Prentice Hall, 1997).

11. Draper Fisher Jurvetson; see: www.dfj.com/resources/index.html.

Chapter 15

1. See Edward Tufte, *Visual Explanations* (New Haven, CT: Graphics Press, 1997).

2. See John Seely Brown and Paul Duguid, *The Social Life of Information* (Boston: Harvard Business School Press, 2000).

Bibliography

Amram, Martha, and Nalin Kulatilaka. *Real Options*. Boston: Harvard Business School Press, 1999.

————. "Strategy and Shareholder Value Creation: The Real Options Frontier." *Journal of Applied Corporate Finance,* Summer 2000, 8–21.

Baron, Jonathan. *Thinking and Deciding*. 2d ed. Cambridge: Cambridge University Press, 1994.

Brealey, Richard, and Stewart Myers. *Principles of Corporate Finance*. 5th ed. New York: McGraw-Hill, 1996.

Damodaran, Aswath. *The Dark Side of Valuation*. Upper Saddle River, NJ: Prentice Hall, 2001.

Dixit, Avinash, and Robert Pindyck. *Investment under Uncertainty*. Princeton, NJ: Princeton University Press, 1994.

Gompers, Paul, and Josh Lerner. *The Venture Capital Cycle*. Cambridge, MA: MIT Press, 2000.

Kidder, Tracy. *The Soul of a New Machine*. Boston: Back Bay Books, 2000.

Luehrman, Timothy. "Corporate Opportunities as Real Options: Getting Started with the Numbers." *Harvard Business Review,* July–August 1998.

Matheson, David, and Jim Matheson. *The Smart Organization*. Boston: Harvard Business School Press, 1998.

Mauboussin, Michael, and Al Rappaport. *Expectations Investing*. Boston: Harvard Business School Press, 2001.

Moore, Geoffrey. *Living on the Fault Line*. New York: HarperBusiness, 2000.

Morrison, David, and Adrian Slywotzky. *How Digital Is Your Business?* New York: Crown Business, 2000.

Myers, Stewart. "Finance Theory and Financial Strategy." *Interfaces,* January–February 1984, 126–137.

Penman, Stephen. *Financial Statement Analysis and Security Valuation.* Boston: McGraw-Hill, 2001.

Seybold, Patricia. *Customers.com.* New York: Times Business, 1998.

Shefrin, Hersh. *Beyond Greed and Fear.* Boston: Harvard Business School Press, 2000.

Shiller, Robert. *Irrational Exuberance.* Princeton, NJ: Princeton University Press, 2000.

Siegel, Jeremy. *Stocks for the Long Run.* 2d ed. New York: McGraw-Hill, 1998.

Skinner, David. *Introduction to Decision Analysis.* 2d ed. Gainesville, FL: Probabilistic Publishing, 1999.

Squire, Jason, ed. *The Movie Business Book.* 2d ed. New York: Simon & Schuster, 1992.

Stevens, Greg, and James Burley. "3,000 Raw Ideas = 1 Commercial Success." In *The Financial Management of R&D,* 4–15. Washington, DC: Industrial Research Institute, 2001.

Vogel, Harold. *Entertainment Industry Economics.* 4th ed. Cambridge: Cambridge University Press, 1998.

Index

About the Author

MARTHA AMRAM is an experienced management consultant specializing in valuation and corporate strategy. She has led strategy consulting teams in a wide range of industries, from consumer goods to energy to high-tech.

Amram is currently CEO of Vocomo Software Corporation, which provides software and services for voice applications. Previously she was Managing Director at Navigant Consulting, where she developed valuation and strategic decision-making methodology for large-scale risky investments and led the design of an employee stock-options exchange program. She was also a cofounder of Glaze Creek Partners, a consulting firm specializing in real options–based strategy and valuation, which she sold to Navigant in 1999.

Amram holds a Ph.D. in Applied Economics from MIT and has served on the boards of several startup companies. She is the coauthor of *Real Options: Managing Strategic Investments in an Uncertain World* (1998), which has been translated into five languages. She can be reached at www.valuesweep.com.